THE KILLING SEASON

A Summer Inside
an LAPD
Homicide Division

MILES
CORWIN

Simon & Schuster

SIMON & SCHUSTER
Rockefeller Center
1230 Avenue of the Americas
New York, NY 10020

Designed by Deirdre C. Amthor

Manufactured in the United States of America

3 5 7 9 10 8 6 4 2

Library of Congress Cataloging-in-Publication Data
Corwin, Miles.
The killing season : a summer inside an LAPD homicide division /
Miles Corwin.
p. cm.
1. Homicide investigation—California—Los Angeles—Case studies.
2. Los Angeles (Calif.). Police Dept.— Case studies.
3. Detectives—California—Los Angeles—Case studies. I. Title.
HV8079.H6C67 1997
364.1'523'0979494—dc21 96-47429 CIP

ISBN 0-684-80235-X

Photographs number 5 through number 18
by Gary Friedman/Los Angeles Times

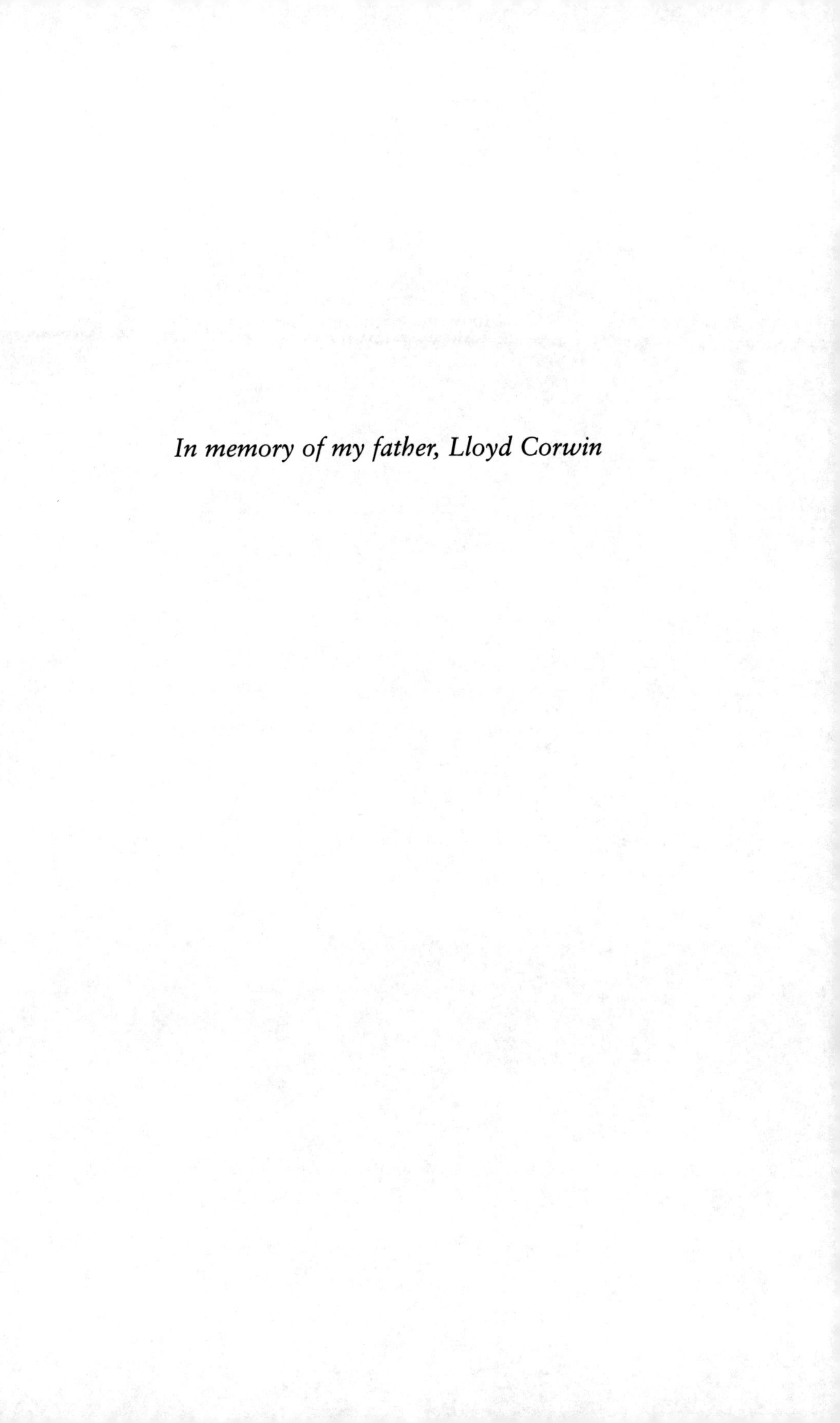

In memory of my father, Lloyd Corwin

Introduction

The genesis of this book was a summer night that I spent with a homicide detective in South-Central Los Angeles. I was the crime reporter for the *Los Angeles Times,* and I followed the detective in order to write about the changing nature of homicide in the city.

On that steamy Wednesday night in August, when the detective was called out to a murder scene, he contacted me. We met at the station and reached the scene at about midnight. A 15-year-old boy had been killed in a drive-by shooting. The boy had been walking home from a friend's house and listening to his Walkman when he was gunned down. He was not dressed like a gangbanger, and he was listening to the love songs of Minnie Ripperton—not the gangsta rap favored by the gangbangers in the neighborhood. The detective talked to weeping relatives, neighbors and witnesses and concluded the victim was just a high-school boy caught in the wrong place at the wrong time.

We were at the scene for about 45 minutes when the detective's beeper went off and he was dispatched to another murder.

As a supervising detective for the Los Angeles Police Department, his responsibility was to assist the lead detectives at murder scenes and oversee the initial investigations.

About a mile away from the first murder we found the body of a woman sprawled on the sidewalk near an alley. The crime scene was a testament to the power of crack cocaine. From the time the woman had struggled with the killer, taken a shot in the chest, stumbled back into a driveway and fallen as she slammed her head on the pavement, she continued to tightly clutch a small glass cocaine pipe in her right hand. We had not been at the scene long when the detective was beeped again and sent to yet another murder. A blue Nissan was abandoned on a ramp leading to a freeway, and the driver was about 100 yards away, lying on his back, beside a concrete wall. He had been shot in the back and the side.

In three hours there had been three murders, all within one square mile. A typical weeknight in South-Central Los Angeles.

Months after the story had run, I continued to be haunted by that Wednesday night in August. I felt as if I had a brief glimpse of a quiet genocide that was taking place.

In more affluent neighborhoods, people whose relatives had been murdered often were unwilling to talk to reporters. But in South-Central families welcomed my presence. Sometimes I would show up weeks after a homicide, and family members would complain that their relative's murder had not merited a single line in the newspaper or even a brief mention on the local news. They felt the news media did not care and the detectives did not care. They simply wanted someone to pay attention to what had happened to their family member, what had happened to their neighborhood. After these interviews, I often thought of the line from *Death of a Salesman* when Willy Loman's wife, infuriated that her husband could so easily be discarded by his firm after a lifetime of service, cried out, "Attention must be paid!"

I decided to pay attention to this mounting murder toll and write a book about homicide in South-Central Los Angeles, about the victims and the killers and the neighborhoods and the detectives.

Introduction

There is a great clamor about how the media overemphasize crime news. But in South-Central, crime news is *under*emphasized. A home invasion robbery in West Los Angeles or a carjacking in the San Fernando Valley often will lead the evening news. But in 1993—when I spent that summer night with the homicide detective—there were more than 400 murders in South-Central, and few had received any news coverage, any attention whatsoever. If 400 American soldiers were killed during a peacekeeping mission, it would be debated at the highest levels of government and lead to major changes in foreign policy. If 400 people in West Los Angeles were murdered in one year, the response by police, city officials and the business community would be unprecedented. But 400 murders in South-Central were considered business as usual. A life in South-Central simply seemed to have less value than a life in other parts of the city.

This cavalier attitude toward murder in South-Central has changed little over the years and is reflected in the 1940 Raymond Chandler novel, *Farewell, My Lovely.* When a South-Central bar owner is killed, a burnt-out homicide detective by the name of Nulty is uninterested in the case because the victim was black.

"Another shine killing," Nulty tells private eye Philip Marlowe. "That's what I rate after eighteen years in this man's police department. No pix, no space, not even four lines in the want-ad section."

Later, Marlowe says, "I went down to the lobby of the building to buy an evening paper. Nulty was right in one thing at least. The Montgomery killing hadn't even made the want-ad section so far."

Media attention is important on a number of levels. When reporters publicize a murder, police department brass usually respond. They often will devote more resources to the investigation, put more pressure on the detectives, scrutinize the investigation more closely. But when hundreds of murders a year are ignored, detectives can lose motivation, and the department leaders, many of whom are highly political, will devote more resources to higher profile crimes.

The murder rate in South-Central and in most major cities has dropped since the early 1990s. But it still remains appallingly high. And the decline is expected to soon be reversed. While the murder rate among adults 25 and older has been falling, the rate among teenage boys and young men in their early 20s has increased sharply. During the late 1990s, and for the following decade, there will be a surge in the juvenile population. As a result, criminologists expect another marked rise in homicides.

It is often the white suburbanites who are the most outspoken about crime, who have the most clout with politicians, who prompt the crime-fighting legislation. But it is the poor, the inner-city residents, who are victimized the most. And when it comes to preventing and solving crime, these residents often receive unequal treatment. They must rely on an overburdened police department and overburdened detectives—just as they rely on a deteriorating school system and crowded public hospitals.

Homicide detectives in South-Central investigate two to three times more cases than homicide detectives in most other LAPD divisions. The two-detective homicide teams in South-Central handle up to 20 murder investigations a year. Former Bronx homicide commander Vernon Geberth, author of *Practical Homicide Investigation,* says this is "totally inappropriate and unacceptable. It is physically impossible for them to be doing everything they're supposed to be doing on their cases." An appropriate caseload, he says, is about six to eight homicide investigations a year.

The onerous caseload has had a profound impact on the overwhelmed, overworked detectives. They, too, are casualties of the murder count.

That August night I tracked the three murders, Pete "Raz" Razanskas headed the homicide investigation of the woman who had been found clutching the crack pipe. I watched him work a few other crime scenes that year, and I enjoyed his sense of humor and was impressed with his ability to spot obscure details that other detectives missed, details that later proved to be significant.

Razanskas seemed like the ideal guide for the book. He treated people on the street with respect; he seemed to truly care when he talked to the families of murder victims. And unlike most homicide detectives who work in South-Central for a few years and then request a transfer to a quieter division station or a high-profile unit downtown, Razanskas has chosen to spend his entire 22-year career in South-Central, as a patrolman, gang investigator, and detective.

Razanskas also supervises detective trainees, and I thought that the best way for me to learn about homicide in South-Central was to follow him as he trained a new detective. I could learn along with his new partner.

But I wanted to make sure he had the right trainee. I wanted to follow someone who cared about South-Central and didn't look upon the stint there as merely another stage in career advancement. I wanted someone who was bright and knowledgeable enough so I could learn from the trainee as well as from Razanskas. And I wanted someone who was open-minded enough to allow a reporter to be, in essence, a third partner. I knew Razanskas was due for a new trainee. If his new partner did not seem like the right choice for me, I had planned on finding another detective team.

I soon discovered that his new partner was a woman named Marcella Winn, a child of South-Central who would now be investigating murders in the neighborhood where she was raised. During her seven years with the LAPD, Winn proved that she had the toughness and the smarts to succeed in a department that traditionally had been white and male. Winn was confident of her abilities, self-assured and very outspoken. She would not be one of those timid trainees who would do something just because Razanskas told her to do it.

As soon as I met Winn, I knew I had found the right detective team. And they assented to my presence because they believed it was important that people learn how the hundreds of murders a year in South-Central take a terrible toll on the residents, the families of the victims, and the detectives.

But while Razanskas and Winn were excellent guides for my journey, I did not want to rely entirely on the two detectives. I did not want to view murder solely from a police perspective.

To get a better understanding of the consequences of murder and its impact on a community, I also spent much time talking to therapists and clients at Loved Ones of Homicide Victims, a remarkable South-Central counseling center. There has been much written about black-on-black crime. The founders of Loved Ones decided to create a place for black-on-black healing. They sought out and hired accomplished black therapists to work with their mostly black clientele, who had lost children, parents, spouses and siblings to homicide.

Every Saturday morning, a group of people gathered at the center's headquarters, behind a Baptist church. They were gracious enough to allow me to sit in on their sessions during the summer and fall of 1994, while they met with a therapist and shared their anguish, their fear, their struggle to survive the loss of loved ones.

I shadowed Razanskas and Winn from March, when Winn investigated her first murder, until October, when she and Razanskas split up. I was there in the middle of the night when they picked up their "fresh blood" cases and began their crime scene investigations. I was with them in the interview rooms when they interrogated suspects. I was with them when they notified parents that their children had been murdered. I was with them at autopsies and when they traveled across the country to arrest fugitives and bring them back to Los Angeles.

Although I followed the detectives' cases from spring to fall, the focus of this book is on one summer in South-Central. A summer in South-Central, in terms of murder statistics, is like a year in many other high-crime neighborhoods. Summer is when there is more than one murder a day in South-Central, when weary detectives lurch from crime scene to crime scene, when the bodies stack up faster than the coroner can pick them up. Summer is the most murderous time of year. Summer is the homicide detective's season.

On the eve of the summer of 1994, Razanskas and Winn became partners, and during this prelude to the carnage that summer brings, they had the luxury of time as Razanskas guided

Winn through her first cases. Once summer began the pace quickened dramatically. And throughout the summer, Razanskas watched Winn carefully because he knew if she could make it through the crucible of a summer in South-Central, she could make it in homicide.

For murder, though it have no tongue, will speak
with most miraculous organ.
—William Shakespeare,
Hamlet

Prologue

Pete Razanskas was a young police officer, just a few years out of the academy, when he and his partner were dispatched to a gang shooting. The homicide detectives at the scene were perplexed by a 3-inch cut on the victim's right palm because there was no evidence indicating a knife had been used.

It was Razanskas who spotted a slight lead-colored smear on the victim's nickel-plated .32 semiautomatic. He told the detectives that when the shooter fired at the victim, one of the bullets probably hit the victim's gun. This could have caused the bullet to fragment, and a sliver from the bullet might have cut the victim's hand.

One of the detectives, an old-timer everyone called Fuzzy, looked Razanskas up and down and nodded. "You got a good eye, kid," Fuzzy told him. "One of these days you ought to work homicide with us."

A few years later, Razanskas picked up his first homicide experience when he was promoted to a specialized unit that investigated Latino gangs. Although nobody in the unit was a detective yet, they were allowed to work gang murders. In the early 1980s, after about ten years with the LAPD, he made detective and was assigned to a station in South-Central Los Angeles where he investigated robberies. This was regarded as the minor leagues then, a training ground for homicide. In those days a lieutenant would approach an up-and-coming young detective and say, "Son, you want to get divorced? How about working homicide?" After a year working robberies, that question was posed to Razanskas.

Years later, he realized that the lieutenant's words had been prophetic. Two of his marriages ended in divorce. The hours had been too long and the pressure too great. He knew he had spent too much time at the station, time he should have spent at home with his family. He had made it to homicide and he had succeeded there. But Razanskas sometimes wonders if the price he paid was too high.

Razanskas' route to the Los Angeles Police Department was an unlikely and circuitous one. His parents are Lithuanian. He spent his childhood years in Venezuela. He went to high school in southern California. And now he wears Western boots, chews tobacco and dresses and acts like a cowboy.

Razanskas, who is 46, has played the part so long he now even looks a bit like a grizzled cowhand. He is lean, has a broad, gray, droopy mustache and deep-set pale blue eyes with crow's feet from too much squinting. At homicide scenes, he slowly saunters about, as if he is reluctantly heading out to the barn on a cold morning.

In the early 1970s, when Razanskas returned from Vietnam as an Air Force explosives expert, he considered going to college and studying electrical engineering. But he was married, broke and needed a job. He decided to become a cop.

After graduating from the LAPD academy, Razanskas was assigned to a South-Central police station, a few miles from the home of Marcella Winn, a junior-high-school student at the time, who, 20 years later, would be his partner.

Prologue

• • •

A year before Razanskas joined the LAPD, Winn, who was 13, moved to South-Central with her family from a small Texas town near the Gulf of Mexico. South-Central was a far different place then. The gangs and drugs had not yet taken hold. Industry had not entirely abandoned the area. The Latino influx had not yet begun.

Winn learned about hard work from her father. He was up at five o'clock every morning, collecting garbage for the city. He worked his route alone; he felt that a partner would slow him down. When he returned home in the early afternoon, he showered, ate lunch and headed off for his second job as a mail handler at the post office. He returned home after midnight, was up at five, and did it all over again.

By the time Winn was finishing high school, her neighborhood had changed. The Rollin 60s began covering the walls with graffiti and doing drive-bys. Some of the boys on her street ran with the 60s, but Winn's parents were strict and would not let their daughters associate with them. Winn was a good student and was known as a girl who did not hang out.

After high school, Winn worked at a law office and attended community college and, later, a state college. When she was 30 units shy of her degree in political science, she quit school. She was bored in college and she wanted to make some money. Winn had considered becoming an attorney but decided she was too restless to spend her life at a desk.

She decided to become a cop, in part because police work was a way for her to protect her neighborhood from some of the forces that were destroying it. She was angry that everyone she knew seemed to have lost a family member or a close friend to homicide, angry that people did not feel safe on their own streets. She wanted to do something to change her neighborhood, to bring it back to the way it once was.

Many of her friends were shocked by her decision to join the LAPD, which had a long-standing reputation in the black community for racism and brutality. Being a black cop in South-

Central adds just one more difficulty to an already difficult job. When she first began working patrol, suspects would ask her, "What you want to arrest a brother for?" She usually deflected comments like this with a quip, "If you can't take the heat, get your ass off the street." It was too complicated to explain to them why she became a cop.

Winn is a tall, imposing woman and can be intimidating when she needs to be. She has spent a lot of time lifting weights in the police academy gym, but she does not have the mien nor the manner of a body builder. Winn, who is 35 and single, can quickly lose the wary cop demeanor and turn on the charm when she needs something from a surly desk sergeant.

Since Winn has joined the homicide unit, she has heard fewer snide comments on the street. While patrol officers, particularly black patrol officers, often are challenged in South-Central, their usefulness questioned, their motives impugned, residents cut homicide detectives some slack because they share a common goal: They both want the killers off the street.

South-Central is not an isolated, monolithic neighborhood of crumbling high-rise tenements, like East Coast slums. Much of the area consists of vast tracts of stucco bungalows, small apartment buildings and palm trees that belie the danger on the streets.

When visitors travel through South-Central, they often ask, "Where's the ghetto?" The answer always surprises them: "You're in it."

South-Central is a microcosm of Los Angeles, and, like the city, it is a pastiche of many neighborhoods. It is composed of working-class neighborhoods with well-kept single-family homes; pockets of dilapidated apartments, rock houses and corner hookers; crumbling commercial strips dominated by liquor stores and check-cashing shops. This is a Los Angeles that is unknown to most residents of the city, a city so sprawling and segregated, it is still possible to spend an entire lifetime in Santa Monica or Encino and never find a single reason to visit South-Central.

More than 500,000 people live here, about a third of the households subsisting below the national poverty level. It is a multiethnic city within a city—once mostly black, now about half Latino—with simmering racial tensions and dozens of warring gang factions.

Razanskas and Winn lived through the changes in the area—he as a police officer, she as a schoolgirl—that created the burgeoning homicide rate that has kept them in South-Central and led to their partnership.

Razanskas and Winn are assigned to South Bureau Homicide, which is responsible for all murders in Los Angeles' killing fields, a jagged strip of streets that runs from South Los Angeles to the harbor. This is such murderous terrain that if it were a separate city it would rank among the nation's top ten for homicides. Razanskas and Winn work the most violent sector in a violent bureau: 77th Street Division, the heart of South-Central.

Razanskas, a supervising detective, and Winn, a detective trainee, are partners. For a while Razanskas also will be Winn's mentor and teach her the rudiments of homicide investigation.

It is no accident, not simply the luck of the draw, that Razanskas, an easygoing good old boy, and Winn, an intense, ambitious black woman, are partners. Lieutenant Sergio Robleto, who heads South Bureau Homicide, often pairs up detectives with disparate temperaments and divergent backgrounds. He believes the partnership will develop a greater range than the sum of its parts. He knows Razanskas has the patience of a hunter who likes to slowly stalk his quarry before making a move. But sometimes Razanskas can be too patient, can approach a case too deliberately. Robleto wants Razanskas to be occasionally prodded by a young, gung-ho detective who will push him and force him to justify any delay.

Robleto knows that Winn is a hard charger, an intense, impatient detective who is eager to rack up arrests and quickly move on to the next case. He wants Winn to work with someone who knows the value of slowing down an investigation.

Razanskas has such a strong personality he can easily intimidate a trainee. But Robleto knows Winn is not easily intimidated. It is not easy for a black woman cop to succeed in the LAPD, where sexual harassment and racism in the ranks have long been a problem. Winn learned that to endure and prevail in the department, she had to follow one factum: Don't take any shit. She does not intend to get pushed around on the street, nor in the squad room.

Homicide in South-Central is a young detectives' game. Most of the detectives are in their 20s and 30s. Razanskas is the second oldest case-carrying detective in the unit. Most of the detectives he started with have retired, or are now supervisors. Most cannot sustain the pace of working 24 hours, even 48 hours at a stretch, juggling dozens of old cases while attempting to keep track of an inexorable wave of new ones. This takes its toll. And a few of Razanskas' supervisors believe it has taken its toll on him.

He still can be dazzling at crime scenes. His knowledge of firearms, trajectories, ammunition types and other nuances of homicide still is highly respected. He still has a remarkable memory and can recall arcane details from ancient cases. But his supervisors have been carping at him lately about late reports and insufficient follow-up work on cases. They believe he is approaching burnout. If he can't convince them otherwise, he may be forced to leave the bureau.

In some homicide units, detectives can go on, year after year, aging gracefully until retirement. Their experience and years of service are looked on as an asset. But these are units where detectives may work only a handful of homicides a year. At South Bureau, detectives have one of the heaviest workloads in the country. Some cannot take the grind. They work a year or two and then request a transfer. Razanskas has been investigating homicides almost 15 years.

As Razanskas and Winn begin their partnership, Winn has to prove she belongs in homicide. And Razanskas has to prove he is still the detective he once was. At the same time, he has to teach Winn how to investigate homicides in some of the most violent neighborhoods in the nation, during the most murderous time of year.

From the overcast days in June when the fog never seems to burn off and the murder rate holds steady, to the sweltering days in July when the homicide toll begins to rise, to the bloody days in August when there are sometimes more than a dozen murders on a single weekend, to the final deadly heat wave of summer when the Santa Ana winds howl down the mountain passes and people begin pulling triggers for no apparent reason, this is a summer in South-Central.

Chapter 1
The First Murder

Friday, March 25

Homicide detectives in South-Central Los Angeles usually do not wait long for a murder. On Detective Marcella Winn's first weekend on call, she spends an edgy Friday evening at home, waiting for the call of death. She watches a video of the movie *Tombstone* and munches on popcorn, but cannot keep her mind on the plot. She keeps waiting for the phone to ring. Before going to sleep she lays out her gold linen blazer, beige blouse and green rayon slacks; she does not want to have to fumble through her closet in the middle of the night looking for the right color combination. Winn has only been in the homicide bureau two weeks and this will be her first murder investigation. She would just as soon get started tonight. But this is a rainy March night, one of the rare Friday nights in South-Central when people are not being battered, bludgeoned, knifed or shot to death.

On Saturday morning, she cancels her pedicure appointment. She is afraid of having to race to a murder scene with wet nails. Winn spends a few hours watching reruns on television, but she cannot relax. Waiting for a homicide call is like waiting for that big sneeze that just won't come.

When the sun goes down, Winn is sure that tonight will be the night. After all, this is Saturday night, the most murderous night of the week. She is number one on the weekend rotation, which means she rolls on the first murder of the weekend. And there is a full moon, which usually kicks the pace of mayhem and murder into a high gear. She bakes a chicken breast and a potato and watches a video of *A River Runs Through It.* At 9 P.M., she turns in, hoping to catch at least a few hours' sleep. She tosses and turns, waking up every hour or two to check her answering machine and her beeper, to make sure she has not slept through a call.

By Sunday morning Winn is a wreck. She buys a paper and discovers people were murdered all over the city this weekend. Just not in South-Central. She takes her beeper and cellular phone to the gym and spends a few hours on the treadmill and weight machines, hoping to work off some nervous energy. It is drizzling Sunday night, and she invites a friend over to play dominoes. After a few games, she tells him, "You better go home now. I may get one." Then Winn thinks for a moment and says, "I don't think so. This is Sunday night."

They watch television for a few hours, he heads home and she crawls into bed. The weekend was a wash, Winn figures. All that worry for nothing. She dozes off at 11.

On this cool, breezy spring weekend, Felipe Angeles Gonzales spends Friday night at home, a small South-Central bungalow that he shares with nine other recent immigrants from Mexico City. He and a few roommates watch a movie called *El Coyote y La Bronca* on the Spanish language television station. On Saturday morning he is up at 5:30. Gonzales and a friend, who both work at a stereo manufacturing company, buy a few car stereos, amplifiers and speakers from the owner and spend the day selling them at a swap meet.

He is separated from his wife, who lives in Mexico with his four daughters, but he sends money home every month. His father drives a beat-up Volkswagen for a taxi company because he cannot afford his own cab. When Gonzales was 16 he, too, began working for the taxi company, and he spent more than 10 years driving a company cab. Gonzales' dream is to save enough money so he can return to Mexico, buy his own taxi and house and live near his daughters.

During the week, Gonzales works 10 to 12 hours a day, gluing fabric on speaker boxes. He attends English classes every weeknight and works most weekends at the swap meet. His one release, his one break from the long hours, the monotonous work, the homesickness, the danger he feels every day on the streets, is dancing. On Saturday night, after working at the swap meet all day, he drives to a friend's birthday party where he knows he can dance to his favorite music: cumbia, an earthy Afro-Columbian sound popular among young Latino immigrants. He begins dancing from the moment he arrives at the apartment, tiring out a number of partners, and dances until midnight, when the party breaks up.

Gonzales returns to the swap meet on Sunday. In the evening he and a few roommates prepare a dinner of *carne asada* with tortillas, salsa and one of Gonzales' favorite dishes—*nopales,* sautéed cactus leaves. They listen to cumbia for a few hours, until two of Gonzales' roommates decide to pick up a six-pack of beer at a liquor store. Gonzales asks them to do him a favor. On the way back from the store, he wants them to stop by the apartment of a woman he knows. He wants to see if she is there. They pick up the beer and drop him off near her apartment, at the corner of 49th and Figueroa.

"Wait for me," he tells them, as he climbs out of the car. "I'll be back in a minute."

It seems to Winn that she had just closed her eyes when the telephone finally rings. She checks her alarm clock. It is a few minutes before midnight. "This is it," she says to herself. "No one else would call this late."

"You got one," the night supervisor tells her.

"What's the story?" she asks him.

"Male Hispanic. Shot in the chest. On the street. Two possible witnesses."

"Where?"

"Forty-ninth and Figueroa."

Winn meets Detective Pete "Raz" Razanskas, who is waiting at a police station parking lot in an unmarked squad car, engine running. Winn is a detective trainee and Razanskas is her supervisor—and her partner. Winn has passed the written detective exam and is waiting to take her orals. She has all the responsibility and authority of a detective. Now she must earn her shield.

Razanskas pulls out of the parking lot and asks Winn, "What you got?"

"One vic," she says. "Forty-ninth and Fig. Two possible wits."

"Did you write it all down?"

"No."

"You got to write down the details," he tells her. "Who told you and at exactly what time."

Winn stares glumly out the window. This night, she thinks, is getting off to a bad start.

Razanskas and Winn pull up to the murder scene, an intersection lined with ramshackle two-story apartment buildings, storefront churches, a used-car lot and an auto repair shop advertising the installation of "Sun Ruffs." A few palm trees break the weathered monotony of the neighborhood, a hint of the tropics in the ghetto. The area is blocked off with yellow crime-scene tape. A handful of bystanders strain against the tape, trying to get a look at the body. There is an eerie quiet on this early Monday morning; the only sounds are the staccato dispatches from the squad car radios and the hissing of the flares.

Razanskas and Winn grab their flashlights and walk to the edge of the flares. He looks off into the distance and impersonates Robert Duvall playing the whacked-out colonel in *Apocalypse Now.* "Ah," says Razanskas, breathing deeply through his nose. "I love the smell of flares at a murder scene. It smells like victory."

Winn still seems half-asleep, but Razanskas is full of energy, laughing and pacing beside the flares. This is the part of the investigation he enjoys the most, when there is just a body and a few possible witnesses who may or may not have seen anything, and he has to search for threads of evidence, vague leads, shades of clues, sort it all out, and ultimately figure out what happened. Razanskas enjoys working with trainees at murder scenes. This is his stage and he is playing his favorite part—the lead.

He and Winn approach a uniformed officer who is leaning against a squad car. The officer tells them he was only able to locate one witness, who is back at the station giving a statement. The witness will be of little use because he saw the killing from a distance. All he knows is that three men in a car were shot in what looked like a botched robbery. Two of the victims, who were bleeding heavily, sped away and left the slain man on the sidewalk. Both victims in the car were shot several times and now are in surgery. One may not make it.

Razanskas turns to Winn and says, "You got one victim tits up. You got another victim circling the drain. If he goes down, you got a twofer."

The detectives have little to go on. Was it an attempted carjacking? Or was it a straight robbery? Did the men resist? Or were they shot anyway? How did the victim end up on the street?

Razanskas starts with the physical evidence. The body is laid out on the sidewalk under a white sheet. Two shell casings, the victim's glasses and a can of beer he had been drinking are all circled in chalk. The drizzle has stopped and the skies have cleared. Shallow puddles by the curb glisten under the full moon, and the white sheet looks like it is glowing.

Razanskas shows Winn how to diagram the crime scene. He tells her to include the location of the street lamps and the flood lights from a storefront church. This will make it difficult for defense attorneys to impeach witnesses—if any turn up. He tells her to record that there is a full moon tonight and to include the temperature. He demonstrates how to record the location of evidence with a measuring tool that looks like a golf club with wheels. She records the data while he calls out, "Shell casings one inch south of the north curb . . . beer can forty-three inches north of the north curb . . . eyeglass fragment fifteen inches east of the east curb." The one thing they cannot do at the scene, Razanskas explains, is go though the victim's pockets and search for clues or identification. In fact, they are not allowed to even touch the victim until the coroner investigator arrives. He has first crack at the body.

"I'm just walking you through this now because it's your first one," he tells Winn after all the evidence is logged. "But you're not my secretary. You're my partner."

A hooker wanders by and tries to climb underneath the crime-scene tape to get to the other side of the street. A uniformed officer berates her. Razanskas calls him off.

"The uniformed guys hate hookers," he whispers to Winn. "But I love 'em. Treat 'em right and they can be a good source of information for you."

He walks over to the hooker and says, "Hey, want a date tonight?"

The hooker, who is wearing a tight black skirt and spike heels, scowls at him for a moment. But as he walks closer she recognizes him and smiles broadly. "Hey, Raz," she says. "Wha's up?"

Razanskas investigated her brother's murder a few years ago and caught the killer. He asks her softly, so other bystanders cannot hear, if she knows what happened. She says she does not, but promises to ask around.

Razanskas and Winn approach the victim's body, and she spots a syringe and a few balled-up scraps of paper. She crouches, shines her flashlight on the syringe and studies it, concentrating intently.

"Don't worry about the needle," Razanskas tells her. "All that crap was left by the paramedics who came and went before we got here."

Winn is embarrassed, flicks off her flashlight and slaps it on her palm. She shakes her head. Everything is so new and unfamiliar to her. She feels self-conscious following Razanskas like a puppy, wandering about in the dark, not knowing what she is supposed to be looking for. And she is worried. Although this is her first murder, Winn is listed as the primary investigator on the case—partners usually alternate—which means she is responsible for solving it. And this case looks to her like a loser. There are no decent witnesses and there is no solid evidence. She bemoans her rotten luck. Why did she have to get stuck with this one? Why couldn't she have picked up a slam-dunker for her first case? Maybe there is more to the case, but she cannot see it.

Winn has been promoted quickly and often during her seven years with the Los Angeles Police Department: from patrol to a gang task force, to vice, to an elite burglary unit, to a detective trainee in bunco forgery, where she investigated a number of complex white-collar crimes. She has been successful in every unit she has worked. But now Winn worries that murder cases might exceed her abilities, that she simply may not have the skills to be a homicide detective.

She decides if she is responsible for solving the case, she is going to take some initiative. She is going to search for some evidence on her own. She wanders off into the darkness in the hopes of finding more bullet slugs.

Ten minutes later she returns. With the first break of the case. She found a witness. A true eyewitness. She is so excited that she stutters and her hands flutter as she tells Razanskas what she learned from the interview. The witness manages the building and lives in the apartment right above the shooting. He saw the three Latino victims pull over to the curb. One went to the apartment building and rang the doorbell. He waited a minute or two and then turned around and began to walk back to the car. Three black men—"kids . . . youngsters," he called them—emerged from the darkness. Two of them had pistols. They demanded money from the victim. They told the other two men to get out of the car. But the three Latino victims did not appear to understand English. They did not resist; they just appeared confused. A robber, angered by the delay, shouted, "Kill him." One gunman sprayed the car with bullets. The other shot the victim in the back as he was trying to escape. The witness yelled at the shooters, to try to scare them off. One of the robbers began shooting at him, and then they all disappeared into an alley.

Razanskas nods at Winn and asks, "How did you get him to open up?"

"I didn't front him," she says. "I just talked to him and told him that this shit has *got* to stop, that we got to work together so the people he cared about didn't get shot on the street."

"Beautiful. We'll talk to him again in the morning. You know, it sounds like our victim didn't present any threat to them at all. They just shot him in the back for no reason."

Razanskas tells Winn she will see murders like this all summer. Random murders without motive. Murders where victims do not resist. Murders that are merely homicidal afterthoughts.

The coroner investigator arrives and Razanskas calls out to him, "Hey, be nice to her." He points at Winn. "It's her first one."

"Don't worry," the investigator says. "I'll take it nice and slow."

The investigator empties the victim's pockets. He pulls out his wallet, counts out $70, and determines the victim's name is Felipe Angeles Gonzales. His death will attract no television cameras, no photographers straining behind the crime-scene tape, no reporters scrambling for poignant biographical details. Gonzales' death is lost in a sea of statistics, just another one of the 25 homicides in the county this weekend.

This same weekend, in another part of Los Angeles, another homicide scene precipitated an entirely different response. Two 19-year-old Japanese exchange students, attending a local university, were shot late Friday night during a carjacking in a supermarket parking lot. They died a few hours before Gonzales was shot, when they were taken off life-support systems. The story made the front page of all the local newspapers and led the evening news. President Clinton called the victims' parents. The governor of California and the U.S ambassador to Japan issued statements. The LAPD yanked the case from overworked local detectives and assigned it to Robbery-Homicide Division, a squad that specializes in complex and high-profile cases.

On a damp sidewalk, about 20 miles north of the San Pedro parking lot where the Japanese students were shot, the body of Felipe Gonzales draws little attention. The handful of rubberneckers have long since moved on. The only ones left are the coroner investigator, Razanskas and Winn.

"You don't have to worry about RHD taking *this* case from you," Razanskas tells Winn.

"Maybe they don't care about this killing, but I do," she says. "My victim's got a mama who's grieving just as much as the mamas of those students. I want the predators who did this off the street. I don't want them walking around jacking people I care about. I still have family in this neighborhood."

Razanskas nods. "Don't matter to me who the victim is. I don't care if he's a shithead or a saint. Every victim deserves a decent investigation."

The coroner investigator removes Gonzales' shirt, lowers his pants and examines the body. He is only a few inches over 5 feet, chubby and looks about 16—even though he is 29. Under his right nipple is a red blotch the size of a dime. The coroner determines that this is an exit wound because of the jagged edges. Gonzales' stomach is distended and drawn tight as a drum. "He has a belly full of blood," the investigator says. The bullet tumbled end over end and caused massive internal bleeding. This is the final indignity of death. Gonzales is sprawled out on the sidewalk, his trousers around his ankles, his blue and white striped bikini briefs pulled down to his thighs.

The coroner turns the body over and Winn flinches when she hears a sudden hissing sound—air escaping from the victim's lungs. There is a neat, perfectly round entry wound just beneath a shoulder blade. Winn and Razanskas crouch beside the body as the coroner works. Razanskas tells her to write down the direction the head is pointing—northwest. He studies her notes for a moment and then tells her not to be so precise when describing the angle of the left arm to the body.

"Always say, 'approximately,' " he says. "Don't just say it's at a seventy-five-degree angle. A defense attorney will have a field day with that at the trial." Razanskas asks, in a parody of a smug, imperious attorney, " 'Detective, how do you know it's exactly seventy-five degrees. Did you measure it out on the street with a protractor?' "

Razanskas tells her that a murder investigation is like a chess game. "You always got to think a few moves ahead. You got to anticipate questions you might have to answer years later at a trial. If you don't, your crime scene report is going to come back and bite you in the ass."

While the coroner investigator examines the body, Winn continues to take notes as the sky fades from black, to gray, to deep blue with streaks of pink on the horizon. At dawn, the anomalous sound of a rooster crowing in South-Central breaks the early morning calm. Before the coroner wheels the body away on a metal gurney, Razanskas takes a Polaroid picture of the victim's face. This will save them time, he tells Winn. Now they don't have to wait for family members to visit the coroner's office to identify the victim.

The detectives then trace the suspects' route, illuminating their way with flashlights, to a dirt alley littered with old sofas and rusting bedsprings. They spot a trail of fresh shoe imprints. He calls over an LAPD photographer, who just arrived at the scene, to take a picture.

"This guy's got a hell of a stride," Razanskas says.

Winn shines her flashlight on the imprints. "He was hauling ass."

"He was beating feet," Razanskas says. Razanskas tromps through the alley in his cowboy boots. He is wearing only slacks and a sports coat and tie, and Winn, who is shivering and hugging herself to keep warm, is amazed that the early morning chill does not seem to bother him.

"It's colder than a well digger's ass," she tells Razanskas. "How do you stay so warm?"

He grins and pats his chest and legs. "I'm wearing my thermal underwear. My hunting underwear. This keeps me warm in Wyoming when there's snow on the ground."

Winn, who is wearing rayon slacks, a linen blazer and crocodile Ferragamos with heels, did not know how to dress for her first murder, so she put on one of her most stylish outfits. As she tiptoes past the muddy spots in the alley, Winn vows she will never again wear heels at a murder scene. And next time she will bring a wool overcoat.

They leave the alley and examine an old Cadillac with a fresh bullet hole in the windshield and glass fragments on the hood. It is parked on the street about one hundred yards from the body. This mystifies them. The errant bullet did not follow the logical path of the suspects' shots. Razanskas tells Winn to make a note of this because it could prove significant later on.

As the streets begin to fill up with commuters and the sun breaks through the early morning fog, Razanskas and Winn drive away from the crime scene. He opens a tin of long-cut wintergreen Skoal, and the smell of mint envelops the car. He deposits a pinch in his cheek, grabs a paper cup from the back seat, spits and places the cup in a wire holder he has jury-rigged under the police radio. Winn eyes the cup warily. She worries about the consequences of a sudden stop.

"We're going to be interviewing some people on this case, and you're going to have to get a sense of who to trust and who not to trust," he tells her. "Sometimes I like to feel people out, ask them questions that aren't critical to the case, just to see how truthful they are. Once they lie to me, I know how to view them. My feeling is, once a chicken-killing dog, always a chicken-killing dog."

"I'm pretty skeptical about most people," she says. "Until they prove otherwise. Like B. B. King sings, 'I don't trust anyone except my mama, and she may be lyin' too.' "

"You're only supposed to be that cynical when you're old like me. How'd you get like that at such a young age?"

"My granddaddy in Texas used to tell me, 'Think the worst of every single SOB you meet. It'll only take him thirty days before he proves you right.' "

Razanskas laughs and spits another stream of tobacco into the cup, with a little more force than usual. Winn edges toward the door.

Back at South Bureau Homicide, an underground, windowless warren at the edge of a high-security mall, a group of detectives are talking about an early morning homicide. This murder is so cold it even jolts these jaded detectives. A 14-year-old girl was watching television with her grandfather. He told her to put on her pajamas and go to bed. She refused. He insisted. So she calmly walked into his bedroom, grabbed his .357 Magnum from the closet and blew him away.

Winn and Razanskas listen to the story as they search Felipe Gonzales' wallet. They then work the phones for a few minutes and finally obtain Gonzales' brother's telephone number. Razanskas tells Winn that he is not going to inform the brother on the telephone about the murder. Relatives often can provide leads and suspects, he tells her, but if they become hysterical after the death notification, you will not get anything from them. When you get them on the telephone, try to keep it vague. Just get them in the office. Interview them first. Then give them the bad news.

Razanskas calls the brother and tells him he has some very important information about Felipe Gonzales and asks him to come to the station. The brother presses Razanskas, who will only say, "We need to talk to you in person." Fortunately, the brother agrees.

When the brother arrives at the station, Razanskas, who spent his childhood years in Venezuela, begins interviewing him in fluent Spanish. After Razanskas obtains the information he needs, he shows the brother the Polaroid picture he took of the victim shortly after death. The brother's expression never changes, but his eyes fill with tears. He nods. "*Si,*" he says softly. "*Es mi hermano.*"

Razanskas offers his condolences to the brother, who looks dazed and in shock. He begins mumbling to Razanskas, in a slow monotone, as if he were talking in his sleep. His brother had been in the United States for only five months. He sent money home every month. He was known by everyone as a good worker. He loved his four daughters.

"Four kids," Razanskas says after he and Winn walk the brother out. "That sucks."

The investigation now has been inalterably changed for Winn. The interview with the brother has transformed the victim in Winn's eyes. He is no longer just another anonymous "vic," the eightieth murder of the year in South Bureau. He is Felipe Angeles Gonzales, a brother, a father, a good worker who only wanted to save enough money so he could return to Mexico City, buy his own taxi and support his children. Winn is angry now. Someone like Gonzales did not deserve to be shot in the back and left to die on the street. She does not want to see his killing go unavenged.

The two detectives finish up some paperwork on the homicide, have eggs, toast and coffee at a South-Central restaurant and then return to the murder scene. Razanskas tells her it is always important to visit the scene a second time, during the day, when it is light outside. You might find additional evidence on the street, he says, and you will have a better sense of the setting.

After they thoroughly examine the intersection of 49th and Figueroa, and retrace the killers' steps, they visit their only witness, John Jones, the apartment building manager. He is in his early 50s, has bloodshot eyes and is wearing black pants, black T-shirt, black boots and a black baseball cap. Jones, like many of his neighbors who spend a lot of time on the street, will only wear black. He knows if he wears anything remotely resembling red or blue—gang colors—he could get shot.

He takes them onto the roof for a better view of the murder scene. The roof overlooks an auto repair lot jammed with the rusting hulks of ancient cars and a small Baptist church with stained-glass windows dulled by grime. The horizon is dotted with rum and malt liquor billboards, the plastic flags of a used-car lot, and rooftop clotheslines, the shirts and underwear and trousers flapping in the wind.

When Razanskas conducts outdoor interviews in South-Central, he often scans the ground for old bullet slugs. It is almost involuntary now, a nervous habit, like a quarterback licking his fingers before taking a snap. Razanskas finds six rusty slugs on this roof within a few minutes and pockets them.

Jones walks to the edge of the roof, looks down at the spot where Gonzales was shot and says, "It was cold, man. Those some cold dudes."

Jones begins telling his story, but suddenly stops and studies the detectives for a moment. He tells them he has something they might be able to use. His building has a video camera by the front door that is always on. Razanskas and Winn exchange a quick glance. They walk down to his apartment, through a hallway littered with cigarette butts and specks of plaster that have fallen from the ceiling, and pop the tape into his VCR. The flickering black and white images show the faint outline of a man ringing the doorbell. Someone comes to the door and tells the man that his friend is not home. The man turns around and leaves. A few seconds later garbled voices are heard in the background. Then a volley of shots. Then more shots.

Razanskas and Winn jump up at the same time to roll the tape back. They both realize that the man who rang the bell was Gonzales, the victim. They replay the tape, again, which picks up only bits and pieces of the audio. They hear: "All right . . . motherfucker . . . give me your money . . . asshole . . . all your money . . . too slow . . . Kill him! Kill him!" They hear 14 shots, fired from three different guns, with three distinct popping sounds. Razanskas rolls back the tape and listens to the gunshots again. One thing bothers Razanskas about the gunshots.

He cannot account for the third weapon.

"Did you see a third shithead with a gun?" Razanskas asks.

Jones shakes his head.

"Was there another suspect out on the street who could have been strapped?" Winn asks.

Jones shakes his head. "I told you everything I know."

It is now midafternoon as they head back to the station. They have been up since midnight. At a stop sign, Winn, who is driving, checks her hair in the mirror and tries to pat it into place.

"This all-nighter is giving me a bad hair day," she says.

Razanskas stares out the window, lost in thought. "I think our wit is holding out."

"Yeah," she says. "He's only going halfway with us."

"He was up on that roof the whole time. He knows more than he's letting on. That's OK. We'll get another shot at him."

Razanskas spits into his paper cup and stares out the window for a few minutes. Then he brings up a delicate subject, a subject he feels that has to be addressed sooner or later. Some people might think he is some kind of racist, he tells Winn, because of his good old boy manner, because he is old school LAPD. But he wants to let her know that he is not. He tells her he would not have voluntarily spent his entire career in South-Central if he were a racist.

"If I was some kind of racist, I'd be out in some West Side or Valley division jacking anyone I saw who wasn't white."

"I asked around about you a while back. My sources told me you weren't a neck" (redneck). She stops at a light and says, "They told me you were too silly to be a neck."

Winn smiles and glances at Razanskas out of the corner of her eye. He chuckles.

"I been on the job twenty-two years and I've seen the whole gamut," he says. "I've worked with white cops who were racists. I've worked with Mexican cops who were racists. I've worked with black cops who treat black suspects like shit. I'd say, 'Don't do that around me. I don't need it.' "

"When I was on patrol," Winn says, "one cop told me that he considered every stop in South-Central a felony stop. I told him, 'You have an attitude like that and these brothers are going to take your gun and stick it up your ass.' "

"In a heartbeat," he says, nodding.

"There's a lot of racists, in the closet and out," she says. "I heard somebody ask this one detective at the station, 'Are you prejudiced?' He said, 'Not while I'm on duty.' "

"I know the type," he says. "I want to clear something else up. I got no problem with women partners. You've got good women cops and bad women cops. Same as men."

He coughs into his fist.

Winn points at him. "It's all that tobacco you been chewing."

"Naw. It's good for you."

He grabs a pinch and holds it out to her. "Here. Have some."

She holds her nose and shakes her head. "That's some vile shit."

He laughs and they head back to the office. Winn finishes up some paperwork and by early evening she is on the freeway heading home, fighting to keep her eyes open, after her first all-night shift in homicide.

During the next few days they attend Gonzales' autopsy and follow police technicians as they lift fingerprints off his friend's car. They visit the department's audio lab where sound experts enhance the quality of the tape. They return to the crime scene and talk to neighbors. They visit the two badly wounded victims, who just had surgery, at the hospital. The victims still have no idea why they were shot. The detectives still cannot identify any suspects.

The preliminary investigation report is due within three days of the murder, and Winn wakes up at 3:30 A.M. on Thursday and rushes into the office early so she will have more time to write. While Razanskas handwrites his reports, she brings a laptop computer and portable printer from home, plugs them in and does it the high tech way. She takes pride in her writing skills and spends much of the day hunched over her computer, writing and rewriting until she is satisfied. In the afternoon Razanskas reviews her report and has a few minor suggestions. She disagrees with one of them. He wants her to put a reference to the victim's property in the middle of the sentence. She has it at the end of the sentence.

"The way you want it sounds awkward as hell," she says.

"Well, that's just the way we do it around here."

"I've written plenty of reports before at bunco forgery, and I don't think it sounds right."

"Sure it sounds right."

"Look," she says, becoming angry. "When you do *your* report, do it any way you want. When I write *my* report, I'll do the way I want."

He stares at the ceiling for a moment and extends his palms, a mock, exaggerated gesture. "Goddamn it. You're fighting me already."

"I'm not fighting you," she says. "I spent a lot of time on my report. I want it to read right."

"Ah, why don't you go back to bunco forgery," he says, smiling. He shouts to a detective sitting behind Winn, "Hey, Carlos. She won't listen to me. Choke her out."

On the whole, Razanskas decides, the report is pretty damn good. One minor point is not worth arguing about.

On Thursday afternoon, as the momentum of the investigation begins to stall, Razanskas decides to ask John Jones, the apartment building manager, to come into the station for an interview. Razanskas wants him to fill out a witness statement form and sign it. But more important, he tells Winn, he wants to get Jones in an interview room, away from the distractions of home. Razanskas decides to conduct the interview in order to show Winn how to handle a witness.

Jones appears tense when he enters the small, windowless interview room, so Razanskas asks him how long it took for police to arrive at the scene—a softball question to loosen him up. Jones says they responded immediately.

Razanskas smiles and quips, "They must have run out of donuts." Jones laughs. They chat for a few minutes, and when Razanskas feels Jones is relaxed, he steers the conversation back to the night of the killing.

Jones gives a few more details about the gunmen. One of them, Jones says, was about six feet tall, had a dark complexion and wore a blue stocking cap and a long dark coat that reached his knees. The other one was wearing a gray coat and was a few inches shorter, with a shaved head. Razanskas brings Jones a cup of coffee. He takes a sip, sets the cup on a table and places his palms on his knees, his four gold rings gleaming under the fluorescent lights. He studies his rings and says softly, "You should look into whether one of the suspects got shot."

"Why?" Razanskas asks.

"Just a hunch."

Razanskas and Winn look puzzled. Then they suddenly realize that the shots from the third gun on the tape were not fired *by* the suspects, but were fired *at* the suspects. Now they know why the Cadillac took a bullet through the windshield.

"You know," Razanskas tells Jones, "we have no problem with this guy firing a few shots."

"What if he's an ex-felon with a gun?" Jones asks.

"We still have no problem." Razanskas leans forward and says earnestly, "I'm going to be up front with you. I look at this guy as a fucking hero. I'd like to give him a medal. Let's just call him an 'unknown citizen.' We'll leave it at that."

Jones stares into his coffee cup. He tells Razanskas he trusts him. He knows the hooker Razanskas talked to the night of the murder. He talked to her yesterday, and she told him, "Raz is straight."

"All right," Jones says. "The unknown citizen," he says, smiling, amused at the phrase, "capped off six rounds."

The unknown citizen fired the shots as the suspects ran down the street toward the alley, Jones says. One shot hit the suspect wearing the long coat in the leg. He began limping and the others helped him escape down the alley.

Razanskas and Winn quickly try to figure out who the unknown citizen was. Maybe the unknown citizen knew the victim and decided to mete out some street justice after he saw what happened. Maybe the unknown citizen was a neighbor who wanted to scare the suspects off. Or maybe the unknown citizen was Jones, and maybe he fired at the suspects after they had fired at him.

Winn and Razanskas do not want to push too hard to determine who the unknown citizen was. They have a good witness, a rare commodity these days at South Bureau Homicide. They do not want to do anything to scare him off.

Jones signs his statement sheet, shakes hands with Razanskas and Winn and says, "This is the first civil conversation I've had with a cop in thirty years." The moment he leaves, Razanskas sends out a bulletin to all area hospitals.

A Latino gang member, whom Razanskas has been trying to reach for weeks, shows up unexpectedly at the bureau. He is wearing yellow pants about six sizes too big and has tattoos on his elbows, arms and neck. His homeboy was shot on the street in a walk-by and Razanskas has been trying to get some leads. First Razanskas assumed a rival gang member was the shooter.

But then he figured it could have been an in-house hit because he was told by a snitch that the victim was sneaking around with another gang member's girlfriend.

This makes sense to Razanskas. The victim was punched in the face twice before he was shot, which is unusual in a gang murder. Razanskas wants to see if he can nail this theory down. Razanskas tries to persuade the gang member to talk by flattering him.

"Look, you're a *veterano*. These peewees respect you. You can find out what went down."

"I don't want no snitch jacket," the veterano says.

"Hey, he's your homie," Razanskas says "If it was you who was hit, wouldn't he be trying to find your killer?"

They banter for a while, until the veterano eventually tells Razanskas that Crazy and Sleepy might know something.

"What's this, Disneyland?" Razanskas quips. "You giving me some of the Seven Dwarfs?"

The veterano scowls for a moment, but when he sees that Razanskas is smiling, he realizes the detective was joking, not dissing him. He smiles too. "Is it possible," Raz asks, "that a jealous homie was the shooter?" The veterano won't answer his question directly. But he lets Razanskas know he is on the right track when he leans back in his chair, crosses his arms and says, "Love is a motherfucker."

Razanskas laughs and pounds a fist on the table. He loves the line. It perfectly encapsulates the murder and a few others he has handled. And for a man who has been married three times, the line has real resonance. He repeats it often during the afternoon. It becomes part of the Raz repertoire.

It is Friday afternoon, the end of a long week, and Razanskas and Winn are in the lobby of Martin Luther King, Jr./Drew Medical Center. They are interviewing a security officer for the hospital who responded to their bulletin.

Yesterday, the officer tells them, four young men pulled up in front of the hospital. One, whose leg was heavily wrapped, limped out and was helped by a friend. The officer approached him and asked what happened. He said he had injured his leg. But when the receiving nurse began to question him about the wound, the man hurried out the door and rode off with his friends. Officers could not detain them or get a license plate number because they had to respond to a fight that broke out in another part of the hospital.

He describes the wounded man as black, approximately six feet tall and wearing a long, dark-colored coat and a stocking cap.

"Damn!" Winn says.

His friend who was helping him was a few inches shorter. Both looked like teenagers.

The detectives head back to the office, frustrated that they just missed the suspects by a day. But they figure if one of them has a festering bullet wound he will show up somewhere else for treatment. When he does, they hope that this time the hospital will be ready for him. All they can now do is wait.

A few weeks after the murder, there is still no sign of the suspects and the trail has grown faint. Winn interviews witnesses again. She revisits the crime scene. She cruises Figueroa, talking to hookers, hoping one of them might have heard or seen something.

Razanskas works the Gonzales murder with Winn, but, at the same time, he is chasing leads on several old cases: the murder of an Ecuadorian travel agent; the murder of an 11-year-old boy killed during a carjacking; the murder of a Guatemalan immigrant killed during a carjacking; a double-murder after a dope-house rip-off and another double-murder committed by a gang member after a street argument. He also is bedeviled by a mountain of paperwork.

Every morning, Winn pores over the case at her desk and mutters to herself, "I hope this trail hasn't gone cold." Then everything changes one morning when she picks up an enormous break, that one golden phone call every detective prays for. A snitch calls the bureau and asks which detective is working the March 27 killing at 49th and Fig. Winn picks up the line.

"You know that Mexican guy who got killed at 49th and Fig?" the snitch asks. "Baby Day Day, a Five-Deuce Hoover Crip, and some of his partners made the move at 49th and Fig. Everything went wrong."

She asks him if he knew the names of Baby Day Day's partners.

"Just find Baby Day Day," he says and hangs up.

"Yessss!" she shouts, clenching a fist.

She checks the department's computerized moniker file. She finds a Baby Day Day, a Five-Deuce currently in county jail. But she is worried. If he had been arrested before March 27, he could not have been involved in the Gonzales killing. She checks the arrest date and is elated—he was arrested April 20. He and two partners were picked up for a carjacking.

Winn and Razanskas drive over to see John Jones, the apartment manager. "Five-Deuce Hoover Crips," Winn says with disgust, as they pull up in front of Jones's apartment. "Shit. You know what Crip stands for? Cowards Run In Packs."

She shows Jones several "six-packs"—sheets containing six photographs, one of whom is a suspect. He cannot identify Baby Day Day. But he quickly identifies the other two carjacking suspects. One, known as Little Day Day, is 19; the other is 18. They are from another set of Hoover Crips. But some of the Hoover Crip sets hang together, Winn learns, so they could have been working together. Winn shows six-packs to the security officer at hospital. He too picks out Little Day Day. Now the case is rolling; everything is falling into place. All Winn needs now is to show the photographs to the two wounded men who had been in the car with Gonzales.

A case is considered cleared when the district attorney files murder charges and a suspect is in custody. Winn does not want to go to the D.A. without at least one of the two wounded witnesses who had been in the car with the victim. But Winn runs into a problem. They have disappeared. They left the hospital and moved out of their house. Their former roommates do not know where they are. They left no forwarding address with the post office or the hospital. She hopes they did not return to Mexico.

Winn spends much of her spring trying to finish off the Gonzales case and learn more about homicide by studying the crime scenes at Razanskas' new cases and tracking the investigations with him. In mid-May, she takes advantage of the calm before the summer storm and plans a month-long vacation in Texas, where she will visit relatives.

Razanskas and Winn walk to the station parking lot after work on the Friday before she leaves for vacation. He tells Winn that working on one case for so long is a luxury. Next month the pace will pick up like a runaway train. Because for a homicide detective, Razanskas says, spitting a stream of Skoal on the curb, summer in South-Central is a bitch.

CHAPTER 2
FAR, FAR AWAY

MONDAY, JUNE 13

Winn returns from vacation and is disappointed to learn there still is no word on her two wounded witnesses. Razanskas gives her an update on the new cases he picked up while she was gone and the progress he has made on his old ones.

She is on call this week, ready for her second homicide. This time she does not wait long. After a few hours of sleep Monday night, she is awakened by the night supervisor who tells her she has a double-murder on Clovis Avenue, near 95th and Central. Even though she is half-asleep, she makes a point to jot down everything he tells her.

At dawn, Razanskas and Winn pull up in front of a rickety, four-unit apartment building—a long, narrow structure that looks as if it could house a bowling alley. The roof is flat and dips in spots, and the pipes atop the water heaters, which are outside each unit, are riddled with rust holes. The building is surrounded by a brown lawn strewn with splintered chairs, cardboard boxes and torn sofa cushions. The outside walls are a patchwork of several shades of yellow—repainted at different times, in different spots, to cover the gang graffiti. Across the street, covering a full city block, is an enormous power station. The conductors, insulators, transmission towers and iron scaffolding loom above the neighborhood like a skeletal cityscape.

Razanskas and Winn walk across the grass and study the side of the apartment building. The wall is peppered with dozens of rounds from a 9-millimeter pistol and an AK-47 assault rifle. There are more than fifty shell casings scattered on the grass and sidewalk. The two victims are inside.

Razanskas, who usually wakes up at 4:20 A.M., got the murder call this morning at 4:10 A.M. "What a rip-off," he quips, studying the shell casings. "I got cheated out of ten minutes sleep."

It is a cool, overcast morning, with high clouds and fog blowing in from the ocean. In some areas of the country, it already is hot by mid-June, with scorching summer weather. In Los Angeles, June often is misty and overcast. The real inauguration of summer, the first stretch of mornings without a hint of mist—hot, sunny summer mornings—may not arrive until July.

As Winn and Razanskas survey the crime scene, the weak, gray light softens the edges of a bleak neighborhood. The only respite from the grim surroundings is the two lush jacaranda trees along the side of the building. They are in full bloom and their brilliant lavender flowers glow against the fog like neon.

Winn, who is the primary investigator on this case, learned well from her last homicide, Razanskas thinks as he watches her confidently take control of the investigation, question the uniformed officers and diagram the area. This time Razanskas just watches her work and occasionally offers suggestions.

They enter the apartment and notice that everything is covered with a fine white dust. The AK-47 rounds penetrated the walls of the apartment and crumbled the plaster inside. Winn discovers in the hallway a path of tiny footprints in the white dust, a woman's footprints. They take a quick look inside, and Razanskas decides to call in the Scientific Investigation Division. There is a lot of potential evidence and he does not want to disturb any of it. While SID technicians search for fingerprints, fibers and blood samples, the two detectives study shell casings outside and interview neighbors.

When SID finishes, Winn and Razanskas enter the apartment. The carpeting is stained, the linoleum floor chipped and the furniture worn. On a folding table in the bedroom, piles of rock cocaine and stacks of plastic baggies tell part of the story. The apartment is a rock house, so the detectives figure the shooting could have been a rip-off gone wrong or the extirpation of business rivals.

A fusillade of bullets shattered the apartment's interior. The walls are dappled with holes and a television set is splintered by rounds. One victim, with a .38 snub nose in his front pocket, is slumped in an overstuffed easy chair. His chin has been shot off. The other victim is sprawled on a red sofa, with a .44 semiautomatic beneath the cushion. He has a bullet hole in his chest above a tattoo: "SCORPIO."

Both victims are middle-aged, with hair flecked with gray. This mystifies the detectives; they are older than the usual rock house entrepreneurs. After interviewing neighbors and a few street people, they are able to piece together a rough scenario. This was the rock house of an enterprising 15-year-old gang member called Li'l Sambo. He employed his uncle and his uncle's friend to run it when he was indisposed. Sambo was a Front Street Crip, and a rival gang did not like the competition. So they decided to punctuate their displeasure with a few blasts of an AK-47. Sambo and a female basehead—who had left the footprints—were in the house at the time and escaped unharmed. The basehead disappeared down an alley. Sambo hopped on his motor scooter and sped off.

On the first day of summer, June 21, the summer solstice, the longest day of the year, Winn is pounding away on her computer when Li'l Sambo and his parents show up for an interview. One of the men killed at the rock house was Sambo's uncle—his mother's brother.

Sambo is a big hulking kid, who looks older than 15. If he had grown up in South-Central in another era, he might have been a promising linebacker with a shot at a college scholarship. But a scholarship today is chump change for a kid with his own rock house. Sambo is wearing the standard gang outfit: oversized pants and baggy white T-shirt.

The detectives, Sambo and his parents crowd into an interview room, a small windowless cubicle lined with white insulation panels. Sambo's mother, who is squeezed into a tight tan jump suit and wearing a leather cap, glares at the detectives. Before Winn can ask a question, the mother pulls a tape recorder out of her purse and says, in a testy tone, "I'm taping this. Do you *mind?*"

Winn shrugs. She asks Sambo, "You familiar with the place where your uncle was killed?" Razanskas sits in silence in the corner of the interview room. He wants to give Winn the chance to conduct the interview on her own.

"I was there once to visit my Uncle Larry. He helped me with my homework," Sambo says, wide-eyed and earnest.

"What kind of homework?"

"Oh, biology and history. I was studying for my finals."

Winn shakes her head. She knows he was absent from school for 44 straight days. "What happened the day your uncle was killed?"

"I don't even be down there then."

Winn knows he is lying because she has talked to witnesses who have placed him at the scene. She also knows this is not the first time he was shot at. A month before the double-murder, Sambo was shot in the leg during a drive-by.

Winn puts down her notebook and pen and sighs heavily. "Let me be straight with you. This is a murder investigation. I don't care about any rock house or any cocaine. All I'm interested in is who shot your uncle. So I don't need you telling me you only been there once. I know you were there the day of the murders. I know what's what. So let me ask you again, what do you know about that shooting?"

"Nothin'."

"OK," Winn says with resignation. "Do they call you Li'l Sambo?"

"No."

"Look, I ran your arrest warrants and you come up in the system as Li'l Sambo. So what you telling me?"

Sambo does not respond.

"I think you need a memory pill," Winn says. "Look, I'm trying to do you a favor. Two different times people have tried to kill you. Your luck may run out the third time." She wags a forefinger at him. "You know what I'm saying?"

For the first time, Sambo seems to pay attention to Winn. He puts his head in his hands and moans softly, "Oh, God." He has his own rock house and has escaped two assassination attempts. It is easy to forget he is only a 15-year-old boy with acne.

Winn turns to the mother. "I'm trying to find out who tried to kill your son. I'm trying to find out who killed your brother. But for me to do that, I need some cooperation."

The mother stares at her, unmoved.

"I get the feeling, we're the only ones who care about your uncle," Winn says to Sambo, "If someone did my uncle, I'd be singing like a jaybird. You'd have to *shut* me up."

Sambo shakes his head and says, "I don't know nothin'."

Winn asks if she can speak to the parents alone. They send Sambo out of the room.

"Look, your son was operating a rock house," Winn says. "He wasn't doing any homework in that room. It was filled with baggies and rocks ready to be rocked up. Witnesses put your son at the scene right at the time of the shooting. I think he knows who is after him. I'm not asking your son to testify. I just want him to give me a few names. I'll do the rest."

The mother turns off the tape recorder. She is worried now.

Winn shows her pictures of the crime scene. "Are all those holes in the wall bullet holes?" the mother asks.

Winn nods.

"Will he be going to court for drugs?"

"I'm not interested in that."

The father, who put on a pair of slacks for the interview, but still is wearing his heavy work boots, says, "He's under a lot of pressure right now. After the funeral, we'll definitely get back to you. Believe me, we'll get back to you," he says with great concern. "We don't want him to snow you."

Back in the squad room, after Winn walks the parents out, Razanskas grins and says, "I'll *bet* he was at the rock house doing his homework. The homework was like, 'I sell three rocks for five dollars each. Then I sell four rocks for seven dollars each. How much more did I make in the second transaction?' "

Winn shakes her head. "Missing forty-four days of school. You couldn't get away with that shit in *my* family."

"If that was my kid," he says, "and he knew who killed my brother, I'd be doing a tap dance on the little fucker's head."

"I couldn't believe it when she pulled out that tape recorder," Winn says. "She's acting like *we're* the enemy. It was *her* brother that was killed. All we're trying to do is solve his murder. She sits there nodding as her son feeds me a line of bullshit. She must think I'm Sally Blankhead."

"Mama is covering her boy like a blanket," he says.

"Yeah. She come struttin' in here in that tight outfit, buttons popping, with that leather hat on her nappy ol' head. She thinks she lookin' *good.* She's acting like she's Miss *It.* Damn. That bitch was born and raised in the ghetto. She never been west of Central Avenue."

Winn is angry now. The woman's son has been shot at twice. He is lucky to be alive. Winn cannot believe the woman will not cooperate. She realizes that, in the end, she and Razanskas are all alone on this one. They are the only ones who seem to care.

Winn is getting a taste of homicide case-juggling. She is trying to find the two wounded witnesses in the Gonzales killing. And she is scrambling to find the basehead with the small feet who was with Sambo when the shooting started.

Winn had a successful stint as a detective trainee in bunco forgery, but as the other homicide detectives like to remind her, a real estate swindle is not a murder and bunco forgery is not homicide. In other words, murder is the ultimate crime. And no matter how successful you've been, you ain't shit until you've cleared a few murders.

Winn has two cases to juggle, but Razanskas has dozens. At South Bureau Homicide, the longer you have been there, the more onerous your workload. Razanskas already is falling behind and the crush of summer—when there are more than 100 murders in South Bureau alone—has not even hit yet. He is hoping for a slow June. He wants to catch up on his old investigations so he can put extra effort into his new ones. He wants to prove to his supervisors that he is not burned out.

The book on Razanskas, his supervisors say, is he will hit the investigation hard in the beginning. If he has some live leads, he is unrelenting until the case is cleared. But if the leads fade, or there is not much to begin with, he will not show the tenacity and doggedness of a younger, more gung-ho detective.

Razanskas contends he simply has more work, more responsibility and less time than younger detectives. He has so many old cases, cases that resurface and demand attention, that he can barely devote enough time to the new ones. In addition to his own heavy caseload, he also supervises the work of Winn and two other detectives.

He still works long hours and logs a lot of overtime. But unlike the old days, he will not automatically place his work before his family. Even though he is behind on his paperwork and it is only June, he will not take reports home with him on weekends. He will not work late every night. His first two marriages failed, he believes, because of the demands of the job. He does not want to screw up the third one. And Razanskas, who already has high blood pressure, does not want to destroy his health. Last year he was rushed to the hospital from the police shooting range with dizziness and disorientation. He thought he was having a heart attack. Although the symptoms disappeared, his wife began pushing him to retire so they can leave California and move to Colorado. She is a nurse who knows what it is like to work a demanding job with maddening hours. But, she says, enough is enough.

Razanskas is not ready to retire. He still loves the unpredictability and variety of homicide cases. And for a flamboyant personality who enjoys being the center of attention, the power and cachet of being a homicide detective are highly satisfying. He will not work a detective table—chasing burglars, muggers and car thieves—at a neighborhood station.

Sometimes, in one of his rare philosophical moods, Razanskas, who has two grown daughters, will talk about all the sacrifices he made as a young cop, all the times he chased leads instead of staying home with his wife and children. He will shake his head and mutter, "This department will use you up like a number-two pencil."

Winn and Razanskas decide to drive over to 49th and Figueroa and study the Gonzales murder scene again. He tells her to take Hoover to 49th and then east to Figueroa. She ignores him and takes another route.

"Hey, you're not taking Hoover," he says.

"That's right," she says. "When I drive, I go my own way."

He flips on the radio and, as usual, turns to a country and western station.

"And I'm sick of listening to that shit-kicking music every day," she says. "When I drive, I should get to pick the station. When you drive, you can listen to that twangy shit all you want."

Razanskas grabs a pinch of Skoal and spits into his cup. She is so adamant and her expression so determined he does not feel like challenging her.

Winn makes it a point to assert herself around Razanskas and the other detectives in the bureau, even on minor issues. She knows that to make it in South Bureau Homicide, detectives have to stand up to their suspects, their witnesses and, sometimes, their partners. South Bureau is a macho environment where detectives ride each other constantly. If you cannot take the scrutiny and the pressure, if you are too timid to speak your mind, you will not last long in South Bureau.

Winn flips the dial to a call-in show that features a female psychologist.

They listen to a call from a woman whose boyfriend has cheated on her a few times but now promises to be faithful. She wants to know if she can trust him.

Razanskas grabs a crime report from the back seat, reads it and pretends to ignore the program.

But Winn is engrossed and shouts at the radio, "I don't think so. Girl, how can you trust that chump?"

"Do you think he'll cheat on me again?" the caller asks.

"What do *you* think, fool?" Winn says.

The caller tells the psychologist that there is another problem with her boyfriend. He has impregnated another woman.

Now Razanskas, who pretended he wasn't listening, pipes in, "I can't believe the bullshit some women fall for."

"Do you think I should marry him?" the woman asks.

"Dump that motherfucker," Winn shouts. "He's *never* going to stop cheating on you. Get a clue, girl."

On Friday, during the first week of summer, as Winn is finishing up a follow-up report on her double-murder, one of the wounded witnesses to the Gonzales killing finally calls the bureau. She is more relieved than elated. She did not want to even contemplate the consequences of losing two key witnesses on her first homicide. They had moved after the killing because they were afraid of staying in South-Central. They now share a small apartment with a few friends near MacArthur Park, a neighborhood populated mostly by Central American refugees. As the detectives drive over to the apartment, Razanskas tells Winn to always watch witnesses' eyes when they look through the photos in the six-packs. Even witnesses who lie to detectives and tell them they cannot identify anyone, will always stare, for a second or two, at a photograph they recognize.

The two surviving victims let the detectives into their apartment, which they share with a number of other Mexican men who are sending money home to their families. The bedroom is lined with cots, and the only furniture in the living room is a sofa and a television set on a cardboard box. Neither of the victims speaks English, so Razanskas explains the six-pack system in Spanish.

One victim, a shy 17-year-old boy, was wounded in both legs. He has not been able to return to his job as a bicycle messenger. Razanskas shows him a sheaf of six-packs. But the victim says too much happened too quickly. He cannot identify either suspect.

The other victim, who is 19, was shot in the chest, ankle and groin. He has returned to work at the stereo manufacturing company where Gonzales also had worked. But because of the injuries he often is in pain. He once was one of the best workers at the company, he says. Now he works slowly and is afraid of losing his job. Razanskas hands him a few six-packs, but he cannot identify the first suspect. Razanskas hands him another one and the victim immediately points to picture number one—the upper left-hand corner. Little Day Day.

Winn grins. "That's the third ID on the little bastard," she says. The chase is coming to a close and she is excited. Winn would have liked both victims to ID all the suspects, but she believes she has enough. The apartment building manager already identified two of the suspects. The officer at the hospital picked out one. And this victim identified the same one. Winn can now take her case to the district attorney.

The 19-year-old victim says he still is plagued by nightmares. Sometimes at work, while assembling stereos, he has flashbacks and sees the shooting all over again. Gonzales was like a big brother to him. They grew up together in Mexico, played on the same soccer team, Vagabundo, worked together at the stereo company. He cannot believe Gonzales' dream ended on a South-Central street corner.

In a gray cinder-block house, at the edge of a hillside barrio about 45 minutes north of downtown Mexico City, Gonzales' mother and father talk about their son. Felipe senior is about five feet tall with a broad, impassive face. His wife, Soccoro, a tiny plump woman, barely four and a half feet tall, is wearing a flowered house dress and an apron. She is a Mixtec Indian with long gray hair that reaches the small of her back. She sits on a small wooden stool and tightly grips a white handkerchief in both hands, frequently pausing to dry her eyes.

Their house is at the outer edges of the Mexico City sprawl, a neighborhood for the working poor set in the smoggy foothills above the city. The narrow cobbled streets have the feel of a rural pueblo. Horses pull loads of lumber; chickens squawk in sidewalk cages; dogs snooze on corrugated metal roofs. The Gonzales family lives in a small house with uncovered cement floors and an open-air kitchen. Each room, separated by frayed cloth curtains, contains small shrines filled with crosses and pictures of saints. The house is immaculate.

Felipe was the oldest of six children, an industrious little boy who began selling newspapers when he was 6 years old to help the family buy food. He dropped out of school at 13 and began washing cars. At 16 he began driving a taxi, working 10 to 12 hours a day, six days a week. He earned the equivalent of $10 a day, but he had to pay half to the taxi company he worked for. He married young and had four daughters before he was 25. He loved his little girls, his mother says, but there were problems with the marriage. They decided to separate. His wife moved in with her sister and he moved back with his parents, a few blocks away. But Felipe was miserable at home. He missed his daughters and was frustrated he could not do more for them.

After about a month at home, he told his parents he wanted to move to Los Angeles. He could make more money and better support his daughters, and when he returned to Mexico he could buy his own home and his own taxi. His parents did not want him to leave. Los Angeles, they told him, was too far away and too dangerous. He argued that they had left their homes when they were young and moved to Mexico City in search of a better life.

Felipe senior is from a village in the state of Tlaxcala. When he was 6 years old, he began planting corn and harvesting cactus leaves with a machete. The agriculture was primitive and the crops were at the mercy of the seasons. There was no irrigation; the corn and wheat plants were watered when it rained. He left the poverty of his pueblo at 13 and took the train to Mexico City. After selling newspapers on buses and street corners, he opened his own newsstand. He later began driving a taxi and saved enough to buy a modest house.

Soccoro is from a tiny tropical village, between the mountains and the sea, in the state of Oaxaca. Her parents could not feed their 11 children, so when she was 12 years old she took a bus to Mexico City, moved in with an aunt and found work as a maid. Every day, on her way to the market, she passed Felipe's newsstand. They soon began chatting. Within a year they married.

Since their son wanted to migrate to Los Angeles for the same reasons they moved to Mexico City, they decided they could not withhold their blessings. Soccoro told him she did not want him to leave, but she understood why he had to go. She told him to better himself and work hard on behalf of his daughters.

In late October, along with his 21-year-old brother, Gerardo, and two friends, he prepared to leave for Tijuana. Felipe carried only a small nylon backpack, a change of clothes and pictures of his daughters. A few hours before he left, he visited his daughters for the last time. He told them, "I will be gone for a while. But even though I will be away, I want you to study hard and behave yourselves." He told them he loved them. He said good-by, began crying and hurried out the door.

Before they boarded the bus that night, his mother handed her two sons a sack of sandwiches and a jug of lemonade. She kissed Felipe and Gerardo, prayed, and whispered, "*Que Dios te acompane.*" (May God be with you.)

They arrived in Tijuana 48 hours later and took a city bus to the border. They waited at dusk with a handful of other *pollos* (chickens) on a plateau overlooking the border. At nightfall, they scurried down the plateau and ran along the base of a rocky canyon. But before they could make it out, they were nabbed by *la migra,* border patrol guards, whose dogs had picked up their trail. They were taken to a holding cell, booked and fingerprinted. Three hours later they were bused back to the border, with a group of others *pollos,* and dropped off at the San Ysidro port of entry.

They hung around Tijuana for a few days and eventually found an experienced guide, a *coyote* from Sinaloa who wore cowboy boots and Western shirts with pearl buttons. He demanded $200 from each of them. They told him if he could get them to a house in South-Central, their friends would pay the money. The *coyote* had shepherded hundreds of *pollos* across the border and he knew precisely where to cross. That afternoon he led them on a long walk, parallel to the border, until they reached an area of steep, brush-covered slopes. It was hot and dry and their throats were caked with dust. Finally, they stopped at a thick clump of bushes and hid.

The *coyote* waited until midafternoon, when the border patrol changed shifts. He motioned for them to follow and he led them on a serpentine trail over rugged terrain. They scrambled over jagged rocks, through mesquite, past cactus and scraggly oaks. They traversed shallow canyons and low hills thick with thorn bushes. Twice the *coyote* spotted *la migra* in the distance, and they hid behind enormous water pipes. When they reached Interstate 5, a highway on the American side of the border, Felipe turned to his friends and said, "*Ya la hicimos.*" (We finally made it.)

They followed the *coyote* to a small house just over the border and waited until night. The *coyote* called the house in South-Central to make sure Gonzales' friends had the money. He then herded them into the cab of a Nissan truck and headed north. He slipped past the border patrol checkpoint by exiting the freeway and taking the side roads. When they arrived in South-Central, their friends gave the *coyote* $800, and he headed back to the border.

It took Gonzales two months to find his job at the stereo manufacturing company. He made $195 a week, and his first few paychecks went to pay off the $200 his friends gave the *coyote* and the back rent and money for food he had borrowed. He soon began sending about $300 to his mother every month. He wanted her to make sure his daughters had everything they needed. His schedule revolved around work, night school where he was learning to speak English and the swap meet on weekends.

A few weeks before his death, his *patron* (his boss) went on a brief vacation and closed up shop. Gonzales and a co-worker spent their mornings at the beach. He was giddy with excitement, suddenly freed from the routine of gluing fabric on speaker boxes all day. Every morning he swam in the surf and played soccer on the sand with his friend. In the afternoon he liked to visit the observatory at Griffith Park and study the stars. This was his time for dreaming, dreaming about what kind of house he would buy in Mexico City, dreaming about being with his daughters again.

On his birthday, a Thursday night three days before his death, he called home. After chatting with his brothers and sisters, he told his mother he would call again on Monday. He wanted to send her a money order for $400, and he planned to call with the details. On Monday night, Gerardo called home instead. He told his parents that Felipe was dead. A few days later, Gerardo returned to Mexico with his brother's body.

A few blocks away from the Gonzales' home, Felipe's wife, Griselda, and their four daughters, are visiting her sister. Griselda recently has moved to a small city in the state of Michoacan. Her uncle is the mayor and he found her a job as a filing clerk so she could support her daughters. The four little girls, ranging in ages from 4 to 8, each have pony tails tied with pink ribbons and are wearing matching pink and white party dresses with lace collars. The two youngest still do not know their father is dead. Griselda just told them that he is "far, far away." The two oldest daughters still cry almost every night.

In the late afternoon, Gonzales' parents visit their son's grave. He is buried at "Cementiero Los Cipreses" (Cemetery of the Cypress Trees), a lush expanse of lawn high above the city. Gonzales' grave is on a shady plot framed by towering eucalyptus and cypress trees. His parents, who spent all their savings to bury their son, buy a dozen red carnations and a half dozen white dahlias. Soccoro, who is still wearing her apron, sits beside the grave and carefully removes the flowers from the wrapping. Her husband fills a plastic vase with water and she arranges the flowers in the vase.

It is cool and serene at the cemetery, a respite from the heat and clamor of the city. The only sounds are the wind rustling through the eucalyptus leaves. When she finishes arranging the flowers, she puts her head in her hands and sobs. Her husband, tears streaming down his face, comforts her. They then kneel and pray.

After about ten minutes, she leans over and kisses the flat marble gravestone, with an engraved cross, that reads:

Felipe Angeles Gonzales
1965–1994

CHAPTER 3
A DYING DECLARATION

MONDAY, JUNE 27

At 9 A.M., Winn drives downtown and presents the Felipe Gonzales case to a deputy district attorney. After she sums up the investigation he says, "For kids so young, these are two bad little bastards." He agrees to file murder charges. This is an auspicious beginning for Winn. She has cleared her first case.

She is elated, but her enthusiasm is soon tempered. She thinks about the victim's daughters and his brother. Gerardo is the first person she attempts to contact. She wants him to know that someone cared about his brother's death, that justice was done. But she cannot locate him and learns later that he has moved back to Mexico.

Winn does not have long to savor her first success in homicide. She was able to compile a strong enough case to satisfy a deputy district attorney. But now she needs to buttress her case further, in preparation for the preliminary hearing, when a judge will determine if there is enough evidence to hold the suspects over for trial.

Winn must arrange live lineups of the suspects, because lineups hold more weight than photo IDs. She needs to tie up various loose ends so she will be prepared to be cross-examined in court. It is too late to interview the suspects because they already have public defenders from the carjacking case. They won't be saying much. But the apartment building manager had said that an "unknown citizen" wounded one suspect as he was escaping. So Winn and Razanskas want to examine the suspects in jail and see if they can spot any recent bullet wounds.

The detectives and a police photographer by the name of Berkowitz—whom Razanskas calls "Son of Sam"—meet at the "super max" facility where many murder suspects are held. Set in the yellow, desiccated hills about 20 miles north of downtown, it looks more like a high-tech prison than the typical dank, dim county jail.

Winn wants to know what these suspects look like. What kind of person blasts a car full of immigrants because they do not move fast enough when robbed. What kind of person shoots a man in the back as he is running away? It is still unclear which suspect actually shot Felipe Gonzales in the back. But with California's "felony murder rule," it does not matter who was the triggerman. If a murder occurs during the commission of a felony—and in this case it was a robbery—everyone involved in the felony is culpable for the murder.

What Winn has determined, from the scenario she pieced together from witnesses, is that Little Day Day is suspected of shooting into the car. Witnesses said the other suspect grabbed Gonzales on the sidewalk, whacked him in the face with a pistol—to intimidate him before the robbery—and, while fleeing, shot at the apartment building manager.

The guards bring Little Day Day into the interview room . He is baby-faced, has a wispy mustache and a wide-eyed smile. He is cooperative and friendly with the detectives. When he strips to his shorts, Winn leaves the room and he chats with Razanskas. He has the tattoo "Smile Now, Cry Later," on his forearm; "Pamela" (his mother) on his other arm; behind one bicep he has a "9" and the other bicep a "2" (Nine-Deuce Hoover Crips); "Day Day 2" is tattooed on an arm just above the elbow.

He has a round scar the size of a nickel below his right knee. Razanskas asks him how he got the scar.

"A guy bit me."

"I hope you kicked the snot out of him."

Little Day Day laughs and says, "I tried."

Razanskas takes a closer look at the scar. He shakes his head. It does not look like a gunshot wound.

Little Day Day dresses, sighs heavily and a guard escorts him back to his cell. He has been in trouble before. But this, he thinks, is some serious shit. How did he end up like this, facing a murder beef, locked down in "super max," standing in his shorts while a homicide cop looks for bullet holes.

Little Day Day, whose real name is Obie Steven Anthony III, was born in St. Louis. His mother and father split up a few years later. His father, a barber who never married Anthony's mother, moved to Memphis. His mother met a man in St. Louis, married him and they had three daughters. When Obie was 7, the family moved to Los Angeles.

Obie has fond memories of these years, the only time in his life when he felt secure and part of a family. The family rented a three-bedroom home, and his mother stayed home with the children. Anthony's stepfather, who had a well-paying job at an aircraft plant, was a good father to the four children. He was from the Midwest, and the ocean was a novelty, so he spent many weekends at the beach with the kids.

Anthony was 9 when his stepfather died. After his funeral there was little money left, and Anthony's mother, who had four small children, went on welfare. When she lived in St. Louis, she had kicked a cocaine habit. In fact, one of the reasons she had moved to Los Angeles was to get away from her fast-living friends. But now it was the mid-1980s and crack cocaine was everywhere in South-Central. This drug was a lot different than the powdered cocaine she had snorted back in St. Louis. These rocks were cheaper, more readily available and much more addictive. She soon became hooked again.

She began spending time with a man she later married, a man the children hated. He, too, was a smoker and the two began spending days away from home, leaving her children to fend for themselves. Anthony was the youngest, and at 10 years old he often was on his own. Many days all he had to eat for breakfast, lunch and dinner was cereal and milk—and there was not always milk. Sometimes he was so hungry at night that he scrounged change from neighbors and ran over to the corner hamburger stand. But he and his sisters often would have to share an order of chili cheese fries because they did not have enough money for a hamburger.

The family was evicted from a series of apartments. One landlord kept all their belongings, even Anthony's most prized possessions—his football trophies from a neighborhood youth league. They soon were homeless. The kids slept in a succession of different houses—the living rooms and spare bedrooms of friends and neighbors. His mother often smoked away the welfare check. Anthony and his sisters had to move into a rusted camper shell that had been removed from the back of a truck and plunked in the backyard of a neighbor's house.

At 14, he joined the gang that hung around his 92nd Street neighborhood—the Nine-Deuce Hoover Crips. His mother was never around. His older sisters were busy with their boyfriends. His father was in St. Louis and had never once visited him in Los Angeles. His homies in the gang were the only ones who seemed to care about him, the only ones he felt he could count on. He soon picked up a long juvenile record and was in and out of youth facilities.

When he was 17, after he was released from a work camp, he returned home to find his mother a changed woman. She had quit smoking crack and began working. She was tormented about neglecting Anthony, she told him, and she wanted to make it up to him. Anthony told her he never had stopped loving her. He told her he knew she had always loved him, even when she was not around.

"She finally got right and she wanted me to straighten out too," Anthony recalls. "One day she said to me, 'Let's work on this together.' " He stares across the jail visiting cubicle and sighs. "We got really tight."

She asked him to stop hanging out with his Crip friends, and he told her he would try to change, try to make her proud of him. He and his girlfriend moved into an apartment. He attended continuation school to obtain his high-school diploma. He eventually enrolled in a professional school and studied to become a dental assistant, while working nights as a janitor at a hotel.

There was a side of Anthony that always surprised his teachers and co-workers. He had a personality that did not jive with his criminal record. When he enrolled at the continuation school, at the age of 18, he was reading at a fourth-grade level. He was bright enough, his teachers believed. But he had missed years of school and had never put in the effort to catch up.

His teachers at Central Adult High School remember Anthony well because he seemed so different from the other students, many of whom were gang members. He did not wear the baggy pants and other gang attire, but dressed neatly in slacks and loafers. His teachers were amused because he looked like a preppie. He was attentive and polite in class and truly seemed interested in learning. After he graduated, his English teacher, Geraldine Davis, was stunned when he took her out to lunch to thank her.

This was the happiest time of Anthony's life, working, going to school, spending time with his mother as they tried to make up for all the lost years. They went to the beach on weekends. They sat around her apartment drinking coffee and talking for hours. They smoked pot together occasionally, as she played her favorite album, "In the Mood" by the Whispers, and he turned her on to rap. But in January his mother developed a serious heart problem and he moved in with her and her husband so he could take care of her. In February she died. But right before her death, she told Anthony that she wanted him to move in with his father in St. Louis.

"The death really threw Obie off track," recalls his father, Obie Anthony, Sr. "He called me after his mother died and told me that he was not yet twenty and he felt deserted. He had no mama, no money, no nothin'. He didn't even have enough money to bury her. He wanted to come to St. Louis. I had to tell him I didn't have any room for him. You see, I have other kids and money is tight here.

"I wish I could have done it," he says softly. After a long pause he says, "You know, out of my three sons, he's the best one. The other two can be mean and might dig the gang scene. But Obie was always such a shy, sweet child. But I guess where he grew up it was a snake pit. And if you're in the snake pit, you're going to get bit."

Anthony slipped into a deep depression. He was 19 years old, his girlfriend had broken up with him and he felt he was all alone. He hated living with his stepfather, but he could not afford to rent his own apartment. His stepfather had smoked crack in the back room the day of his mother's funeral. A few weeks later his stepfather began bringing prostitutes into the house and smoking with them. Anthony could not move in with his father in St. Louis, and he was not getting along with his sisters. His mother, he felt, was all he had. Now that she was gone, he did not care about anything. He quit his job. He looked up his old gang friends. He began selling crack in front of a motel on 101st Street. And in April, two months after his mother died, he was arrested for carjacking and, later, charged with a murder.

The other suspect in the case, Reggie DeShawn Cole, is brought out to the interview room and he strips down to his shorts. Cole, unlike Anthony, does not have a long juvenile record nor any gang tattoos. He is just a skinny kid with acne on his shoulders who looks very frightened.

"What's this all about?" he asks Razanskas.

"It's about a murder."

Cole shakes his head and sighs. As Razanskas examines him, Cole begins talking rapidly, sounding extremely nervous. "I ain't done no murder. No way I done any murder. Why you come after me? You trying to do me. You trying to railroad me like you do."

Razanskas ignores him. He is too busy examining Cole's legs for scars.

"Bingo," Razanskas says. He spots a jagged scar on the side

of Cole's left shin. It looks to Razanskas like a gunshot wound. The photographer takes a few pictures of the scar.

Winn is waiting in a hallway, pacing. "Well?" she says, when she sees Razanskas. He gives her the thumbs-up sign and tells her about the scar.

"Yessss," she says excitedly. They head back to the city. Cole is sent back to his cell.

Cole has had a few brushes with the law, but he never has been in a jail like this before. He has a background far different from Anthony and many of the others in super max. He grew up on West 71st Street in a tan clapboard bungalow with a manicured lawn bordered by rose bushes. The street is lined with small, well-kept homes and shaded by palm and eucalyptus trees.

Anthony is from a South-Central where the hookers, gangbangers and drug dealers control the streets. Cole is from a South-Central, only a mile or two away, where residents are trying to keep these encroaching forces at bay. Cole's mother is a religious woman who made sure her children attended the nearby Concord Missionary Baptist Church every Sunday. His mother runs the church's nursery school. His older sister, a bus driver, is the choir director, and his younger sister, a college student, sang in the choir for years. His oldest brother, an equipment mechanic at a hospital, was a church usher. When Reggie was in junior high school, he too was an usher. His mother was strict, and when the children were young they knew better than to violate her cardinal rule: *Be inside the house when the street lights go on.*

Cole's stepfather, who worked at an aluminum factory, raised his wife's children as his own. He was a soul food cook of some renown in the neighborhood. Cole and his brothers and sisters looked forward to Sunday supper when his stepfather, who was from a small town in Louisiana, often made red beans and rice, neck bones, black-eyed peas and collard greens. He and Reggie's mother separated a few years ago.

The family moved to West 71st Street when Reggie, the youngest son, was 10. But John, the middle son, kept returning to the old neighborhood on 98th Street to hang with his friends. He soon was immersed in the gang life there. At the age of 15,

John was killed in a drive-by. After John's death, Reggie's mother became protective of her youngest son. Overprotective, Reggie thought. Reggie had been a good student in school and spent weekends involved in church activities. He had no juvenile record. But his last year in high school he began hanging out with some of John's friends from the old neighborhood. He dropped out of school and began "dressing down" in oversized clothes. At 18, he was arrested for the first time, for evading a police officer who was trying to pull him over. A few months later he was caught carrying a weapon.

After Reggie left high school, he worked occasionally for his brother-in-law, who owned a plumbing company. He moved into a shed behind his mother's house. His mother's neat, tidy living room is filled with photographs of her children and their basketball and baseball trophies. Two large Bibles flank the coffee table. Pictures of Jesus fill the house, and in the dining room there is a large framed prayer: "God Rest His Hand Upon My Door And Bless This Home Forevermore." On one wall there is a picture of Reggie, as a grinning schoolboy in a white T-shirt. Next to it is a high-school prom picture of Reggie, who is wearing a white tuxedo, and his date.

Behind the house, in front of the shed where Reggie lived when he was arrested, there are two large marijuana plants. Inside, the shed is messy, strewn with Reggie's shoes, jeans and socks. A high-school report card is under the bed. He earned almost all "Ds" and one "A"—in basketball. One of the walls is filled with gang graffiti from the neighborhood gang, the Seven-Four Hoover Crips, and a set from the old neighborhood, the Nine-Deuce Hoover Crips.

While Anthony has little contact with his family and has not had a visitor in months, Cole's family visits him in jail every weekend. Several times a week he calls home collect from jail. Pastor William Hemphill, who heads the Baptist church the family attends, has visited him in jail many times. A number of his parishioners' sons have been in trouble, and Hemphill is all too familiar with the consequences of gangs and drugs.

In suburban areas, gang members are some vague and terrifying force, but in South-Central they are omnipresent. They are the boys you grew up with, the boys you played ball with as a kid. In some South-Central neighborhoods if you want to hang out, you hang out with gang members. If you do not want to hang out with gang members, you stay inside. In the suburbs, a boy can go through a rebellious streak, hang around with the wrong crowd for a while and eventually straighten out with few lasting consequences. Not in South-Central.

Razanskas and Winn return to the squad room, after their trip to the jail, and begin arguing about a case that they picked up in early May, another dopehouse double-murder. He is the primary, but she worked the investigation with him.

They have identified a suspect by the name of Larry Charles Gary. Everyone in the neighborhood knows him by his middle name or by his street name, C-Loc. C for Charles, Loc for loco. Winn wants to arrest Charles immediately. Razanskas wants to wait, continue the investigation and try to obtain more evidence against him. He tells Winn he has set up an interview later in the afternoon with Charles' girlfriend, in the hopes that she can tie him to the murder.

"Forget the girlfriend," Winn says. "Let's nab this guy right now."

"I want to build a stronger case before I get a warrant," he says.

"You got a good motherfucking case now."

"You telling me what to do, woman?" he says, smiling. "Look, if we go out half-cocked, it'll come back to bite us in the ass when the case comes to trial."

"Leaving this guy on the streets don't fly with me. He's a time bomb. It's only a matter of time before he kills someone else."

"You want to get the guy off the street *now.* I want to convict the SOB and make sure he's put away *for good.* All we've got, at this point, is circumstantial evidence."

"It's good enough."

"I don't want any Teflon on the son of a bitch. I want this case to stick. You haven't seen a first-degree murder case fall apart in court. You haven't seen a killer walk. We're not talking about a little forgery here. We're talking about a murder."

She looks hurt and shakes her head.

"Anyway," he says, "the girlfriend's statement could be the icing on the cake."

"Probably be hearsay."

"It's important."

"Won't be admissible."

"We might be able to slide it in." He stands up, puts his hands on his hips and looks down at Winn. "Your personality is abrasive and caustic," he says, smiling to let her know he is not altogether serious.

Winn, who is about the same size as Razanskas, stands up and glares at him. "Coming from an asshole like you, I consider that the ultimate compliment."

He looks exasperated now. "Why are you so goddamn bitchy?"

"I'm not bitchy. I'm just standing my ground."

"Look, I'm the primary on this one. We're going to wait on him. And we're going to interview the girlfriend."

She returns to her desk, grumbling, and begins leafing through the crime report on her own dopehouse double-murder.

After working together for three months, Razanskas still has not established a comfortable rapport with Winn. He is accustomed to communicating with the young detectives he trains through humor and kidding and sarcasm, the thrust and parry of typical cop talk. But Winn is so touchy, Razanskas is reluctant to kid her and subject her to his usual jibes.

When Winn worked vice in the Southeast Division, she occasionally saw Razanskas wander through the station. He was boisterous and he would unmercifully razz the cops he knew and play practical jokes on them. When Winn joined South Bureau Homicide she decided she did not want to be kidded and embarrassed in front of the other homicide detectives. As a woman and as a trainee she felt this would undermine her authority, and the other detectives would not take her seriously. She decided to let

Razanskas know right away that she was not going to take it. And she decided she wanted to be treated like a partner, not a hireling. She was not going to play the role of the timorous trainee. If she had an opinion, she would state it. And she would not back down.

At this stage in their partnership there are a number of questions yet to be answered. Winn wonders whether she can ever learn to trust a good old boy who chews tobacco and listens to country music. And Razanskas wonders about her. He and his previous partner had guns pulled on them at crime scenes. They had to chase fleeing suspects down alleys late at night. Razanskas wants to know how Winn reacts under these pressures. He knows his life may depend on it.

Razanskas sifts through the paperwork on the Larry Charles Gary case and prepares for his interview with the girlfriend. The two victims in the case were murdered on a sunny May afternoon, in a small South-Central house surrounded by apartment buildings. A 68-year-old woman and her 34-year-old son were shot to death. The son had been selling marijuana from the house, and baggies and piles of pot were found in the living room. The killer got away, but he made one mistake. Both victims briefly survived the shooting—long enough to tell three neighbors that they were killed by a man named "Charles."

When a patrolman arrived, he briefly interviewed the 34-year-old victim before he died. The victim told the officer, "He asked for my money. I told him I didn't have any money and he started shooting. He ran out the back door. I ran out the back door after him and I collapsed." The victim identified the shooter as Charles. He told the officer he did not know his last name.

Another neighbor told the detectives that Charles had stopped by his apartment on the afternoon of the shooting. Charles sat on the couch and set his chrome .380 semiautomatic on a seat cushion. Five minutes after Charles left, the neighbor heard a series of shots. A friend rushed over and told him about the shooting. "I ran to help," the neighbor told Razanskas and Winn. "I saw Anthony had been shot. He was in the driveway. He said, 'Charles shot me. Charles shot me. Check my mother. Why did Charles have to shoot me?' "

A dying declaration is admissible in court, so the detectives caught a break. But no one in the neighborhood knew Charles' last name or where he lived.

After canvassing the neighborhood a second time, a day after the murder, Razanskas was able to pick up a few leads that enabled him to identify Charles. He gained the trust of a neighbor, who told him that Charles' girlfriend bought him an Oldsmobile Cutlass. Razanskas then convinced another neighbor to talk and learned that the girlfriend purchased the Cutlass at a used-car lot at 83rd and Figueroa. Razanskas sifted through all the paperwork at the lot and found a receipt for an Oldsmobile Cutlass. This led him to the girlfriend. He searched motor vehicle records and discovered that a male driver, Larry Charles Gary, picked up a traffic ticket while driving the Cutlass. The physical description of Charles fit the suspect in the shooting. Razanskas later learned the suspect was a 118th Street East Coast Crip and was known by his middle name.

The victims making the dying declaration did not give a last name. And Razanskas knows that a good defense attorney can raise a lot of reasonable doubt with a name as common as Charles. So Razanskas has been searching for other ways to tie Larry Charles Gary to the murder.

He still is hoping for the murder weapon. There was a mini-mart robbery a week after the murder and the suspect fit Charles' description. Since Charles is 6 foot 6, with arms covered with tattoos, he is easily identified. And the weapon used in the robbery, a chrome .380, fit the murder weapon. Because it appears that Charles did not dump the weapon right after the murder, Razanskas figures he still has it. If police can catch Charles with the weapon, Razanskas knows the case against him will be unassailable. Razanskas has an LAPD surveillance detail monitoring Charles' mother's and girlfriend's apartments. If they can catch him near one of the two apartments, Razanskas would have enough probable cause to get search warrants and check the two apartments for the gun. But Charles has not yet been spotted.

So, for now, Razanskas will interview the girlfriend. Maybe he can get something from her that will tie Charles to the murder. The girlfriend, a heavy young woman wearing turquoise stretch pants, shows up at the bureau with an attitude. She is surly and makes it clear she does not want to be interviewed. She has long pink fingernails and her dyed hair swirls atop her head like a honey-colored cumulus cloud.

Razanskas points to Winn and says, "She hates me. So I want to get along with you, so you don't hate me too."

Winn fixes Razanskas with a look of exaggerated boredom. "You got to care to hate someone. I don't care enough to hate you."

The girlfriend ignores both of them. She starts off the interview by either grunting to his questions or giving monosyllabic replies.

"Look," Razanskas says, "if you've been protecting this guy, knowing what he's been into, you could be in *big-time* trouble," he says. "We might have to get you into court. And not as a witness. As a *defendant.*" He lowers his chin and stares at her over his bifocals.

"You *know* what I'm saying?"

She is nervous now. She licks her lips.

"I'm not threatening you. That's just a fact of life."

"I understand," she says.

"OK. Let's start with his tattoos. Describe them."

She thinks for a moment. "On his chest he has '118th Street'—his gang. On one arm he has 'Pooky'—his mom's name. And on the other arm he has 'Fuck A Snake Bitch.' "

Razanskas removes his bifocals. Winn raises an eyebrow.

"Fuck a snake bitch?" Winn asks. "You're with a guy who's got that tattooed on his arm?" She shakes her head in wonderment. "Like my mama always said, 'What I don't understand would make a whole new world.' "

The girlfriend looks down, embarrassed. "He didn't act like the kind of person who'd have that kind of tattoo. When he was around me he was a totally different person. He treated me very well."

"What did he do for a living?" Razanskas asks.

"Nothing. That was a problem. But when I was at work he always kept the house very clean. At the end of the day, he was good to me," she says, trying to present him in the best light. "He wouldn't actually cook. But he *would* take the meat out of the freezer to thaw."

"Big deal," Winn mutters.

"Now the car he was driving is registered to you," Razanskas says.

"Yeah. I bought the car and gave it to him."

"That's what *I* want in a woman. Someone who will buy me a car."

"I got it for him so he could go on job interviews."

"But he never got a job, did he?" Razanskas asks.

She shakes her head.

"Do you know where Charles is now?" he asks.

"No. We haven't even talked in a while."

"Are you sure? You sure he hasn't called and asked you for money?"

She shakes her head.

"This may be a little blunt," Razanskas says, "but I got to tell you. This guy's been squeezing you like a lemon. Can't you see that?"

Before she can answer, Winn chimes in. "He killed a sixty-eight-year-old woman. That pisses me off. He's a very big dude. Six-foot-six. She posed no threat to him at all. Maybe I could understand him killing the guy. But an old lady? That just don't set right with me."

The girlfriend is nervous now. She hugs herself and begins shivering. "I already broke up with him. We not even together now," she says weakly.

Razanskas, sensing she is ready to break, asks, "Did you ever see him with a gun?"

"Yeah. I always asked him why he had to carry a gun. I told him it'll lead to nothing but trouble. He just said I didn't understand what it was like on the streets. We always fought about this."

Razanskas leans forward, stares at her for a moment and says, "What did he tell you about this murder?"

She does not answer. She just shivers and hugs herself.

"Don't you take the fall for his mistakes," Winn says.

"This ain't no game," Razanskas says. "You could go down, too, if you don't level with us."

She nods and emits a long, slow sigh, as if slowly relinquishing all resistance. "He called me and acted like it was all my fault. He said that I shouldn't of left him, that he knew if I left him he'd get into trouble."

"What exactly did he tell you?" Razanskas asks.

She begins rocking in her chair. "He was crying when he told me about it. He said he was sorry. He said he didn't mean to do anything." She pauses and her eyes fill with tears.

"He was hysterical. He said, 'I shot someone and I may have killed them.' I told him to calm down and tell me what happened. He didn't want to talk any more about it. I left it alone after that."

She begins crying. Razanskas nods. He has what he needs now.

Razanskas is grateful this has been a slow June for homicides. The World Cup soccer tournament is in Los Angeles now and the police department has flooded the streets with extra patrol officers. And there have been fewer people on the streets to patrol because much of South-Central's Latino population has been spending the nights watching the games on television. If you are in your living room watching television, you will not be shot in a street robbery, during a drug transaction, in a carjacking, or at a liquor store holdup. Although there have not been enough murders to put Razanskas and Winn back into the rotation, this does not mean all is quiet on the streets. A slow week at South Bureau would keep most other homicide squads hopping.

Razanskas had hoped a slow June would give him a chance to catch up on all his paperwork. Four of his 60-day reports—extensive updates on unsolved homicides—are long overdue. A lieutenant has been pressuring him to finish them. Razanskas hates to write 60-dayers because they are almost an admission of defeat. If a detective has not cleared a case in 60 days, the odds are the case never will be cleared. The 60-dayers detail everything a detective has done on a case, take up to three days to complete and can be as long as 30 pages.

Every time Razanskas is about to work on one of his 60-dayers, something seems to come up, some pressing business from an old case that demands attention. Every morning when he sits at his desk, covered with subpoenas, murder books, witness statements and suspect interviews, he feels like the Sisyphus of South-Central, forever filling out reports that never end.

Most mornings Razanskas lugs a stack of heavy murder books from the office to his unmarked car. A murder book is a three-ring, blue plastic binder that summarizes a homicide case. It contains everything the detective gathers during the course of an investigation, from crime scene diagrams, lists of evidence and preliminary reports, to statements from witnesses, suspects and patrol officers. The murder books he removes from the office dictate his agenda for the day.

Razanskas is a creature of habit. Although he is not scheduled to begin until 7 A.M., he arrives at the squad room every morning at 6 o'clock sharp. His desk is festooned with pictures of his hunting trips and gag cards from his cop buddies in other units, with messages such as: "Jesus Loves You. But Everyone Else Thinks You're An Asshole." He lives in a suburban tract about 45 minutes south of the city, and he leaves home early to beat the freeway traffic. He buys a newspaper, quickly scans the headlines, saves the section with the crossword puzzle and throws the rest of the paper away. He unwinds at his desk, after the commute, with a cup of coffee and the puzzle. Filling out the puzzle, wracking his brain for leads and clues, gets him in the right frame of mind for homicide.

The new homicide detectives in the bureau often are mystified by Razanskas. They wonder why a Lithuanian-Venezuelan-American detective chews tobacco, listens to country music, spends all his vacations hunting and dresses like a cowboy.

Razanskas loved watching John Wayne movies on television as a child in Venezuela and was enchanted with the cowboy culture. But his first exposure to the real thing was with his first wife's family. His mother-in-law was from Texas and his father-in-law was an Okie who had drifted out to California. He was a truck driver and he played guitar on weekends in a country band. He introduced Razanskas to country music and hunting. Razanskas began chewing tobacco during the 1984 Los Angeles Olympics, when he was on rooftop sniper duty. Another cop, who spent many long, boring afternoons with him, chewed. Razanskas tried it, liked it and found it pepped him up during all-night homicide investigations. Now, despite LAPD regulations, he often has a plug of Skoal set between his cheek and gum.

Winn, who sits opposite Razanskas, is grateful that at least he does not chew when he is in the bureau. Their desks are only a few inches apart.

Winn arrives at the squad room every morning about a half hour after Razanskas, sets up her laptop computer and printer and gets right to work. On the corner of her desk, she has a drawing of a black cat, and underneath it, in large block letters: "I HAVE PMS AND A 9-MILLIMETER HANDGUN WITH 16 ROUNDS. ANY QUESTIONS?"

Her life revolves around her job, and she often works 12-hour days and then fights the traffic home. A few years ago, Winn moved out of South-Central to a suburb about an hour east of Los Angeles. It was not that she wanted to leave the city. It was simply a matter of finances; she could buy a new town house in the suburbs for the price of a shotgun shack in Los Angeles.

She makes dinner when she gets home and tries to stay awake through the four soap operas she tapes. The soaps help Winn lose herself in a fantasy world of romance and passion and tortured love; they help her forget, for a few hours, the bodies and the despair she sees every day.

While the detectives spend many of their nights on some of the city's most dangerous streets, they spend their office hours in the antiseptic environs of a mall. South Bureau Homicide is housed in a cavernous underground office at the south end of the Baldwin Hills Crenshaw Plaza. The LAPD created the bureau in 1989 to take over homicide investigations from four neighborhood stations because the division detectives were overwhelmed by the increasing number of murders.

The bureau does not have the dingy, frenetic ambience of the stereotypical homicide squad room. It is carpeted, the desks are lined up in even rows, the fluorescent lights glow overhead, the old murder books in their shiny blue binders are neatly lined up in metal cabinets. This could be an office for a telephone sales team pushing retirement property in Arizona.

A few days after Razanskas and Winn interview Larry Charles Gary's girlfriend, he plans to present the case to the D.A. Winn has work to do on her own double, so they will meet up later.

He struggles to balance four thick murder books and hauls them to his chocolate brown 1989 Chevrolet Caprice squad car. The sides are dented and dappled with flecks of white, where the paint has chipped off. He has the murder book from a November double—he has to interview a reluctant witness and make sure she will testify at the preliminary hearing. He has the murder book from a May carjacking—he plans to talk to the victim's wife. He has the murder book from a January homicide inside a travel agency—he just received a tip that a merchant next door may know the suspects. And he has the murder book for the Larry Charles Gary case. The district attorney's office is his first stop of the morning.

Razanskas pulls onto the freeway on a hot, dusty morning. The days of June gloom are over. In the distance an adobe-colored strip of smog stretches across the horizon. Only the faint outlines of the downtown skyscrapers are visible, a flat, spectral skyline silhouetted against the smog.

He takes advantage of Winn's absence by flipping on a country-western station. At the D.A.'s Hardcore Gang Unit, which specializes in homicides involving gang members, Razanskas drops his Larry Charles Gary murder book on the desk of a deputy district attorney.

"You got a good one?" she asks.

"This is a double-murder," he says somberly. "I got a video tape of the whole thing. It clearly shows the killer entering the house. It shows him pulling out his gun. And it shows him blowing away two people."

Her jaw drops. "Really?"

"Naw," Razanskas says. "It's all circumstantial."

She shakes her head. "Same old Raz."

"But I do have a dying declaration."

"*That's* interesting."

He explains the case to her. He tells her about his interview with the girlfriend. She confers with a supervisor. They decide to file murder charges against Larry Charles Gary.

"I like the fact that he calls up his girlfriend, crying and talking about the murder," the DA says. "I like that a lot."

The case is filed, but Razanskas does not get credit for a cleared case. The suspect has to be in custody. As long as Charles is on the lam, Razanskas has an open file.

When he returns to the office he checks with the LAPD surveillance unit. No one has seen Charles. Razanskas slaps a palm on his desk in frustration. He figures Charles has skipped town. He drives over to Parker Center, LAPD headquarters, to do a background check on Charles' mother. She was arrested oncc for shoplifting. He studies her booking sheet in order to find out her hometown: Shreveport, Louisiana.

Back at the office, he contacts an FBI unit that tracks fugitives for local law enforcement agencies. He tells them what he knows about the case, the phone numbers and addresses of Charles' friends and family and his mother's hometown, in case he decides to hide out there. Now all he can do is wait. And hope Charles does something stupid.

Chapter 4
The Ways of Death

Friday, July 1

At the beginning of the July 4 holiday weekend, Razanskas is on call. A detective trainee's partner is on vacation and he needs a substitute partner for the weekend. Razanskas fills in.

A few hours after midnight, Razanskas gets beeped. He meets Vic Corella at the 77th Street station.

"That didn't take long," Razanskas says, as they drive to the crime scene. "This is going to be a long weekend."

" 'Tis the season," Corella says.

It is a hot steamy night and the two night watch detectives, who are in their shirtsleeves, are at the scene when Razanskas and Corella arrive. The night watch detectives roll from the bureau and help secure evidence and do anything necessary to make it easier for the investigating detectives.

"We got the killer right here waiting for you," one of the detectives says to Razanskas, putting an arm around his shoulder. "You want us to drive him to the 77th or the Southwest station so you can interview him?"

Before Razanskas can answer, he and Corella realize they have been had.

"Find your own fucking suspect," the night watch detective says. "We don't have shit."

It looks like another anonymous street shooting. They do not have a suspect in custody. They do not even have a suspect. All they have is the body of a small-time crack dealer known as K-Mac. He is sprawled on the sidewalk in front of the Two & One Liquor Store. A white sheet is draped over him. Small rivulets of blood are flowing down the sidewalk, from the body to the gutter.

Corella is short and stocky and is wearing a short-sleeved shirt and a tie. He talks to the uniformed officers and a few street people behind the yellow tape. Razanskas gravitates to the crime scene. The night watch detectives told him that K-Mac was shot twice in the head as he walked into the liquor store and that one of the wounds was a "through and through." So Razanskas tries to trace the flight of the bullet. A bullet slug could be worth something down the road if a gun is recovered. If ballistics can match the bullet with the slug, this may be all the evidence he needs.

The liquor store is closed now, and it is oppressive inside, sweltering and stuffy with a faint smell of disinfectant. He interviews a store clerk, who fans himself with an invoice sheet. Razanskas discovers the clerk has just been discharged from the Army, where he had been an artilleryman.

"A cannon cocker, huh?"

"Yep."

"Those motherfuckers kept me awake every night in 'Nam. But they did a number on Charlie."

"Charlie?"

"You don't know who Charlie is?" he asks incredulously. "Vietnam must seem like a hundred years ago to a kid like you. Hell, I was in 'Nam before you were born."

Razanskas borrows a hammer and a screwdriver from the clerk and then walks up and down the store, trying to visualize the path of the bullet. He stops beside the entrance, removes a chipped panel and digs around with his screwdriver. He unearths a mangled bullet slug.

Outside winos and baseheads wander by the yellow tape and gaze at the victim. Usually passersby will offer some faint expression of sympathy for even the lowliest bagman. But the street people who pass by tonight mutter a variety of imprecations when they discover it is K-Mac under the sheet.

"Nobody like the dude," says one man pushing a shopping cart.

"He try to jack everyone around here," says a man in house slippers who shuffles by. "He jack me once."

A uniformed officer at the scene says everyone in the neighborhood was afraid of K-Mac. He sold crack and picked up some cash on the side by robbing people.

"Today's suspect is tomorrow's victim," the officer says. "This guy was a knucklehead."

"He was an asshole-and-a-half," his partner says.

K-Mac had so many enemies, the officer says, it is going to be hard to narrow down the suspect list. He is surprised that a guy as street-wise as K-Mac ended up at 48th and Normandie and got caught looking. In the past month, he says, there have been seven shootings, three of them fatal, near this corner.

The corner is in a played-out neighborhood of boarded-up homes, aging duplexes with the addresses spray-painted on the front and struggling storefront businesses with heavy metal security doors. The businesses reflect a changing neighborhood: Archie's Louisiana Sea Food, Nails by Wang, Vueltas Auto Sales. Across the street there is an empty lot where a grocery store, burned down during the riots, once stood. It is now used as the neighborhood dump and is littered with ragged sofas, empty diaper bags and rusting shopping carts. One of the walls of the brick liquor store, which has been painted purple, is pocked with dozens of bullet holes, including large chips from the megarounds of an AK-47.

The detectives interview a few street people, neighbors and the liquor store clerk and have pieced together a rough scenario. The Rollin 40s, who control the crack trade in the area, did not like K-Mac freelancing. So a Rollin 40 crack dealer—whose name the detectives are unable to obtain—decided to eliminate his competition. When K-Mac was shot he was with a strawberry, a woman who exchanges sex for crack. She grabbed a gun from his pocket and split.

When the coroner investigator arrives, Razanskas takes him aside. The investigator does not have too much time on the job, so he still takes Razanskas seriously.

"You're not supposed to be here," Razanskas says in a concerned whisper.

The investigator looks perplexed.

"We have a new policy. Didn't anyone tell you?"

He shakes his head.

"You don't have to come to the scenes anymore. We just toss the bodies in our trunk and *we* bring 'em to *you.*"

The investigator finally realizes Razanskas is kidding, shakes his head sheepishly and turns his attention to the body. He lifts the sheet and dabs K-Mac's hands with a sticky aluminum tab that will be tested later for gunshot residue. He empties K-Mac's pockets. The $275 in his front pocket rules out a robbery. As the investigator examines the large, star-shaped exit wound on K-Mac's forehead, a heavyset man in an old Mercury screeches to a halt in front of the yellow tape. He tells the detectives he is K-Mac's brother-in-law. He is a minister, he says, and the victim's mother is a "Christian lady."

While no one on the street has a kind word for the victim, the minister, who has known K-Mac since he was 4, has a different perspective. In a brief street sermon, he reminisces and succinctly sums up the life and death of K-Mac. He remembers him as a chubby, affectionate little boy who was called "Teddy Bear" by everyone in the neighborhood. "When he was four, I gave him his first haircut," the minister says wistfully. K-Mac's mother could not afford to buy him a bicycle, so the minister bought a used bike, painted it, polished the chrome and put streamers on the end of the handlebars. He recalls how happy K-Mac was, riding down the street on his new bicycle, grinning, streamers flying.

K-Mac wanted to play football in high school, but he was too chubby. So he ran and lifted weights and dieted and did push-ups and sit-ups until he was in good enough shape to make the team. He eventually became an all-conference tailback, attracting interest from a few college coaches.

But K-Mac married after high school and began working as a counterman at a fried-chicken restaurant. The chain transferred him to Fresno and promoted him to manager of his own restaurant. He missed Los Angeles, but the firm would not allow him to transfer back to Southern California, so he quit and moved back home. His wife picked up a crack habit, left him, and he and their four children moved in with his mother. He could not find a steady job. An occasional dalliance with crack soon became an obsession. And a profession. When he was shot in the back of the head, few were surprised.

"There was one thing he wasn't—he wasn't no murderer," the minister says, struggling for something good to say about his brother-in-law. "He never killed anybody and he never would.

"People around here don't remember him like I do. I remember him singing in the church choir. I remember him when he would help me feed the homeless. I talked to him. I scolded him. I lectured him. I told him he had to *stop* that kind of living that he do," the minister shouts. He paces back and forth behind the yellow tape, mopping his brow with a handkerchief.

"I used to quote a passage from Proverbs to him. And now it looks like those words have come to pass. I told him, 'There is a way that seemeth right unto man. But in the end, thereof, are the ways of death.'

"This neighborhood ain't nothin' but one big cemetery, nothin' but one big funeral home," he says, flicking his head toward K-Mac's body. "So many of our people moved here for a better life. They left the hard times of the South, from Mississippi to Louisiana, traveled all the way to California with big dreams, only to see their children end up dead on a street corner like this boy here."

Southern blacks began migrating to Los Angeles because of the same trinity of forces that attracted most people to Southern California—weather, real estate and opportunity. Unlike cramped midwestern and eastern cities, with their slums jammed with tenements, land in Los Angeles was plentiful and cheap. These new residents, many of whom had been laboring under the fetters of the sharecropper system, had a rare opportunity for home ownership.

From 1910 to 1920, the black population in Los Angeles doubled to about 15,000, but compared with many eastern cities, the population was still relatively small, less than 3 percent of the city's total. Many blacks, attracted by the availability of inexpensive land, began moving into Watts, a community abutting South-Central. But white residents, including a group of Ku Klux Klan members, were so outraged that blacks would soon be the majority and gain political control of the city that in 1926 they prevailed upon Los Angeles to annex Watts.

During the 1920s and 1930s, the increasing number of blacks migrating to Los Angeles alarmed the citizenry, who pushed for restrictive housing covenants. Soon, most new black arrivals were confined to a fast-growing South-Central neighborhood, a 30-block stretch surrounding Central Avenue.

"The Avenue" evolved into a black cultural hub, the center of the West Coast jazz scene. Billie Holiday, Cab Calloway, Duke Ellington and other black stars performed there. They stayed at the Hotel Summerville—later renamed the Dunbar Hotel—known as the "Jewel of Central Avenue." A black dentist built the Summerville because so many black visitors were turned away by the city's white-owned hotels. The Avenue soon became famous for its music and its nightclubs, including The Club Alabam (where "Saturday night is whooperino nite"), The Apex Night Club, ("where mirth, pleasure and happiness reigns supreme") and the Kentucky Club, with its elaborate horse-racing decor.

"Some remember the Avenue as a miniature Harlem, where musicians and literati gauged the community's pulse by day and transformed that energy into rhyme and music by night," Lonnie G. Bunch wrote in *Black Angelenos.* "Others recall with pride the offices of the Black physicians and dentists, the storefronts of

Black businesses. . . . The Avenue became an eclectic mix of stately homes representing the cream of Black society, rentals and apartments that housed the new southern migrants, and the business and professional offices of the Black middle class. In essence poverty and prosperity existed side by side on Central Avenue."

After the outbreak of World War II, blacks poured into Los Angeles, seeking work in the shipyards, aircraft plants and other war-related industries. But hiring policies were discriminatory and many were turned away. In 1942, A. Philip Randolph, president of the Brotherhood of Sleeping Car Porters, demanded that defense contractors end discrimination or he would call for a march on Washington. President Roosevelt, concerned that a march would give Germany and Japan a useful propaganda tool, issued an executive order requiring that defense contractors end discriminatory hiring practices.

The population continued to multiply after the war as black servicemen, who had been stationed at California bases, decided to stay. By 1965, the black population in Los Angeles was about 400,000. And the handful of traditionally black neighborhoods were becoming intertwined.

During the early 1960s, the economy was booming in southern California, and Lyndon Johnson was pushing antipoverty legislation through Congress. Many black immigrants, who had been raised amid the segregation and shantytowns of the rural South, found the pastel bungalows and stucco apartment buildings of South-Central a vast improvement.

But life in South-Central had deteriorated over the years, for many of the same reasons that inner-city neighborhoods across the country had deteriorated. The unemployment rate in South-Central was double that of the rest of the city. Much of the housing was in disrepair and owned by absentee landlords. Many of the small businesses were owned by outsiders. The schools were so understaffed and overcrowded that many students were forced to attend half-day sessions.

This was a Los Angeles far from the movie studios and television lots, where shows such as *Leave It to Beaver* and *Father*

Knows Best were being filmed, shows that portrayed a serene, suburban white America. This was a Los Angeles far from the offices of the real estate developers, the people who had first idealized, packaged and sold the southern California dream to the nation.

Attempts by local civil rights groups to address job and housing discrimination in the 1960s were strongly opposed by many white residents. Congress passed the Civil Rights Act in June of 1964, but five months later California residents overwhelmingly approved a proposition that overturned state and local antidiscrimination housing laws. While newly arriving blacks were funneled into South-Central and Watts, the police made sure they stayed there. And the LAPD officers they encountered were not the polite, "Just the facts, ma'am," types portrayed on *Dragnet.* Residents complained for years about police harassment, about police beatings following arrests. And the beatings were not the worst of it. From 1963 to 1965, 60 black Los Angeles residents—25 of them unarmed—were killed by police.

All the indignation and rage simmering beneath these placid neighborhoods, with their postage-stamp front yards and palm-lined streets, erupted on a sweltering August night in 1965. A highway patrolman pulled over a 21-year-old man in Watts on suspicion of drunk driving. A routine stop led to an arrest, a confrontation and then the arrest of the suspect's brother and mother, who had arrived at the scene. A crowd gathered. Angry words led to scuffles and then to rocks and bottles. More police arrived. A riot broke out. When it was over, six days later, 34 people were dead, more than 1,000 were injured and the damage was estimated at almost $200 million. After the riots, commissions were formed, grants awarded, the causes of the riots explored, the efficacy of government programs examined. Although President Johnson's antipoverty legislation received much attention, comparatively few jobs were created in Los Angeles. Soon the Vietnam War was diverting funds that could have been used in the War on Poverty. The problems of Watts and South-Central were forgotten.

In the years following the Watts riots, gleaming glass and steel towers were constructed downtown on Bunker Hill. But as the skyline was taking shape, South-Central neighborhoods continued to deteriorate. During the late 1970s and early 1980s, while heavy industry declined across the country, numerous large industrial plants in the area were shut down, resulting in tens of thousands of lost jobs. Later, recession and competition from foreign imports led to more plant closings and more jobs lost by black workers.

Longtime white residents of South-Central began to flee to the suburbs following the Watts riots. During the 1980s, the confluence of gangs, drugs and violence precipitated black flight, and almost 75,000 blacks moved out of South Los Angeles during the decade. Those who left were mostly the middle and working class black families, the people who volunteered at church, who were active politically. They felt their neighborhoods were being abandoned by government and business leaders and saw more opportunity in outlying areas that had safer streets and better schools. The community was being drained of its most active and prosperous residents. The people who remained often were those who could not afford to move—the unemployed, the growing number of single mothers, the elderly, the welfare cases. Those who left were being replaced by an influx of Latinos, who were fleeing a crumbling economy in Mexico and civil wars in Central America.

Blacks began competing with Latinos for increasingly scarce blue-collar jobs. Adding to the racial tension—and the resentment—were Korean merchants, who began buying up small markets and liquor stores.

During the 1984 Olympics, Los Angeles was touted as a multicultural model, an urban exemplar. But beneath the surface lay deep fissures that would be exposed to the world during the next decade—in the aftermath of the Rodney King beating and the most destructive urban insurrection in modern American history. South-Central became the symbol of antagonism between the populace and the police, the embodiment of the lawless inner city.

• • •

During the July 4 weekend, South-Central lives up to this lawless image. There are six other homicides after the murder of K-Mac. One basehead stabs another basehead in the chest at a rock house. A member of the Easy Riders gang is shot in a drive-by. A liquor store security guard shoots an unarmed man who he suspected was involved in a robbery. A woman who is seven months pregnant stabs her stepbrother, a crack dealer, after an argument over the family's dope supply. Detectives in the squad room quip that they do not know whether to classify this as a business or a family dispute. The woman claimed she did not murder her stepbrother. She was just holding out the knife, she told detectives, "and he ran into it." The coroner's report, however, showed a deep wound to the aorta, a wound too deep for an accidental stabbing.

The last homicide of the weekend—a double—makes the detectives in the bureau nervous. They are concerned the murders could precipitate a full-blown gang war. Two Diamond Street gang members pay a visit to the home of a Harpy gang member. The two are connected to the Mexican Mafia, one of California's most notorious prison gangs. The Mexican Mafia collects drug-dealing taxes from some street gangs. If the members do not pay they know they will face serious consequences when they eventually, inevitably, return to prison.

The Harpy had paid the tax a few times, but he finally decides it is getting too high. He pulls out his 9-millimeter, blasts both Diamond Street gang members in the head and disappears into the night.

On the morning after Independence Day, Razanskas and Winn are back at their desks. She still is trying to find the basehead with the tiny feet. He is still juggling his stacks of murder books and homicide reports.

Every morning Razanskas has the same breakfast, at the same time, at the same restaurant. It is always steak and eggs at Pepy's Galley. The restaurant adjoins a bowling alley not far from the airport. He and a few old-timers head out there in the morning and grab a table in the dim, empty cocktail lounge behind the coffee shop, away from the morning breakfast crowd. They can remove their jackets and do not have to worry about the 9-millimeter Berettas in their shoulder and belt holsters disturbing the other diners. Razanskas has been eating at Pepy's since he was a young patrolman and would start every afternoon shift with steak or chops, baked potato, and finish it off with a big piece of banana cream pie and coffee.

Winn is a careful eater and has a piece of fruit at her desk while Razanskas is at breakfast. She has lunch later in the morning. She always is fashionably dressed, with her Italian pumps and designer suits. Razanskas dresses in a generic fashion, wearing either gray or blue suits and ties he buys for $5 at a downtown clothing factory. Every day he wears a pair of black Tony Llama elephant-hide boots.

Winn pounds away at her computer most mornings, oblivious to the din in the squad room, while Razanskas, the squad clown, keeps a line of patter going. The kidding was rough in the old squad rooms where Razanskas picked up his detective training. It was personal, often brutal, and it was guaranteed to be politically incorrect. Razanskas has continued the tradition at South Bureau. If you are Italian, he will kid you with a Mafia reference. If you are Greek, he will accuse you of backing into doorknobs. If you are Japanese, he will slip in a few sushi jokes.

This morning, a balding detective walks across the room and Razanskas yells to him, "You better get your prescription for Rogaine before it's too late."

A detective with a shaved head wanders by and Razanskas grabs his sleeve and says, "Hey, do you use Armor All and a buffer to get your head that shiny?"

The detective stops and says to Razanskas, "How come your mustache is gray but your hair is brown? You use that Clairol For Men or Mr. Breck?"

He walks off, chuckling, before Razanskas has a chance to respond. Razanskas spots a chubby detective, who is heading out the door, and he teases him about his gut.

Winn watches the exchange and says, "I think you hurt his feelings."

"Naw. He was laughing."

"He may have been laughing. But you should have looked at his eyes. His eyes weren't laughing. His eyes looked hurt."

He throws up his hands in resignation, mutters, "Women," and returns to his murder books. Later in the morning, as Razanskas and Winn drive over to interview a witness in the Larry Charles Gary case, he complains that Gary still has not turned up. She flashes him an I-told-you-so look.

He ignores her and talks excitedly about his annual hunting trip that he takes every September. This trip serves as an important milestone, he tells Winn. It is his signal that the summer is finally over. Every fall, for the past ten years, he and a few friends, most of them cops, hunt antelope and deer in southern Wyoming.

"Man, it's great," he tells her. "It's a world away. We set up camp in this beautiful spot. Right in some rolling hills covered by aspens. We live in tents. Hang our meat to dry on poles. We don't shower or shave for two weeks."

"Two weeks without a shower? That's ugly. Must be a guy thing."

As he drives through the bleak city streets, without a patch of green or a tree on the horizon, he tells Winn how much he loves Wyoming in the fall. The pungent smell of sage in the morning. The changing leaves of the aspens, burning golden in late afternoon sunlight. The dramatic sunrises after an early-morning snow. The herds of wild horses galloping across the valley. Summer is only a few weeks old, he says, shaking his head. Hunting seems a long way off.

His reverie is broken when he drives through a neighborhood where he has investigated numerous murders. "See that meat market. Had one there. . . . See that old motel. Had a few there. That place used to be like the OK Corral. We haven't gotten called out there in a while. They must of run out of ammunition."

He points to a duplex. "Had one there. The suspect tells me he didn't mean to shoot the guy. He tells me, 'I shot in front of the dude to scare him. I can't help it if the dumb motherfucker ran into the bullet.' "

As Razanskas heads east on Florence, Winn points out the

window and says, "I grew up pretty close to here. When we moved out here our street was real nice. No drive-bys. No helicopters. Makes me sad now to see people afraid to leave their houses. It hurts me to see these little old ladies get killed because a bullet flies through their front window. You can't talk to a kid now who hasn't seen a dead body or who hasn't had a friend or family members killed.

"I was talking to a detective who grew up around here, like me. Her mama has a red hat, but it's gotten so bad that she's afraid to wear that hat now. Afraid some fool driving by will see the flash of color and shoot her. That's a damn sad example of what's it's come to."

"Yeah," he says. "When I started out on patrol here, I got to know a lot of nice folks. But the shitheads have made life tough for all of them."

"On my street, there were a bunch of guys who hung out," she says. "We called them poo-butts. I knew them when they were little boys. One day they started calling themselves the Rollin 60s. My parents wouldn't let any of them come to our house. My sisters and I couldn't go to their houses.

"In the mid-seventies, a family moved to our block from the east side. One of the boys was a Blood. Next thing we knew the 60s shot up their house. That was the first drive-by on our block. Before long, we started getting drive-bys all over the neighborhood, helicopters flying low every night, the whole routine."

He nods. "I was working those same streets, chasing those same 60s."

"There's all these killings now, but nobody outside of South-Central seems to give a damn," she says. "These people are ignorant. They don't realize these predators are mobile. They've got cars. They're not confined to the 'hood. They're already taking their gangbanging, gun-toting, carjacking shit to other parts of town."

He pulls in front of the witness's house, but it is an uneventful interview and lasts only about 20 minutes. Razanskas drops Winn back at the bureau. She has some calls to make.

He is also working an old carjacking murder and drives over

to the Southwest Station because he wants to sift through some crime reports. He walks through the squad room to the robbery table.

"Hello, beautiful," he says to a secretary. "Go easy on that coffee."

"Keep it down," he says to another, who does not look up when he arrives.

"You're lookin' good," he shouts to an officer in shorts, ready for a run. "You going out to hustle some money?"

He points to a detective across the room and shouts, "There's an asshole who betrayed the faith of his friends. He's going to Internal Affairs."

He walks over to a lieutenant and asks, "When you look out over this entire room, do you see one competent detective?"

The other cops seem to enjoy his shtick. A few bristle, but most of them are eager for a laugh, a break in the grim routine.

Razanskas wants to study all of the station's carjacking reports during the past year. In his carjacking case, two gunmen flanked the victim's car at a stop sign. One tried to pull the driver out, but he was wearing his seat belt. The gunman was irritated by the inconvenience. So he shot the driver. "I understand that, shooting his ass because he was wearing a seat belt," Razanskas says, sarcastically, to another detective. "That driver was damn inconsiderate."

Razanskas could not figure out why the driver, a Guatemalan immigrant, was in that neighborhood. He was far from his job and apartment. But when Razanskas sifted through the car trunk he found pictures of the driver and a young woman. Razanskas discovered that the man was sneaking around on his wife and was on his way to visit his girlfriend when he was killed. There is a moral to the story, Razanskas tells the detective, a moral he learned last spring when he interviewed a *veterano* after the murder of a gangbanger.

He raises a forefinger and intones somberly, "Love is a motherfucker."

When he finishes sifting through the carjacking reports, he drives back to South Bureau and picks up a young officer, John Kielbasa, who is visiting the bureau for a month to pick up some detective experience. A South Bureau supervisor wants Kielbasa to learn interviewing techniques from Razanskas, who has a reputation of knowing how to get even the most taciturn witnesses to open up.

"You married?" Razanskas asks Kielbasa.

"Yeah."

"Happy?"

Kielbasa nods.

"Don't worry," Razanskas says, laughing. "It won't last long."

They drive over to East 78th Street, near Main, the site of a double-murder from November. The suspect in the shooting is a gang member by the name of Glenn Mason, who is known as No Neck, for obvious reasons. His head sits squarely atop his broad shoulders like a cantaloupe on a cutting board. On the night before Thanksgiving, No Neck was engaged in a heated argument with an acquaintance named Tony Black. Samuel "Mike" Morris, a neighbor, tried to separate them. No Neck was so enraged he shot Mike for interfering. Then he killed Tony. The officers who arrived at the scene learned that before the killings, as No Neck pulled his pistol out of his pocket, he accidently shot himself in the leg. A short time later, police received a call that a man with a gunshot wound had shown up at an Inglewood hospital.

"Uniformed officers responded and discovered that the male black sustained a gunshot wound to the upper thigh," according to the police report. "Officers also noted the male black to have a distinctive physical feature of a shortened neck."

No Neck was a member of the Swans, a Blood set that is a bitter rival of the Crips. The Swans motto is, "When a Swan flies, a Crip dies." No Neck was taken into custody at the hospital and Razanskas began his investigation. Although few witnesses would cooperate, he compiled enough of a case to get a murder charge filed against No Neck. Still, the deputy DA was not sure the case was strong enough to get past the preliminary hearing. Razanskas told the deputy D.A. when she filed murder charges, "This case is a piece of shit. But it will get better. I promise you." More work needed to be done, but Razanskas soon was inundated with other cases.

The preliminary hearing, however, is coming up, so Razanskas has to hustle. In some homicide squads, detectives can spend weeks, or months, on a single homicide, working the case, lining up witnesses, chasing every lead. But detectives at South Bureau Homicide are so busy that they do as much as they can, as fast as they can, until the next homicide. They have to tie up the loose ends somewhere down the line. Like a MASH unit, South Bureau detectives lurch from one dead body to another, from emergency to emergency.

One key witness in the No Neck case has been reluctant to give a statement. Razanskas decides to try again. Her name is Joann and she lives on the second floor of a run-down four-unit apartment building across the street from the shooting. He and Kielbasa walk up the dank stairwell speckled with stucco chips on the steps. Joann, who is in her mid-40s, is sitting at her kitchen table, drinking water from a jam jar. Her mother is in the living room watching *The Montel Williams Show.* Joann has bloodshot eyes, is missing two teeth and has a white kerchief wrapped around her head. She has improbably long red fingernails and large gold hoop earrings. After eyeing him warily, she tells Razanskas she does not want to talk.

"Look at all the work I've put into this case," he says, patting his thick murder book. He smiles and says, "You probably thought the only thing us cops did was sit around Winchell's, eating donuts and drinking coffee."

He tries to read the murder book, squints, and then, in an exaggerated pantomime, holds the book at arm's length and tries again. Finally he sighs, shakes his head and pulls out his bifocals. He usually is self-conscious around the younger detectives about having to wear bifocals, but sometimes, with witnesses, they can be a helpful prop. He turns to Joann and says, "You ever talk to a cop who's so old he has to wear these granny glasses?"

She smiles. He is encouraged. He asks her if she knew No Neck.

"I use to do Neck's hair."

"One of those guys killed, Mike, was pretty well liked around here, wasn't he?"

"Oh yeah. He sweet. If anyone had any trouble with their car, he fix it for free."

He sees an opening and decides to work it. He tells her how it was not right that Mike was killed, that law-abiding citizens should not have to live in fear of gangsters like No Neck, that No Neck has to be put behind bars, that Mike's family deserves that peace of mind. He pauses, fixes her with an intent gaze and says, "I need your help."

"Can I get in trouble if I answer your questions?"

"I won't let you get in trouble." He grins rakishly. "How could I let you get into trouble? I love you."

She turns her head and peers at him out of one eye. "You a player. You like to flatter the ladies."

They banter for a while, until she finally says, "That No Neck had a fucked-up personality." She agrees to tell him what she saw. It was her birthday, so she remembers the night well. She heard Tony and No Neck arguing. She looked out her window. They began "duking." Mike stepped in to break up the fight. She heard two or three shots. She saw Mike go down.

"It's a cryin' shame," she says. "That Mike was a wonderful person. And now his son is so tore up. His daddy's gone." Tears stream down her face. She takes a sip of water. "I sure could use a smoke."

Razanskas gives Kielbasa two dollars and tells him to get Joann a pack of cigarettes from the corner market.

When he returns, she takes a cigarette from the pack, taps the end on her palm a few times and lights up.

Razanskas pulls out a six-pack, and she immediately picks out No Neck. He writes up her statement and persuades her to sign it. He asks her if she will testify at the preliminary hearing.

She lights another cigarette and takes a deep drag. "Do I got to go to court?"

"If everyone does their part, No Neck won't be getting out of the pen and killing anyone else."

She nods. "Get rid of *that* shit."

"Will you testify at the prelim?"

This is a critical moment. Most witnesses are afraid to even talk to detectives. Those who will talk are even more reluctant to sign a witness statement. And the few who will sign a witness statement usually are terrified about having to testify in court. Testifying can invite retaliation.

"Oh, Lord," she says. She plays with her hair. She stubs out her cigarette in the ashtray.

"OK. I'll do it."

Razanskas looks relieved. He explains to her what kind of questions she might be asked at the preliminary hearing.

She takes a sip of water. "Let me ask you something. Do the court buy me lunch?"

"I'll make sure you get lunch."

As he walks out the door, she waves to him and calls out, "Be sweet."

He climbs down the steps of the apartment and struts to the car, smiling broadly. He is elated the interview went so well and is in a talkative mood. "Man, her statement was dynamite," he tells Kielbasa. "It might not seem like much, but it puts No Neck right at the scene. The D.A.'s going to love it."

"I didn't think she was going to talk to you," Kielbasa says.

"I had to do some ass kissing. Some *major* ass kissing. Remember, if you can't kiss ass, you ain't going to make it as a homicide detective."

One element from Joann's statement, however, was missing, Razanskas tells Kielbasa. She heard the shots but she never actually saw No Neck shoot the two victims. Things happened too fast, she said. But one witness did see No Neck shoot Tony and Mike. And that witness is Mike's son, Samuel Morris III, known as Li'l Boy. But he has refused to give a statement. No Neck's Swan homies have intimidated him.

"It's brutal these days to get people to testify," Razanskas tells Kielbasa as he drives over to where Li'l Boy works. "Especially here, in the south end. People are scared to death of retaliation by gangbangers. You go out to crime scenes these days and nobody sees nothin'. It's gotten bad. Can you believe this shit? Li'l Boy is afraid to help us put away his own father's killer.

"I had a case where a guy gets shot in a bar. The place is packed that night, more than sixty people inside. Everyone I interviewed told me the same thing: 'I was in the bathroom. I didn't see a thing.' I'm shaking my head after this. I turn to my partner and say, 'This is one bathroom I got to see. It's gotta be the biggest bathroom in L.A.' "

This reminds him, he tells Kielbasa, of another case where nobody wanted to get involved. He arrived at an apartment and found two bodies in the living room riddled with bullets. A man who lived in the apartment—a witness, not a suspect—told Razanskas he had no idea what happened.

"It was a war in there," Razanskas says. "Rounds fired all over the place. And this guy expects us to believe that he was sound asleep the whole time and didn't hear a thing."

Razanskas and Kielbasa pull up in front of the machine shop where Li'l Boy works. Li'l Boy comes to the front office, grease up to his elbows. He is not happy to see Razanskas waiting for him with a subpoena. He is in his early 20s, but his street name still fits. He nervously stares at his shoes and looks like a shy, skinny little boy.

"I can't emphasize how important you are to this case," Razanskas tells him. "Without you the whole thing falls apart. I don't want to see No Neck walk."

"Will he be right out there in the courtroom? Will he be able to see me?"

"I ain't going to lie to you. He'll be at the defense table. Look, I want to make sure everything goes OK. Can I pick you up and take you to court?"

Li'l Boy nods and slowly, wearily, walks back to work.

A few days later, at 7 o'clock in the morning, Razanskas knocks at Joann's door. There is no answer. He knocks again. He checks his watch. He continues to knock, and after about 10 minutes she comes to the door in a nightgown. She rubs her eyes, steps over two of her sister-in-law's children sleeping on the floor, and lets Razanskas in. A few minutes later she returns, wearing a long black wig, jeweled sandals, sweat pants and a T-shirt. They walk across the street to pick up Li'l Boy. Razanskas knows he is scared and is uncertain about how truthful his testimony will be.

Driving to court Razanskas wants to make sure Joann and Li'l

Boy do not get too nervous, so he tries to keep them talking. He tells them about a new 62-ounce bottle of malt liquor now on the market.

"Ever try it?" he asks.

"Oh yeah," Joann says.

"All by yourself?"

"Oh yeah."

"Can you down one of those things and still get up and dance?"

"Oh yeah. . . . You drink?"

"I try not to overdo it."

"Me neither," she says. "I'm a Christian."

Razanskas keeps her and Li'l Boy amused by showing them what he calls, "The white boy high five." He raises a palm, but instead of slapping Joann's palm, he clumsily misses.

"I bet your wife enjoys the hell out of you," she tells him. "How long you been married?"

"This time?"

"How many times you *been* to that ol' altar?"

"Three times."

"You a Romeo."

"I ain't no Romeo. I was just working all the time."

"I understand *that.*"

"I wish my first two wives did."

The three of them arrive at the courthouse and fight through the crowds lining up for a hearing in the O.J. Simpson case. Hundreds of T-shirt salesmen, cameramen, reporters and rubberneckers line the sidewalk. Razanskas has little interest in the Simpson case. "Big fucking deal," he tells Joann and Li'l Boy, negotiating his way into the courthouse. "I'm working on three double-murders right now. And it's just me and my partner. We don't have a team of detectives at our disposal to canvas the neighborhood and interview witnesses. We don't snap our fingers and get DNA results whenever we want it. I requested DNA on one case. I got my results all right. Six months after the guy was convicted."

Razanskas and his entourage check in with the deputy D.A.

who is handling the case. She works out of a small office crowded with three desks, metal file cabinets and files scattered on the floor. "Didn't I tell you right from the beginning that this case was a piece of shit, but would get better?" he says. "Well, did I lie to you?" She agrees that the case is solid now. In an aside, away from Joann and Li'l Boy, she tells him she is amazed he got two witnesses to talk.

At the hearing, No Neck, wearing an orange jail jump suit, is escorted into the courtroom by sheriff's deputies. He sits down and puts his elbows on the table, a hulking, menacing-looking figure. Li'l Boy avoids his gaze as he steps up to the witness stand. He slumps in his chair and speaks so softly the judge tells him to talk louder.

"I was sitting in a car and my father came from the porch to talk to me . . ." He points to No Neck. "He came riding up on a bicycle. He and Tony started arguing. . . . My father pulled Tony aside . . . he tried to break it up . . . No Neck . . . pulled a gun out of his right pocket. My father was right next to Tony. He shot my father. No Neck and Tony started wrassling on the ground. He shot Tony. . . . I ran inside and called 911."

Li'l Boy's testimony dooms No Neck, and the judge holds him over for trial. Things look so bad for No Neck, his attorney approaches the deputy D.A. and tells her, "I'm ready to deal. Just don't deal me a death." While they talk, Li'l Boy walks into the hallway, collapses onto a bench and puts his head in his hands.

After a few minutes, he slowly lifts his head and explains why he was reluctant to testify against his father's killer. "I was real nervous. I never been around no killing before. I was afraid of the gang members. They would come up to me—friends of No Neck's—and ask, 'How you going to handle this?' I was afraid they would shoot me or my grandfather."

He stares at the ceiling for a moment. "He killed my pop for nothing. I started thinking about this over and over. All the time. I got real mad. Even though I was scared, I knew I had to do something. The right thing. For my pop."

He takes a deep breath and says softly, "He killed my pop. For nothing."

Chapter 5
One Punch

Friday, July 8

The weekend after July 4, Razanskas is on call again. He and Winn are number three on the on-call list, which means they will pick up the third homicide of the weekend. But the other team he supervises is number one. He does not expect to get much sleep.

Razanskas is the leader of Squad 3, which consists of Razanskas and Winn, and another team—Armando Reyes, a detective trainee, and Detective Paul Masuyama. Squad 3 investigates homicides within the boundaries of the 77th Street Division. Whenever Reyes and Masuyama roll on a homicide, Razanskas rolls with them. He supervises their work at crime scenes and usually stays up all night with them until the first thrust of the investigation is completed. In LAPD bureaucratese, Squad 3 is referred to as "ethnically diverse." The squad is composed of a black woman, a Latino, a Japanese-American and a Lithuanian-Venezuelan-American.

This weekend, supervisors at South Bureau are worried about a gang war. Last Sunday, the two gangbangers collecting drug taxes for the Mexican Mafia were killed. Three nights later, the payback went down. A Harpy gang member named Marco and his 17-year-old niece, who had a 4-month-old daughter, were gunned down. Marco was shot in the street. His niece ran and hid behind an apartment building, but the gunmen tracked her down. Detectives found her body, riddled with bullets, beneath a stairwell. She was huddled in the fetal position, as if she were desperately trying to make herself small enough to avoid the bullets.

The two Diamond Street gangbangers were killed last Sunday. The two Harpys were killed on Wednesday. This weekend, detectives figure, Diamond Street is the target.

Razanskas leaves work Friday afternoon at 3:30, stops by the video store and rents *Tombstone* and *The Pelican Brief.* He plans on having an early dinner with his wife, watching *Tombstone,* and later in the evening, he figures, he probably will get beeped. But before he has a chance to eat dinner, before he has a chance to see the movie, before he even has a chance to change, he gets the call. At 6 o'clock he is back on the freeway, fighting traffic, heading toward South-Central. An hour later he is in his squad car, driving north on Broadway, toward the crime scene. He drives past the forlorn hookers in their miniskirts who are just beginning to gather on the street corners, past groups of men drinking wine in front of the liquor stores, past the skinny, wasted-looking strawberries hanging out in front of the hot sheet motels that rent rooms by the hour, past the check-cashing stands where people are picking up money for the weekend, past the Mexican bars, doors open to the street, the sounds of salsa and cumbia mingling with the purl of traffic and the horns, and the car radios, and the barking dogs and the screeching brakes.

Razanskas pulls in front of the crime scene at West 79th Street, meets up with Reyes and Masuyama and tells them, "This is too damn early to get the first call. Looks like another weekend shot to hell."

This section of West 79th Street, just west of Hoover, is composed of mostly narrow, single-story shotgun flats with patches of dead grass in front and sliding metal security gates, and small, weathered apartment buildings, their railings covered with damp clothes left out to dry. Between the apartments there are stands of banana plants with broad, rubbery leaves that cast enormous shadows. Neighbors are oblivious to the activity surrounding the crime scene; a homicide is not an unusual event on this street. Next door, kids play soccer in their dirt yard. Across the street two little girls hit a tennis ball back and forth with Ping Pong paddles. Alongside the yellow tape, a child rides his tricycle.

Masuyama and Reyes brief Razanskas on the case. A 20-year-old man by the name of Clarence was about to enter a single-story apartment building with splintered wooden siding. It has a stained white gravel roof and a carport with a sagging wooden frame. Clarence was about to buy some pot, but he was ambushed in front of the carport by three men, who shot and robbed him. Miles, a friend of Clarence's, is back at the station. He claims he was in the car the whole time and did not see anything. Both are members of the By Yourself Hustlers, a Crip set.

"Are you the primary on this one?" he asks Masuyama.

"This one's mine," Reyes says.

"Congratulations," Razanskas says. "The case is a piece of shit."

Razanskas sees an old-timer, one of the uniformed cops he used to work with. "Well I got it," Razanskas says. "I finally got it." He tells the cop that he just received his deer hunting tags from Wyoming. They talk hunting for a few minutes, until Razanskas spots a police helicopter in the distance. He tells the cop to make sure the pilot checks the rooftops for handguns that might have been tossed by the suspects.

South-Central is beneath the Los Angeles International Airport flight pattern, and jets frequently roar overhead, their landing lights twinkling in the distance. On nights like this, when the loud *whop-whop-whop* of the police helicopter reverberates overhead, the jets roar in the distance, the occasional staccato of automatic gunfire can be heard and police sirens wail every few minutes, it feels like the edge of a battlefield.

Razanskas yells at a jet overhead, "I want an air strike and I want it now! And drop some napalm right in front of me!"

At dusk, Razanskas joins Masuyama and Reyes and they survey the crime scene. The sun glows a deep red as it drops into the sea, and the sky is streaked with swaths of purple, the color of a bruise. The smell of fried chicken is in the air. The three detectives study footprints in a dirt alley and trace the pattern of .25-caliber shell casings, circled in chalk on a driveway. They try to follow the path of the bullets and end up rooting through an old man's house, filled with bowling trophies, in their search for slugs. Across the street, right outside the passenger's side of the victim's car, Razanskas spots a live round. He picks up the 9-millimeter bullet and rolls it around his palm.

"This was just jacked out of the fucking gun," he tells Reyes. "These guys learn about guns from the movies. They lock and load and usually lose one round from the chamber. I'll bet that's what this is."

On the sidewalk, across the street from the car, the victim is on his back. He is a nice-looking young man with high cheekbones, long eyelashes and eyes that are wide open. There is no blood around the body, just neat round bullet holes on his chest and right bicep. "The bullets must have taken out an aorta," the coroner investigator says, because there is so little bleeding. But internally, he figures, the bleeding must be extensive.

Right by the victim's head, Razanskas spots a cryptic message. Someone scrawled it onto the cement years ago when the cement was wet. In a flowing script are the words: "Dead the Lover." Razanskas gets a kick out of the message. He points it out to the others and announces, "That's fucking irony for you."

At about 10 P.M., Razanskas leaves the crime scene. A minute after getting into his car, two reports crackle over his police radio. A baby is shot at 73rd and Hoover. A patrol car is fired on a few blocks away. But these are not his cases, so Razanskas drives over to the 77th Street Division station where Miles, who was with the victim shortly before he was killed, is waiting in a tiny interview room. Big chunks of tile are missing from the walls and the ceiling is a patchwork of glue splotches, water-stained tiles and chipped paint. Miles, whose street name is "Hump," also is a member of the By Yourself Hustlers. He is in his early 20s, has long, Jeri-curled hair and is wearing baggy jeans, cut off at the calf, and a baggy white T-Shirt. He grew up with the victim and they were close friends.

"Did your friend have a gun?" Razanskas asks him.

"No," he says, looking through Razanskas.

"Did you have a gun?"

"No."

"I got to tell you, we found a live round right by the door of the car. Was that yours?"

"No."

Razanskas leans back in his chair. "We're trying to catch the guys who killed your friend. If we get them into court and it turns out you're holding out on us, it will make everyone look bad. These guys will walk. So let me ask you again, do you know anything about that bullet?"

"No."

Razanskas taps his pencil on his notebook and sighs. He does not want to push too hard because this is not his case. He is just helping out while Reyes and Masuyama pursue other leads. "Detectives Reyes and Masuyama will be talking to you soon. If you care about finding the guys who killed your friend, I want you to be honest with them."

But Miles will not cooperate with them, either. After the interview, they lead him to a detective's desk at the edge of the squad room. As soon as he is alone, Miles drops his head to his knees. He begins crying. He sits up and his tears fall onto a plastic blotter. When a teardrop hits the plastic, it makes a pinging sound. "It keeps coming back to me," he sobs. *Ping. Ping.* "I can't get it out of my mind." *Ping. Ping. Ping. Ping.*

There are a few more murders on Friday night in South-Central, but Saturday night is slow, and Razanskas finally is able to have dinner with his wife and watch *Tombstone.* On Sunday morning at 8 o'clock, he is about to make some bacon and eggs when he gets the call. The third homicide of the weekend has gone down.

As the sun begins to peek through the morning fog, Razanskas and Winn arrive at the scene. The body is in the middle of an oil-stained parking lot behind a boarded-up restaurant with a chipped metal sign advertising "Soup-Grits-Chili." Behind the parking lot, on the other side of the alley, are a few sooty brick buildings housing small manufacturing companies. This is an industrial stretch of Western Avenue, filled with auto body shops, printing plants and salvage yards.

A few blocks away, there is a string of storefront churches. So on this Sunday morning, about 20 feet from the body, the sidewalk is filled with people walking to church. Women in broad pastel hats, men in dark suits and a group wearing matching lime green outfits, a church choir, hurry past the victim.

Lieutenant Faryl Fletcher, who is waiting at the scene, tells Razanskas and Winn that a man was walking down the street this morning when he spotted the body and called 911. The uniformed officers, Fletcher tells them, wanted to keep the 911 caller at the scene until the detectives arrived. He is in the back of their patrol car, snoozing.

Fletcher, who is second in command at South Bureau Homicide, joined the unit a few months ago. He has spent most of his career in patrol, as a patrol officer, patrol sergeant and watch commander. But he knows that to advance in the LAPD he needs more investigative experience, so he volunteered to work at South Bureau, a unit many lieutenants avoid because of the long hours and frequent 24-hour shifts. He has gained the respect of the homicide detectives because he has been honest with them about his dearth of detective experience and has not tried to throw his weight around simply to let them know who is in charge. He rolls on all of Razanskas' homicides and about half of the other detectives' cases. Lieutenant Sergio Robleto, who heads the bureau, responds to the other calls. It is helpful to have a lieutenant on the scene, particularly if there are unruly crowds, angry family members or disputes between a patrol sergeant and a detective, times when the clout and experience of a lieutenant are needed.

Fletcher tells Razanskas and Winn that he is going to take the measurements of the crime scene.

"I'll give you a hand," Winn says.

"I see you're brown-nosing again," Razanskas says, teasing her.

Winn snaps, eyes blazing, "You got your nose so far up his ass he can't shit. You're the biggest damn brown-noser around."

Razanskas is taken aback by the vehemence of Winn's response. He had just been kidding, but she seems genuinely angry, indignant at what he considers an innocuous quip. He shrugs, shaking his head, walks over to the body and lifts the sheet. He sees grass blades and grass stains on the victim's lower back. "Son of a bitch," he mutters. That's all he needs to see to know the case is a loser. A dump job. A homicide detective's nightmare.

The grass means the victim was killed in one location, dragged into a car and dumped at another location. Body dumps might be the toughest cases to solve. There usually are no witnesses, no nosy neighbors, no fingerprints, no shell casings. Killers know that body dumps allow them to simultaneously eliminate a victim, a trail and a crime scene. Razanskas cannot remember the last body dump that was cleared. He is particularly unhappy because he is the primary on this one.

A bagman pushing an overflowing shopping cart stops at the alley and checks out the action. He shouts to the detectives, with a hint of commiseration in his voice, "Body dump, huh?"

While they wait for the coroner investigator to arrive, Razanskas interviews, in Spanish, a security guard who works at one of the manufacturing companies across the alley. Winn stays with the uniformed officers. "Raz," she says, "is doing his Spanish *thang.*" The guard says he has no idea what time the body was dumped, nor who dumped it. He pulls out his wallet, sifts through some papers and removes a business card. He smiles. It is Razanskas' card.

Razanskas studies the guard for a moment. He is in his late 50s, unshaven, pudgy and wearing thick glasses. Razanskas recognizes him. Two years ago the guard was involved in a homicide Razanskas was investigating. The guard was on duty when two men burst into the building, yelled, "This is a jack!" and tried to rob him. But he did not bring any cash to work that day. The robbers, outraged by the guard's thoughtlessness, shot him.

He took one bullet in the leg, whipped out his snub-nosed .38 and blasted away, killing one of the robbers and scaring away the other. The D.A. called it justifiable homicide.

Razanskas walks back to the parking lot, and he and Winn wake the man sleeping in the patrol car. He is tall and lanky and he stretches outside the car. He tells the detectives his name is Dederick, he is from Aurora, Colorado, and is visiting relatives in South-Central. He was walking down the street this morning, looking for a bus stop, when he saw the body in the parking lot.

"I'm thinking the guy was drunk. So I walk over and say, 'Yo, dude. Wake up.' He doesn't move. I look a little closer. That's when I call 911. Damn," he says, slumping against the patrol car. "I've had it with L.A.

"Last night some dudes pull up in a car across the street from me. They yell to a guy, 'Hey, cuz,' and fire on him. Later, some ten-year-old kid missing his two front teeth pulls up on his bike and says to me, 'Hey, homie, I got some cavy [caviar] rocks at a sweet price.' Now this morning I come across a dead body.

"I seen a drive-by, a ten-year-old crack dealer and a stiff, since last night. Y'all can have this town. I'm going home."

By the time the coroner investigator arrives, the sun has burned off the last of the morning mist. It is now clear and hot, in the mid-90s, and even hotter in the center of the parking lot. There is no shade and the asphalt is sizzling. The investigator wipes his brow with a handkerchief and pulls the sheet off the body. The untrained eye sees just a battered and bloody body, and the hows and the whys and the whens are impossible to determine. But Razanskas sees a tableau of action and reaction. A homicide scenario. He sees how the disparate elements—the fibers, the wounds, the body position, the ligature marks—conjoin to create a pattern.

A few tiny twine fibers remain on the inside of the victim's wrist. Razanskas figures he probably was tied up before he was killed. His left foot is on top of his right foot and there are a few fibers on the seat of his pants. He probably was hog-tied. The ligature marks on his wrist are faint. He probably was not tied up long before he died. There is vomit on the pavement. He probably had been gagged. There are abrasions on his knuckles and his left forearm is badly bruised and swollen. He put up a fight. Instead of a belt, a long string is in his belt loops. He probably was a street person. His pockets are turned inside out. He was robbed.

"Keep an open mind on the pockets," he tells Winn. "The suspects could have robbed him. Or it could have been a freebie. Some guys wandering by might have seen the body and ripped him off. On this case and every other case you work, be flexible. Don't lock yourself into one way of thinking."

The coroner investigator checks the victim's back pockets, but he cannot find a wallet. More bad news for Razanskas. This means he will be spending valuable time, not in search of suspects, but merely trying to identify the victim. "This is getting worse all the time," Razanskas says. "Anyone know how to spell John Doe?"

After the investigator removes the victim's shirt, Razanskas shades his eyes with a cupped hand, to cut the glare, and studies the wounds. The victim is covered from his chest to his head with deep wine-colored bruises and deep gash marks. He has a bizarre expression on his face, with his right eye closed and left eye open, as if he is winking at death. He has a broken nose, a black eye, and his hair is matted with blood. Nobody can figure out what kind of weapon was used. Was it a pipe, a baseball bat, a machete, a hammer? The investigator removes the victim's shoes. His feet are filthy.

"When was the last time he washed his feet?" Razanskas asks. "When it rained. At least he doesn't have maggots between his toes. I've had a few like that before."

If there is evidence on a body, detectives call in a criminalist from the coroner's office. If there is evidence at the scene, detectives call an LAPD criminalist. Because this victim had been tied up, and because there is no homicide scene, the criminalist from the coroner's office takes the case. He crouches over the body and removes twine fibers with clear tape. While he clips the victim's fingernails—in case there are remnants of the suspects' tissue or blood—he talks about a great rib joint on Slauson Avenue.

"You go to the counter and the guy asks you," he says laughing, "if you want your ribs hot or if you want them white-boy style." This reminds Razanskas and Winn that they missed breakfast.

"Man, I'm starving," he says.

"I'm hot and thirsty *and* hungry," Winn says. "How 'bout some Mexican food? I'd like some good cheese enchiladas."

When they finish up at the scene, they cruise over to a Mexican restaurant a few miles south of downtown and ease into a booth, relieved to be out of the broiling sun. Winn gets up to wash her hands and when she returns to the booth Razanskas is sipping a glass of ice water.

"Aren't you going to wash your hands?" she asks him.

He shrugs.

"You've been at this job too damn long. I'm not eating with you until you wash your hands. With soap. You were all over that body."

"OK, OK," he says, reluctantly walking off to the bathroom. When he returns, they order lunch and he tells her about an undercover operation he once worked where he posed as a counterman at a fried-chicken restaurant.

"I worked an undercover operation when I was at bunco forgery," she says. "People who were ordered by the court to do community service went to this state agency down at Eighty-eighth and Main. The agency was supposed to set them up with community service jobs. But the agency was taking bribes and forgetting about the jobs.

"I go in there pretending I'd been ordered by the court to do eighty hours of community service. This guy running the place takes a liking to me. He's telling me, 'Don't worry about the community service, baby. We can work it out.' He moves in on me, trying to grab a cheap feel.

"I'm wired, so when he turns away, I whisper into the wire, 'If this guy touches me again, I'm going to kick the shit out of him.' I end up forking over forty bucks to him and a hundred-twenty bucks to a lady there so they'll sign off on my community service. I'm ready to leave, but I can't get rid of this guy. He wants to walk me to my car.

"He asks me how much I had to pay the lady, and I tell him a hundred-twenty bucks. He says, 'I wasn't going to do you like that. She's a greedy bitch.' We get to my car, and now he wants a ride back to the office, so he crawls inside and is on me again. I have to pretend to giggle and be shy and say, 'Oh, I don't kiss on the first date.' I finally get this guy off me and out of the car.

"A few days later, me and a few other officers come in with a search warrant. I'm pointing people out and they're arresting everyone. When I point out the guy who was after me, he's real surprised.

" '*You* the police?' " he asks me.

" 'That's right, baby,' " I tell him.

"The guy looks real disappointed and says, 'Does that mean we can't go out?' "

She slaps her hand on the table, throws her head back and laughs.

"I hope you let the guy down easy," Razanskas says, smiling.

"I told him if we had a date, it would have to be at The Gray Bar Hotel."

A waitress brings their lunch and they eat in silence. Razanskas finishes his coffee, grabs a pinch of Skoal and spits into the empty cup. He tells her about his first exposure to homicide. "I was a boot, just out of the academy. I was still on probation and working patrol. A couple of homicide detectives needed a Spanish-speaker to interview some witnesses. I was loaned out to them for two weeks. These guys were old-timers, seasoned detectives. In those days you couldn't get to homicide unless you'd put in some real time on the job. Not like today. The homicide detective was a god then. He called the shots.

"I dug my only sports coat and tie out of the closet and met up with them in the morning. We started the day by going to breakfast at some old coffee shop. There were four of us there. The waitress came by and puts shot glasses in front of us. I didn't know what the hell was going on. She poured us each a shot of Jack Daniels. I was still on probation and I could get fired if word got around that I was drinking on the job. But if I didn't drink, these guys were going to think I was a snitch and they wouldn't trust me.

"Well, it was a hell of an eye opener. In those days, you were tested in a lot of ways. When my two weeks were up with them, I was impressed as hell. I was thinking, 'Wow. This isn't some chicken-shit investigation. This is murder. The most serious crime anyone can commit. Yeah. One of these days, maybe I can do this.' "

He spits and says, "It was a lot different when I came up. Today, you've got a lot of candy asses coming on the job. No military experience. They live with mommy and daddy. The first time people yell at them, they can't handle it. If you get in a fight on the street, you don't know where they'll be."

She glares at him. "I assume you're talking about women cops?"

"No I'm *not* talking about women cops." He spits again. "I know one thing. If we're in a fight on the street, I don't have to worry about you."

He tells her that he heard she used to compete with the LAPD weight-lifting team.

She nods. "I was on the job a year or two and was in the academy gym working out. This captain who was coaching the lifting team spotted me. He told me I should join. So I started training and competing with them."

"How'd you do?"

She tells him she is retired now, but when she was competing, she won the women's power-lifting gold medal at the California Police Olympics.

"So you can take care of yourself."

"Yeah. I can definitely take care of myself," she says flatly.

"I used to compete for the department—the pistol shooting team," says Razanskas, who is a Distinguished Expert, the LAPD's highest ranking for marksmanship. "But I got pissed off. I'd pay for my own ammo, my own entry fees. At competitions I'd pay for my own lodgings. Then I'd see these guys from other cities. Their departments paid for everything. They'd practice on city time, get free ammo, get days off for competitions. And I had to beg to compete. I finally said, 'Screw it.' "

After lunch, Razanskas and Winn return to the bureau. As he fills out the first page of his murder book, Winn tells him she is going to call some stations and check the major disturbance calls last night. Maybe they will have some connection to this victim.

"Good thinking," he says. "A woman isn't supposed to think of that before me."

She files away the jibe, waiting for her chance to get back at him.

They cannot do much more on the investigation until the victim is identified. And for that, they have to rely on the coroner investigator. He will fingerprint the victim, run the prints and hope the prints will connect to a name somewhere in the system. But the investigator went straight from the body dump to an apartment where a 78-year-old woman was raped and murdered. Because of recent budget cutbacks and layoffs in the coroner's office, detectives have to wait much longer at homicide scenes for bodies to be picked up. And they have to wait longer for victim identification. Razanskas and Winn wait all afternoon and into the evening for the coroner to call. The weekend is almost over now, and Razanskas and Winn are happy about one thing. It has been quiet in the Harpy and Diamond Street neighborhoods.

While they wait, Razanskas begins the onerous task of writing the multitudinous reports the LAPD requires on every homicide. He writes the preliminary investigation report and the death report. He writes a report for Robbery-Homicide Division, which is apprised of every murder in the city. He writes a major incident report. He writes an evidence report and a press release. Later on, he will write an autopsy report. If the case is not solved, follow-up reports are due; if the case is solved, close-out reports are due. Detectives spend an inordinate amount of time filling out reports—many of which are redundant or unnecessarily complicated—time that could be spent investigating homicides. But the LAPD is an enormous bureaucracy, requiring enormous amounts of paperwork. Everyone complains about it, but the system remains unchanged.

Razanskas and Winn wait seven hours for the coroner investigator to call, wasting precious time. Finally, at 8:45, he calls, gives them the victim's name, and they run him in the police computer. His name is John Robert Elliot, he is 38 years old, and he has been arrested numerous times since 1980 for crimes ranging from car theft to drug possession.

They have a name now, but not much else. All Razanskas knows is that the killer was extremely pissed off at the victim. He sifts through the victim's arrest record and mutters to Winn, "This is what you call a miracle case. It's going to take a fucking miracle to clear it. I can see myself writing the sixty-dayer on this one right now."

As they walk to the parking lot they talk about the son of a celebrity who is a flamboyant drag queen.

"If that was my son, I'd kick his ass," he says.

"You just got to love 'em and accept 'em," she says. "Your parents loved and accepted *you*. Even though everyone knows *you're* a big asshole."

Winn knows if you display a weakness in front of Razanskas or are sensitive about something, he will hone in and gleefully needle you about it. A good offense, she figures, is the best defense. So she decides she will put the needle to him when she has the chance, to make *him* respond to *her* jibes.

She learned to stand up for herself shortly after moving to South-Central, when she was 13, from Robstown, Texas, a small farming town in the Rio Grande Valley near the Gulf of Mexico. The South-Central neighborhood where Winn was raised with her three younger sisters was predominately black, with a smattering of white families, a working-class area where most people owned their own homes and single parents were rare. Winn's family lived in a two-bedroom, beige stucco house with a broad front porch bordered by rose bushes and daisies and a backyard filled with collard and mustard greens that her mother had planted. Winn and her sisters spent every Sunday at the Pilgrim Missionary Baptist Church on East 45th Street and their summers at the vacation Bible school.

Winn missed her large extended family in Texas and she missed the calm and comfort of small-town life. She was shy and thought the kids at her new junior high school were "too citified." They were unfriendly to newcomers and they teased her about her stuttering. A girl named Hiawatha, who was particularly cruel, and her friends stole Winn's lunch money and taunted her.

One afternoon during gym class, as Winn sat in the bleachers, Hiawatha and her friends began teasing her again. She ignored them. Hiawatha hauled off and punched her in the back. Winn lost her temper, grabbed Hiawatha and tossed her off the bleachers. That ended her problems with Hiawatha.

Years later, when Winn was working the back-up car on a hooker task force, Hiawatha was arrested. While she was in a police station holding tank, Winn briefly interviewed her.

"You remember me?" Hiawatha asked Winn.

"I sure do."

"Well," Hiawatha said, "you always were a goody-two-shoes."

After Winn solved her problem with Hiawatha, she vowed that if anyone ever tried to bully her again, she would put an instantaneous stop to it. This lesson later proved invaluable when she joined the LAPD, a department where sexual harassment has long been a problem.

She breezed through the police academy, was assigned to an East Los Angeles station and began work as a rookie patrol officer. It was not easy for a woman in the LAPD during the mid-1980s. The year Winn joined the department, two LAPD studies found widespread complaints among female officers about discrimination and harassment. Only recently has the LAPD seriously addressed the problem.

A 1993 study sponsored by the Police Commission described a work environment where women clearly were unwelcome. "Women told of being constantly tested and baited, or deprived of the usual network of officer support," the report stated. In some police stations, according to the report, women officers were humiliated by being segregated during roll call.

The LAPD also has been criticized for tolerating racism. An independent commission, formed in the wake of the videotaped beating of Rodney King, concluded that minority officers often are subjected to discriminatory treatment, slurs and racist comments.

Winn's first exposure to racism in the department was when

she was working as a trick decoy. Another female cop recruited for the trick detail was a young woman who looked like a sorority sister. Her first night, she showed up with her long, light brown hair in a ponytail, wearing stone-washed jeans and a University of Southern California sweatshirt. She looked so ridiculous the lieutenant made her turn her sweatshirt inside out.

Her first john pulled over at the corner and said, " 'Hey, baby, how you doin'?"

"Fine, thank you," she responded enthusiastically. "How are you?"

The lieutenant had heard enough. "Get her off the street," he said. That same weekend Winn and another female cop made 85 arrests.

Later, when there was an opening in vice, both Winn and the woman with the ponytail applied. The captain offered the job to the woman with the ponytail and told Winn it was because she had more time on the job. He did not realize that Winn knew this was untrue. Winn and the woman had joined the department at the same time, and they had gone through the police academy together.

When Winn first began working patrol, some cops would ignore her. Others would refuse to talk to her in the patrol car. One told her, "I won't work with cunts." She felt like she was constantly being tested, in the station and on the street. One night on patrol, she pulled over a car of gang members for reckless driving. One drunk gangbanger in the back of the car, clutching an open bottle of beer, began swearing at her. She was afraid he might toss the bottle at her, so she told him to get out of the car. She asked him for his license.

"I'm not giving you any motherfucking license," he said as he crawled out of the car.

She asked him again.

He reached for his wallet, whirled around and took a swing at her.

She decked him and broke his nose.

After that, some of the patrol officers began calling her "One Punch." And the Neanderthals in the squad room backed off a bit when she came around. Lieutenant Robleto, who now heads South Bureau Homicide, was a watch commander at the station and that was his introduction to Winn. He decided to keep an eye on her. She was his kind of cop.

Sexual harassment might have remained entrenched at the LAPD, but few cops wanted to get in Winn's face. It was not just her physical prowess that impressed Robleto. He noticed that when anyone razzed her, she always had a comeback. He knew that women cops needed that ability, too, if they were to succeed. He filed away her name and decided if he ever had his own unit, he was going to give her a call.

Robleto is not part of the LAPD's old boy network. He was born in Nicaragua and was called a "greaseball" by his first watch commander. He does not care about a detective's race or gender; he just wants to know if the detective can solve murders.

The stakes are higher in homicide than in any other unit because suspects face the ultimate punishment—the death penalty. And because detectives at South Bureau deal with the hardest cases around—killers—Robleto was looking for detectives who were hard cases themselves. At South Bureau, it is not enough to simply be a smart detective. Robleto wanted detectives who were tough enough and ruthless enough to, as he calls it, "back their play." He knew Winn had backed her play a number of times on the street and in the squad room. When Robleto took over South Bureau Homicide, he recruited her.

Chapter 6
Stairs to Nowhere

Tuesday, July 12

John Robert Elliot is laid out on a metal autopsy table, two days after he was found in the parking lot. Winn, who is standing beside the body, is wearing a powder blue scrub suit with surgical mask, booties and protective cap. Razanskas has to miss the autopsy because a fugitive in one of his old homicide cases has just been caught in Oregon. Razanskas hopped a plane Monday. He will conduct a brief investigation in Oregon and bring the suspect back to Los Angeles on Wednesday.

South Bureau detectives try to attend all of their victims' autopsies, because they can occasionally gain invaluable insights. If, for example, a suspect tells detectives that the victim came after him with a knife and he fired his gun in self-defense, the detectives will want to know the trajectory of the bullet. If the pathologist determines the weapon was fired downward, at a 45-degree angle, and the victim probably was on his knees when he died, the suspect will be booked for murder.

Winn hopes the autopsy on Elliot will determine the kind of weapon that was used. That, at least, will be a start. The pathologist performs an autopsy to determine three things: cause of death, mode of death and manner of death. Cause of death might be strangulation. Mode of death might be homicide or suicide. Manner of death might be a gun or a knife or a candlestick. Winn knows the cause and the mode of death. She is at the autopsy to determine the manner—the type of weapon used.

The color scheme of the coroner's office could have been designed for a little boy's room. Everything in the corridors is blue: powder blue walls, navy blue doors, glowing purple-blue fluorescent lights on the walls, "zap" lights designed to kill insects drawn to the corpses. Even the plastic body bags stacked on metal racks in the "cooler" are pale blue. Only an occasional set of red toenails peeking through the bags interrupts the color scheme.

In the autopsy room, Elliot is naked, on his back, as the pathologist studies the deep gash marks on his head. A pathologist at another table glances over and is intrigued by the gash marks.

"Machete?" he asks.

"Don't think so," says Elliot's pathologist.

An autopsy technician wanders by and asks, "How you doing this morning?"

"Better than him," the pathologist says, pointing to Elliot.

He studies a few of Elliot's head gashes and says to Winn, "These are lacerations, but they are not cutting wounds. Maybe a pipe." He probes a 4-inch long gash with a scalpel. The crack in the skull is faintly visible. "No, not a pipe . . . it had a bit of an edge. This is interesting."

He studies a bruised and swollen forearm. He splits it open with his scalpel to get to the bone. "Compound fracture of the left forearm. Defensive wound." He looks at the other arm. "Holy shit! Look at this." He cuts open the arm and sees another break. "This guy was stopping some big-time blows."

After the pathologist finishes his external examination, he picks up a scalpel and makes a large Y-shaped incision in Elliot's chest. An autopsy technician, using a huge tool that looks like a hedge clipper, cuts through Elliot's ribs and removes his sternum.

Winn winces at the loud crunching sound that reverberates in the autopsy room. Now Elliot's internal organs are visible. This is a particularly useful view when trying to determine gunshot trajectory. A pathologist will follow the bruising and bleeding of the organs to trace the path of the bullets. Pathologists also use a fluoroscope, a type of x-ray machine, to locate bullets and bullet fragments.

After the pathologist examines Elliot's internal organs, he removes them and looks for signs of disease and trauma. The organs are not badly bruised; the blows to Elliot's head were the fatal ones. He weighs the organs, takes small tissue samples and places the organs in "hold jars."

Sometimes a detective trainee needs a break midway through an autopsy. The technicolor view of a victim's internal organs and the nauseating smell of moldering flesh mingled with formaldehyde can be overwhelming. But Winn is impassive. She takes notes, asks questions, and is engrossed in the job at hand. But when the autopsy technician fires up the power saw and zips off the top of Elliot's skull, Winn swallows hard and takes a few steps back. The technician folds back the skin of Elliot's scalp. The skull is exposed and the fractures clearly visible, like cracks in a hard-boiled egg. The pathologist runs his pen along a long sinuous crack and says to Winn, "This is what we refer to as H.S.O."

"H.S.O.?" she asks.

"Head split open," he says, chuckling.

He removes Elliot's brain, holds it in his hand and examines it. He shows Winn a few wine-colored splotches—contusions from the blows. "Cause of death," he pronounces, "is brain injury from skull fracture." He weighs the brain and turns to Winn. "I think the weapon used was made of wood and had an edge. But not a real sharp edge. My guess would be something like a two-by-four."

After the autopsy, as Winn drives back to the office, she still is immersed in the case. She theorizes why a two-by-four would be used. She wonders what the victim could have done to have precipitated the beating. She recalls the bagman asking them if the case was a body dump. She wonders if he may know something. To Winn, Elliot is not just some wino ex-con who got what he deserved. He is from South-Central, where she was raised, where she graduated from high school, where her parents still live, and the person who killed Elliot is still out there, posing a threat to the people she cares about, to *her* neighborhood.

The day after the autopsy of John Robert Elliot, Razanskas returns from Oregon. For the next day and a half, he fills out extradition paperwork, arrest reports, close-out reports and expense reports, all from the Oregon case. He drives back and forth from the office to police headquarters. He turns in his expense paperwork to city clerks. He turns in extradition paperwork to state clerks. Friday morning, five days after he picked up the body dump case, he can finally begin his investigation.

"The trail is getting cold," he says to Winn, opening up the murder book. "I haven't done a fucking thing."

After time for paperwork, vacations and court appearances are subtracted, South Bureau detective teams have about eight working days for each homicide—before the next one comes around. On this body dump, Razanskas spent valuable time—as his precious eight days began to tick away—not pursuing suspects, but working a four-year-old case. He has no suspects in the body dump case. He has not even located Elliot's next of kin.

In the afternoon, Winn follows a few leads on the rock house double-murder she picked up in June, but she has to work the case without the help of Li'l Sambo. His parents have not persuaded him to cooperate. They have not even called her back.

But another homicide detective's snitch, who is plugged into the gang scene, agrees to talk to Winn about the murder. He had called his contact at South Bureau and told him he was angry that the killers knocked off two 50-year-old men. Gangbangers versus gangbangers was OK, but killing the two old guys was out of line. They were not running the show. They were just trying to pick up a few extra bucks watching the store.

Winn meets the snitch behind a hamburger stand. He has

wild, unkempt hair, is wearing jeans and sneakers and is shirtless. He tells Winn the name of the female basehead who left the footprints at the scene. He tells her that Sambo, a Front Street Crip, was running a rock house in Nine Seven East Coast Crip territory.

"Nine Seven didn't want another rock house in their territory," he says. "They felt that motherfucker Sambo was disrespecting their hood."

"Who was the shooter?" Winn asks.

The snitch tells Winn his name. "He's an O.G. [original gangster—a veteran] from Front Street."

"Wait a minute," Winn says, shaking her head in confusion. "Sambo is Front Street."

"Front Street wanted to join forces with Nine Seven. They wanted the two sets to be united. Control more action. Sell more drugs. But Sambo's not going along with the program."

"He's not interested in sharing," Winn says.

"Right. And as long as he's in business, the two sets can't get together. But Sambo's some new booty. He's a hard-headed youngster. He's like, 'Fuck y'all. I'll do what I want.' So one of his homies, who's trying to get in good with Nine Seven, takes care of him."

"You know of any witnesses to the shooting, anybody else who can give me some information?" Winn asks.

He shakes his head. "I'll keep my ear down and if I hear anything, I'll let you know."

Winn slips the snitch a $20 bill.

"That's enough to buy me a forty-ouncer and a burger," he says.

"A forty-ouncer and a burger is no twenty bucks," she says, smiling. "If I'd known that's all you wanted, I'd have only given you five."

Winn heads back to the station with two names, two leads. But she cannot locate the basehead. She is a street person, has no permanent address and seems to have disappeared without a trace. And Winn does not have enough on the shooter to force him to talk. All she can do now is track the two trails and hope something breaks. She is beginning to understand why South Bureau Homicide detectives are so chronically frustrated.

Razanskas is still grousing about the disappearance of Larry Charles Gary. He calls a producer from the television show *America's Most Wanted* and tries to interest him in the case. A national television audience often can locate fugitives faster than any task force, and the show has helped South Bureau locate fugitives in the past. But the fugitive needs a certain cachet to interest the producers. So Razanskas pushes the angle of how this is not just another sordid drug hit, how Charles killed a defenseless elderly woman, how the victims, in a dramatic fashion, identified Charles in dying declarations. The producer tells Razanskas he will get back to him, the old "Don't call me, I'll call you," routine.

Razanskas and Winn decide to check some old crime reports and see if they can pick up any leads on John Robert Elliot, their body dump case. Razanskas pulls out of the dim underground lot, into the glare of a broiling July afternoon, and drives to the 77th Street station. This is where Razanskas first worked as a detective and where he often coordinates the initial stages of an investigation because it is closer to the action than the homicide bureau. He peruses gang records and crime reports here and checks with patrol officers and gang investigators.

Razanskas parks in the back of the station, and he and Winn walk through a hallway where jagged holes have been kicked into the walls. The station, built in the 1920s, is the LAPD's oldest and most dilapidated. In 1940, when Raymond Chandler was describing the 77th in *Farewell, My Lovely,* the station already was in a state of disrepair. Chandler described the station's "worn stairs," the "dirty brown linoleum," the "mud-colored hall and stairway," "the smell of old cigar butts . . . in the air."

Today, the station is in even worse shape. Ceiling tiles are kept in place with duct tape and large chunks of tile are missing from the linoleum floor. The roof leaks and roaches scurry under desks. Bare bulbs and exposed pipes hang over a row of dim, dank jail cells. In the winter, the ancient basement boiler always seems to go out and frigid air blows down from the ducts. In the summer, the doors often are thrown open because the air conditioner breaks down.

There is a stairway that leads straight into a brick wall, "the stairs to nowhere," officers call it. The stairs used to lead to a second floor, but there is no second floor now. It was torn down because of fears that it would collapse during an earthquake. The station will be razed next year and rebuilt. But, for now, the officers just have to make do.

The 77th, Razanskas believes, is a metaphor for the plight of LAPD detectives. Because of tight city budgets during the 1980s and 1990s, the LAPD, to cut costs, has put off purchasing equipment. The department does not provide homicide detectives with beepers, which they are required to carry. The detectives pay for their own. They buy their own cellular phones and camera kits. They pay $48.49 for the plastic name tags they wear at crime scenes. They pay $53.50 a box for the business cards they pass out to witnesses.

Although South Bureau Homicide is housed in a relatively new building, all the office equipment is out of date. The bureau's fax machine, which was donated, is frequently broken. There is no voice mail at the bureau and detectives do not have their own phone lines. There are not enough secretaries, and detectives frequently are interrupted by the ringing phones and have to play receptionist.

The LAPD does not even have a computer network that links its 18 geographic divisions. The handful of computers in the various divisions are not compatible. The LAPD hopes to obtain the funds—through private donations—to install a department-wide computer system. But until then, South Bureau Homicide detectives cannot obtain, by computer, crime patterns and trends and other information from divisions throughout the city. Because of the antiquated equipment, LAPD officers spend much of their time manually completing crime reports and other paperwork.

When South Bureau detectives need to obtain files from other divisions, they often have to hop in their cars and pick the files up themselves. The detectives drive worn-out squad cars, some with well over 100,000 miles. The bureau's only video camera and answering machine were donated. Some detectives, including Winn, buy their own printers and laptop computers to write their reports. They are overworked, understaffed, and ignored. Clearing cases is hard enough; the odds against them already are long. The inadequate equipment is just another obstacle in a job fraught with obstacles.

Razanskas and Winn pick up at the 77th Street station some of John Robert Elliot's previous addresses, and they decide to do some door-knocking. Maybe they will get a lead from an ex-wife or girlfriend. Razanskas stops at a liquor store, buys a few tins of Skoal and takes a pinch. He heads west on Manchester Avenue and complains about having to go to his wife's 20-year high-school reunion.

"You're lucky she's showing you in public," Winn says.

He talks about another homicide detective, a longtime friend of his, who married his high-school sweetheart and is still married to her. "I respect that," he says.

"You'd still be married once if you weren't such an asshole."

"I gave more of myself to the job than to my family." He spits into his cup and shakes his head. "I learned the job's not that important, after all."

They drive in silence for a few minutes and he says, "This marriage is going well."

"I should hope so. Damn. You've had three of them."

"Hey, I just bought my wife some roses and a card. So, you see, Raz isn't such an asshole, after all."

She stifles a smile. "I'm glad my influence is finally starting to pay off."

Chapter 7
Dead the Lover

Monday, July 25

The World Cup is over, the extra police patrols are off the streets, the crowds are back on the streets and the murder rate is climbing fast. Things are returning to normal at South-Bureau Homicide.

On this last week in July, the other team of detectives that Razanskas supervises—Armando Reyes and Paul Masuyama—is on call again. They are far down the list, however, so Razanskas is hoping he will have time to catch up on his own cases. There still is no sign of Larry Charles Gary, and Razanskas has not heard from the FBI's fugitive task force or the producer from *America's Most Wanted.* He still is working the body dump, the carjacking, the travel agent murder.

Reyes finishes writing a 60-dayer and Razanskas has to review and edit it before he sends it on to the lieutenant. When Razanskas reaches the section that explains why the homicide is still unsolved, he reads out loud, "Due to the paucity of witnesses."

"Hey, you stole that phrase from me," he tells Reyes.

"Well, that pretty much says it all about the case, doesn't it?" Reyes asks.

"Yeah," Razanskas says. "This case and about a thousand others."

Reyes updates Razanskas on the case they worked a few weeks ago where the victim, Clarence, was shot on the street by the sidewalk scrawl, "Dead the Lover." This case, too, Reyes says, can be summed up by the line, "Due to the paucity of witnesses."

Reyes knows several neighbors can identify the three men who ambushed Clarence, but he cannot convince anyone to talk, so it does not do him much good. The men involved in the killing are hard-core gangsters, 83rd Street Hoover Crips, and everyone in the neighborhood is afraid of them, afraid to sign a witness statement, afraid of repercussions. Even Clarence's best friend, Miles, who was with him when he was killed, still refuses to cooperate.

Reyes knows that a 14-year-old neighbor got a good look at one of the suspects. He brought the boy to the station with his mother, but the boy told him he only saw the suspect from behind. Later in the interview the boy said the suspect was wearing a green shirt with only three of the buttons buttoned. Reyes pointed out to the boy that if he knew about the buttons, he must have seen more than the *back* of the suspect. The boy gave him a blank stare and said flatly, "No. I only saw him from the back."

This is Reyes's third case in which he knows who the suspects are but cannot make any arrests because witnesses will not cooperate. Sometimes, finding the killer is easy. The hard part is finding the witnesses.

The victim's father, Clarence, Sr., has done some door-knocking in the neighborhood and talked to some of his son's homies. He, too, knows who the killers are. He stops by the bureau to talk to Reyes. Clarence, Sr., who is wearing work pants and a powder blue work shirt with his name over the pocket, is heavyset and balding. Since no one will testify, he suggests the police set the killers up. If the police can plant drugs on the killers and send them to jail, he says, "I can have these guys done on the inside. In a minute."

Reyes tells him, contrary to what he may have heard, the LAPD does not operate like that.

"I gotta tell you somethin'," Clarence says to Reyes. "My past ain't nice. But I straightened out my stroke. I'm tired of sitting up at San Quentin, Folsom and Soledad. When I left Soledad, the guard says to me, 'You be back. We put your name on the wall.' I just told him, 'You seen the last of me.' And this time I meant it."

He extends a palm toward Reyes and says, "I'm asking for your help. I want you to get those boys who shot my son off the street. Before I do something to hurt myself. With this three strikes law, I don't want to be no ex-con caught with a gun. Or a baseball bat. You know what I'm sayin'? I got two other boys. I got to be there for 'em. If you don't do something, you putting me against the wall. Even the boy's mama want me to do something. She call me a coward and a punk. She want me to take care of bidness."

Reyes warns him not to take matters into his own hands. As Reyes walks him out the door, he tells him the most constructive thing he can do is to convince Miles to cooperate with police.

Reyes was Razanskas' partner before Winn joined the homicide unit. He also was a detective trainee. When Reyes was growing up, he had no burning desire to be a cop. He joined the department because he had been delivering office supplies for seven years, and he was bored.

His parents were from California's Imperial Valley, where they grew up picking melons and lettuce. After his father, who was driving a tractor in the fields seven days a week, asked for a day off and was refused, he quit. He moved the family to Los Angeles, found a job driving a water tanker truck and earned enough to buy a small two-bedroom house in a working-class neighborhood near the harbor. There were gang members who lived in the neighborhood and on the block, but Reyes's parents kept a close eye on their children. They stayed in school and off the streets.

After high school, Reyes enrolled in a carpentry program at a trade school, but he dropped out because he had just bought a new Camaro and he needed a job to make the payments. He spent seven years delivering office supplies. A friend suggested they both join the police reserves, so Reyes signed up and worked two days a month on patrol. He liked the work—and the pay—and decided to make it a career. At the academy, he realized he had a flair for police work and was named a squad leader. He spent less than three years in patrol before he was promoted to vice. He later became the first member of his academy class to be named a training officer. After less than five years on the job, he made it to South Bureau Homicide as a detective trainee, where the lieutenant was on the lookout for bright, bilingual cops.

Reyes is so friendly and easygoing that suspects underestimate him and make the mistake of saying too much in the interview room. When they do, his smile disappears, his eyes harden, and he pounces on the inconsistencies in their statements. The rattled suspects often provide him with the leads he needs before they regain their composure.

Razanskas taught Reyes to think beyond a suspect's arrest, all the way to the trial. He taught Reyes to be meticulous at crime scenes, so defense attorneys could not undercut his testimony. Reyes knew about Razanskas' failed marriages, and he learned from that, too. He learned how to keep his cases from consuming him, how to balance the demands of the job and still make time for his wife and two children.

Reyes and Razanskas had a few close calls when they were partners, including one confrontation last winter they are still talking about. They were called to the scene after a gangbanger shot and killed a boy who was a passenger in a car that was driving by. Razanskas approached the driver, who was sitting on the curb, next to his car, which was riddled with bullet holes. He asked the driver to show him the exact spot where the shooting took place.

The driver, Razanskas and Reyes walked a few blocks down a side street. It was just after midnight on a cool, damp December night, when two gang members turned a corner and appeared out of the mist. Razanskas noticed that one of them had a pistol in his hand. "He's got a gun," he yelled to Reyes. As the gangbanger began to raise his 9 millimeter, the two detectives grabbed their guns. But just as Razanskas was about to pull the trigger, the gangbanger tossed his gun high in the air and it landed on a nearby rooftop.

It turned out that when Reyes pulled his coat back, reaching for his gun, the gangbanger saw the detective's shiny gold badge on his belt, gleaming under the street lamp. He did not want to shoot a cop. The gun was recovered from the roof, and ballistics matched it to the one that killed the boy in the car. The case was cleared that night.

Although Reyes and Masuyama are far down the on-call list, on Tuesday night a supervisor decides to move them up to the number-one spot. A film crew from a Polish television station is in town to do a story on homicide in Los Angeles. A supervisor asks Razanskas if he speaks Polish. He tells him he does not.

"Why not?" the supervisor asks. "Isn't Polish like Lithuanian?"

"No," Razanskas says sharply.

"Well, you're the closest thing we've got to a Polack. So your team will be up tonight."

With the fall of Communism came a rise in the Polish homicide rate, so murder now is a hot topic in Poland. The film crew contacted LAPD officials, who immediately sent them to South Bureau Homicide. If you want a murder and do not have long to wait, South Bureau is the place to be. They have been given permission to film one murder scene, from behind the tape.

Razanskas is willing to help the crew, he tells a few detectives in the squad room, because Poland is no longer a Communist country. "I still have a heavy, heavy beef against Communists," he says.

During World War II, when the Russians rolled through Lithuania, most of his mother's relatives, including her parents, were executed in their backyards. They were teachers, part of the intelligentsia, people the Soviets considered a threat. His mother and father escaped to Germany, where his father hid during much of World War II to avoid serving in the German army. After the war his mother worked as a civilian nurse for the U.S. Army. The family tried to immigrate to the United States, but there was an endless number of refugees and it might have taken years, so they left for Venezuela, where his father found work as an electrician. In the early 1960s, his father, concerned about political instability in Venezuela, brought the family to the United States.

After high school, when Razanskas was attending community college, the Vietnam War was raging. He had a student deferment and probably could have ridden out the war in college. But he decided to enlist in the Air Force. Because of what happened to his mother's family in Lithuania, he felt an obligation to fight Communism.

The Polish film crew talks to Razanskas on Tuesday afternoon and asks if they will have to wait all week for a murder. He laughs and says, "Not around here." He is true to his word because a few minutes before midnight residents of West 22nd Street hear gunshots and call police. Patrol officers discover a dead body in the middle of the street.

When Razanskas shows up at 1:30 in the morning, Reyes and Masuyama are working the crime scene, and the Polish film crew is behind the tape, smoking cigarettes and filming the detectives. This neighborhood is outside Razanskas' territory, but his team picked up the murder because the supervisor wanted to get the film crew out with Razanskas tonight. This street is at the northern border of the bureau's territory, and the neighborhood is more affluent than the typical South-Central murder site. Down the street, at the edge of the West Adams district, turn-of-the-century mansions with expansive lawns, Craftsman-style bungalows and small Victorians are undergoing renovation. This was once one of Los Angeles' most desirable neighborhoods, and silent film stars, including Roscoe "Fatty" Arbuckle, owned mansions here.

The body is across the street from a new apartment complex, its terraced garden dotted with purple rose bushes, bird-of-paradise plants and yellow daisies. The street is lined with palm and ficus trees, and a faint breeze carries the smell of jasmine. This is a more serene neighborhood than Razanskas is used to, and none of the residents has even ventured outside for a peek at the action.

Razanskas walks to the middle of the street and crouches beside the body. The victim is gagged with a strip of blue cloth and his head is lying in a pool of blood. His hands are bound behind his back with a belt, and his feet are tied with a white extension cord. He has been shot several times.

"Damn," Razanskas mutters. "Another dump job."

Most body dump victims are killed in one location and dumped at another. But this victim has been shot and dumped at the same location. There are no witnesses, but at least detectives have some evidence to work with. They find seven .380-caliber shell casings and a few bullet slugs, which flattened out on the asphalt. A few feet away from the victim's head is an arresting sight: a single, shiny white tooth encircled by drops of blood. It looks like a tiny white flower with red petals.

A criminalist from the coroner's office removes fibers and hair samples and then examines the bullet wounds. One of the bullets hit the victim in the back of the head and shattered a few teeth, which flew out onto the street. He also was shot in the ear. The criminalist notes that the victim's pants are pulled down around his ankles. "This guy," he says, "might have been screwing someone else's girl."

The victim has no wallet and only 30 cents in his pocket. When the criminalist turns him over and the detectives study his face, they are confused. They cannot determine his nationality. His features and coloring are a multiethnic melange.

The detectives are becoming increasingly discouraged. They have no witnesses, no name for the victim, no address, no identification of any kind. They do not even know his nationality.

When Razanskas returns to the squad room he tells Winn, "Somebody up there doesn't like me. I get two cases in the last two and a half weeks. Both are dump jobs."

The number of body dumps he has been seeing, he tells Winn, highlights a troubling trend. Detectives are seeing more homicides where there are no eyewitnesses. Homicides where there are few leads. Homicides that are so tough to investigate that the solve rate has been steadily dropping.

"The fact of the matter is," Razanskas says, "more people are getting away with murder."

In 1965, 91 percent of the nation's murders were cleared (a law enforcement term for a homicide investigation that is closed, in most cases, by a suspect's arrest or death). In 1980, the figure dropped to 72 percent. By the mid-1990s, the clearance rate hovered around 65 percent. And because not all cases stand up in court, even fewer killers pay for their crimes. In Los Angeles County, for example, only one in three killings resulted in a conviction for murder or manslaughter, according to a *Los Angeles Times* study of the county's murders from 1990 to 1994.

People are so frightened by crime today partly because the nature of homicide has changed so dramatically. There has been an "unprecedented shift in national homicide patterns," according to a 1993 FBI study.

In the past, most murders were committed by a spouse, a family member, a friend, an acquaintance. Police did not have to go far in their search for suspects. Police still clear most domestic cases—what they call "Ma and Pa Kettle murders." But while nearly one out of three homicides was family-related during the mid-1960s, by the mid-1990s the figure had dropped to a little more than one out of ten.

In the early 1990s, for the first time, more than half the nation's murders were committed by strangers or unknown persons, according to the FBI. These are the types of murders that compose the bulk of Razanskas' caseload: drive-by shootings, drug-related hits, robbery-murders, body dumps. Because most of these homicides take place on the street, detectives often cannot obtain any physical evidence, so they are even more difficult to solve.

In addition to the rise in stranger homicides, detectives are further hamstrung by the code of silence on the streets. The phrase "Due to the paucity of witnesses" is so prevalent in homicide reports today because people know that gangbangers and drug dealers are not reluctant to kill witnesses.

During the past 15 months, a dozen witnesses to homicides in South Bureau have been murdered, five of them by one street gang. Numerous other witnesses have been attacked, assaulted and intimidated.

The LAPD has purchased a moving van, and, during the past year alone in South Bureau, has helped 39 homicide witnesses and their families move out of their neighborhoods. Simply moving victims, however, is a woefully inadequate response to the danger witnesses face.

Lt. Sergio Robleto of South Bureau Homicide acknowledges that more needs to be done by the LAPD. A comprehensive witness-protection program should be established, he said, and a special LAPD unit is needed just to protect witnesses. But given the current funding shortages of the LAPD, it is unlikely programs such as these will be implemented anytime soon.

Families of murdered witnesses have lambasted South Bureau detectives for not informing them right away about all the other witnesses who have been killed.

"The deaths of these witnesses is eating me up inside," Robleto says, sighing and shaking his head. "But we've got hundreds of murders a year. If we scare off our witnesses, we're not going to solve any of them. The streets will be even more dangerous.

"I care deeply about these witnesses. In my mind, they're incredibly brave—true heroes. But all I can do now to protect them is to make sure that my detectives are trained in how to hide witnesses and to do everything in my power to make sure these witnesses get hidden."

Although more blacks than whites in the U.S. are arrested for murder, the changing nature of homicide is not simply an inner-city problem. The number of white murder arrestees has increased during the past 25 years at a greater rate than that of blacks. And during this time, the number of white juveniles arrested for murder has increased by 224 percent—more than double the rate for black juveniles, according to FBI statistics.

Despite all the concern about crime, it is a myth that a wave of violence is sweeping the country. In fact, the crime rate for a number of serious offenses, including homicide, has gone down since the record-setting year of 1980. This was a time when the population of young males, who commit the most crimes, was at a peak. The truth is, crime in America is a jumble of contradictory statistics.

During the early 1960s, the nation's homicide rate was relatively low—about 4.5 per 100,000 people. By the mid-1970s, it had doubled. In 1980 it had reached a peak of 10.2 per 100,000—still the record high—and then began to dip. With the emergence of crack cocaine and the growth of gangs in the mid-1980s the rate began to climb again. Cocaine created turf wars, which quickly raised the level of violence on the street.

By the mid-1990s, the homicide rate began to drop, with significant declines in a number of major cities. Criminologists attribute this to a number of factors, including a soaring prison population, a possible decline in the use of crack, more effective police work and, most important, demographic changes. The number of young males in the population was lower than during the baby boom years. Still, there are more than 20,000 murders every year in the United States. And the prospects are bleak for the coming decade. The teenage population is expected to increase sharply, and law enforcement officials are bracing for yet another surge in the nation's homicide rate.

So, despite people's fears, there is not more murder today. Just a different kind of murder. Killers today are younger. More of them do not know their victims. They are more likely to use a gun. The murders are less likely to be solved.

In the past, people could make some sense of murders stemming from love triangles or family disputes or barroom fights. But now, because murder is so random, so seemingly senseless, people feel more vulnerable. And more frightened.

People also are frightened because they feel the rules on the street have changed. They know that even if they cooperate during a street robbery or a carjacking or a home burglary, they may be killed anyway. Razanskas knows the rules on the street have changed because the criminals have changed. This new breed of criminal Razanskas and Winn are pursuing has an ethic, a modus operandi and contempt for life that is different from criminals in previous decades.

The older career criminals tell Razanskas they are mystified by the crimes they see today. When they were young, the professional criminal's goal was to get in and out of a crime scene as quickly as possible, with as much money as possible, with the least amount of violence possible. If you held a merchant up and he gave you the money, if you wanted a car and the driver turned it over, if you clipped someone's wallet and they did not resist, you did not shoot them. But crimes that used to be simple street robberies or car thefts or store heists now end up as murders. And Razanskas and Winn are left to make some sense of these senseless murders.

Razanskas gives Winn and another detective a few details about Masuyama and Reyes's body dump case and mentions that the victim was shot in the ear. The detective tells him he once had a case where his victim was found lying in a carport, naked. The coroner investigator could not find an entry wound, an exit wound, blood, or any sign of trauma. At the autopsy, the fluoroscope, a type of x-ray machine, solved the mystery and revealed a .22 slug. The man, who had crossed a Jamaican drug dealer, had been shot in the anus.

Masuyama walks over and begins discussing his case with Razanskas. "It's very strange," Masuyama says. "We still don't know what the guy is. He has dark skin, but he doesn't really have black features . . ."

"There's no such thing as black features," Winn interrupts. "That's a damn ignorant thing to say."

Masuyama tries to explain what he means, but Winn is not in the mood for debate. Masuyama shrugs and returns to his murder book.

Her mood brightens when she and another female detective drive downtown to police headquarters to run an errand. They begin swapping yarns, and Winn tells her about the time she was loaned out to vice and worked as a trick decoy. She wore tight jeans and a T-shirt and stood on street corners ensnaring johns. She was wired and the vice cops in a nearby van could hear everything.

"These fools would pull up in their car and I'd ask, 'What you want?' One guy says to me, 'I just want to watch.'

" 'Who you think you are?' I ask him. 'Jimmy Swaggart?'

"When the guys in the van stop laughing, they yelled, 'Work him, Marcella. Work him.'

"Sometimes I could hardly keep a straight face. One guy pulls over and tells me he doesn't have any money. He says he's going to give me a lottery ticket and a rock.

"I say to him, 'A lottery ticket and a rock? You must be kidding.' " She rolls her eyes. "This guy looks up at me and says, 'Not a rock. A *half* a rock. We can share it, baby.' "

She and the other detective exchange a glance and burst out laughing.

Masuyama is on the phone, calling division stations, in search of kidnapping reports. At 8 A.M., the coroner returns his call. He has matched the victim's fingerprints with a name. The victim is a 19-year-old man named Bernard from Belize. Masuyama obtains the victim's sister's address and heads out with Reyes to make the death notification. He is dreading the moment. This is the part of the job he hates the most.

Masuyama is quiet, introspective and rarely joins the boisterous squad room bantering. This summer, in addition to his homicide cases, he is consumed by an investigation of a more personal nature. He is trying to find his father, whom he has never met, whose name he does not know. Later in the summer, Masuyama plans to visit Japan and track down some of his distant relatives in the hopes that they can lead him to his father.

His father was an American serviceman in Japan, a member of the post-World War II occupation force. His mother, Sumiko Minoguchi, was Japanese. In 1947, they met and married in Sapporo and moved to Sendai, where Masuyama's father was stationed. Two years later his army unit shipped out from Japan and Minoguchi never heard from him again. In 1950, she gave birth to a son, whom she named Mitsuru.

Minoguchi returned to Sapporo and, a few years later, married again, to a Japanese war veteran who adopted Mitsuru. A few weeks before his fifth birthday, his mother died of heart disease. Mitsuru's stepfather and his mother's relatives had difficulty supporting him during the early 1950s, a time of great poverty in Japan. And they were concerned that, because he was half American, he would be subjected to much prejudice. They decided he would have a better future in the United States and put him up for adoption.

One morning when he was 5, he took a bus to the airport with his stepfather and his mother's relatives. He boarded the plane, feeling alone and frightened. He had never even been in an automobile before. As the plane slowly pulled away, toward the runway, he watched his relatives wave good-by in the distance. When the plane landed in Tokyo, he was met by his new parents.

Hisao Masuyama and his wife Elsie were American-born Japanese who met in a Colorado internment camp during World War II. They married, Hisao enlisted in the army and was assigned to military intelligence. After the war, when he and Elsie were stationed in Tokyo, they heard about a 5-year-old Japanese-American boy whose family could not care for him. They adopted the boy and named him Paul.

On his first night with the Masuyamas, the first night he had ever spent in a bed—he was used to sleeping on a futon—Paul cried as he thought about his family. He realized he would never see them again. He has a strong memory of his birth mother. The pain of losing her and the rest of his family hardened him, he later felt, made him more introverted and reflective than the other detectives in the squad room.

Whenever Masuyama has to make a death notification, and he is confronted with the family's tears and the grief, it always brings back memories of his mother. He recalls being brought to the hospital, where he saw her body for the last time, a lifeless figure on a futon, swaddled in a blanket. He recalls his own feelings of pain and loss.

Now, as he and Reyes drive across town to tell Bernard's sister that her brother has been killed, Masuyama is silent and somber. He can identify with the victim, a man with a difficult-to-determine nationality. Some suspects call Masuyama a "chink motherfucker"; others call him "whitey"; a few just assume he is Latino and address him in Spanish.

Masuyama and Reyes park in front of Bernard's sister's small house at 9 A.M., on a cloudy morning with a brisk breeze blowing from the ocean. The sister is not home, so the detectives talk with a next-door neighbor on her front porch. The neighbor points to the street and says, "That's her." The sister pulls up in a red Volkswagen Jetta and parks in her driveway. As she climbs out of the car Masuyama asks if she is the sister of Bernard. She nods.

"Can we go inside and talk?" he asks.

"Is he dead?" she shouts.

"I'm very sorry, but we have some bad news."

"Is he dead?"

"I'm afraid so."

"NO! NO! OH, MY GOD. NO!"

She collapses into Masuyama's arms and sobs. He gently leads her into the neighbor's living room, where she falls onto a sofa and buries her head in her hands. She lifts her head up, tears streaming down her face, and says, "It was that guy who did it. It was Alton. He killed him."

She tells Masuyama that Alton robbed Bernard's girlfriend last night, and she gives him the girlfriend's address. They pick her up, bring her back to the station and Razanskas joins them in the interview room. The girlfriend is in her early 20s, has a diamond stud in her nose and a tattoo of two red roses on her ankle. She is wearing denim shorts, a low-cut lace top; and her dyed apricot-colored hair, held in place by a double dose of hair spray, is splayed atop her head like a bouquet. She dabs her eyes with a tissue and tells them that she and Bernard left Belize a few weeks ago. He brought $3,000 with him and was going to borrow a few thousand more from his sisters. He planned to buy a pick-up truck, drive it back to Belize and start a construction business.

"How much cash did he have on him when you last saw him?" Razanskas asks.

"About twenty dollars."

"You sound just like my wife," he says, smiling. "You got the three thousand. He's got twenty bucks."

She tells them, in a lilting Caribbean accent, that Bernard was beeped at about 11 o'clock last night, made a phone call and left the apartment. About 15 minutes later, a Belizean man by the name of Alton knocked on the door and asked to use the phone. She told him Bernard did not like anyone in the house when he was not around. She was surprised when he pulled out a key to the apartment and attempted to let himself in. She tried to shut the door but he grabbed her by the throat, threw her against a wall and pulled out a black semiautomatic pistol. He threatened to shoot her if she screamed.

Alton was with two other men, members of a gang called the Belizean Blood Posse. They ransacked the apartment while Alton held the gun on her. After a few minutes, the two Bloods returned to the living room and said, "We got everything. Let's go." After they left, she discovered the $3,000 was missing.

"That Alton," she says, "he a bad dude. He do a lot of robbing and jacking in Belize." It turns out Alton has been active in Los Angeles, as well. He has a two-page rap sheet. Razanskas scrounges up a booking photo of Alton, and the girlfriend picks him out of a six-pack. In the photograph, Alton stares straight ahead with cold, vacant eyes. His black T-shirt is covered with dozens of copulating skeletons.

A few of Bernard's sisters show up at the station, along with one of his friends. The detectives interview them and discover why his nationality was so difficult to determine. His mother's family came to Belize from India and his father is part Indian and part black. A sister asks the detectives, "If you don't catch Alton in a few days, you just going to forget about this case?"

"Hell no," Razanskas says. "I just came back from Oregon and picked up a suspect on a case that's four years old."

"How long you been up?" she asks Masuyama.

"Since last night."

"When you going to sleep?"

"We'll work all day on the case and go to sleep tonight."

"I appreciate that," she says. "This is very important to our family."

"I know it is," Masuyama says softly. "That's why we're pushing so hard."

The detectives return to the squad room, lean against their desks and discuss the case. They believe the girlfriend was ripped off by Alton, but they have questions about the $3,000. Bernard has been arrested several times, during a previous stay in Los Angeles, for selling drugs. Another detective in the bureau, who once arrested Alton, tells Masuyama the murder probably is the result of "a Belizean drug thing."

The detectives are amazed how the body dump suddenly came together, how they now have a a few leads and a suspect. Razanskas says to Masuyama, "You never can tell. Sometimes a pile of shit turns into a pile of roses."

The detectives take Alton's picture and create a makeshift wanted poster. They figure he might try to blow town and head back to Belize. They want to make sure that the airport police and the patrol officers in his neighborhood know what he looks like.

Razanskas works all day on the body dump case with Masuyama and Reyes and returns home late in the evening. He has missed a night's sleep, but he is back at the bureau at 6 A.M. the next morning. His eyes are hooded and bloodshot.

He already has missed quite a few nights' sleep this summer because of homicides, and he has sleepwalked through a number of shifts. In addition to the murder calls, every few weeks since June, just when he begins to catch up on his sleep, he and Winn have to get up at two or three in the morning and provide backup for detectives who serve murder warrants or conduct weapons searches in suspects' apartments.

Razanskas has not had a vacation in nine months and he is starting to wear down. He knows he better pace himself because the murderous days of August and September, the hump of summer, still lie ahead.

Chapter 8
What Is Death?

Wednesday, August 3

The trail is growing faint on Winn's dopehouse double-murder. She still cannot find the basehead who left the tiny footprints in the dust, and she still has not heard from Li'l Sambo's parents, who she had hoped would finally persuade their son to tell the truth. Winn is ready for a new case, a "fresh blood" case, a case that will help her forget the frustrations of her double-murder.

She gets her case a few hours after midnight. When she and Razanskas arrive at the crime scene, it is still dark, just before dawn, with a hint of a moon. The detectives open a gate and feel their way past a single-story strip of apartments. A patrol officer, who is talking to Lieutenant Fletcher in the alley behind the apartments, briefs Winn and Razanskas. The victim, a 24-year-old man by the name of Hector Hernandez, was in the alley with his girlfriend and his 5-year-old son. Hernandez was held up by a teenager, who stole $10 from him. The suspect shot Hernandez in front of his son, and he died en route to the hospital. When patrol officers arrived the little boy was crying, "I want my daddy."

The girlfriend and the little boy are inside their apartment. The detectives decide to work the homicide scene before interviewing them, but there is not much to go on. There are no shell casings. There are no visible footprints. There is no body. All that remains are a few bloodstains at the edge of the alley.

The alley runs behind a section of South Broadway, a neighborhood of hot sheet motels and rickety apartments. Rusted shopping cars and the hulks of stripped cars are scattered along the length of the alley. Nearby, on a patch of dirt, there is a station wagon, missing a few wheels, with "God Is Love" scrawled on a dusty window. Crickets thrum in the bushes and, as dawn breaks, a car alarm pierces the early morning calm. The faint susurrus of the first commuters on the Harbor Freeway can be heard in the distance.

Above the gravel rooftops of the apartments, above the telephone poles and power lines that crisscross the horizon, a spectacular sunrise graces the city. The sky is a canvas of the palest blue, set off by broad swaths of gold and purple and orange. Wispy clouds filter the colors of the sunrise, and the crescent moon fades out against the lightening sky.

When inexperienced detectives arrive at homicide scenes, they swivel their heads about, looking for leads at eye level, their noses parallel to the ground. Razanskas keeps his eyes on the ground. Before he is distracted by the action on the street, he studies bloodstains, shell casings, bullet holes, mangled slugs, shotgun wadding. Within minutes, based on the roughest of scenarios, he can visualize where the shooter stood, how the victim fell, the path of the bullets.

After he and Winn talk to the patrol officer in the alley, Razanskas spots the first lead. He walks to the victim's car, an old, dented Cadillac, and crouches by the trunk. "Looks fresh," he says, fingering a small round bullet hole. He finds another bullet hole in the tail light. He finds a slug by the side of the car. He finds another slug in the alley, with shadings of red from the tail light. Inside the garage he spots a bullet hole in the plaster and begins rooting around for the slug.

Winn and Fletcher watch him work. He is in a rhythm now,

putting it all together, locating the bullet holes, imagining the trajectory, tracking down the slugs. When he stops for a break, he struts over to Winn and Fletcher and says, "Damn I'm good."

She looks at him, askance, and fingers his tie, which is extra-wide and garish, with a red and blue seashell pattern.

"That has got to be *the* ugliest tie I've ever seen."

"Hey, don't knock it," Razanskas says. "It only cost me five bucks."

"Ain't worth more than four," she says, as Fletcher cackles.

Razanskas fingers his tie, pretending he is hurt, and shuffles down the alley. He picks up a rusted hanger, straightens it out, clips off an end with a wire cutter, reaches into the garage and sticks the hanger into a bullet hole. This will highlight the hole and the trajectory of the bullet for the police photographer.

"We are definitely high tech at the LAPD," he says, tapping the rusted wire. "Like the brass tell us, 'Nothing is too good for our boys.' "

The victim's girlfriend does not speak much English, so Razanskas will interview her and the boy. Winn heads over to the Southeast station, another cramped, decrepit LAPD station, near the corner of 108th Street and Broadway, only three blocks from the murder. The local gang is the 11-Deuce Broadway Crips, and she wants to check police gang records.

Inside the girlfriend's apartment, looming over the living room, is a three-foot plastic crucifix, blood dripping from Jesus' hands and feet. The 5-year-old boy is lying on a cot, a Mickey Mouse blanket covering him, staring wide-eyed at the wall. The girlfriend tells Razanskas that Hernandez was planning to drive his son, who has the flu, to the boy's mother's house in Porterville, about three hours away. Hernandez had a $10 bill in his hand and was about to give it to his girlfriend, when a teenager with a gun approached them.

The gunman punched Hernandez in the face. Hernandez said he did not want any trouble because he had his son with him. He implored the gunman to calm down, assured him that he would cooperate. The gunman shouted a few things, which the girlfriend could not understand because her English is poor. He grabbed the $10 bill out of Hernandez's hand, shot him and ran down the alley.

The girlfriend pounds a fist on her thigh and sobs. When she regains her composure she tells Razanskas that the shooter had a shaved head and was young, maybe 16 or 17 years old. She leans over and asks the boy if he can talk to the detective. He does not move. He just stares at the wall, tightly clutching his Mickey Mouse blanket.

Razanskas meets Winn at the Southeast station and tells her about his interview with the victim's girlfriend. A few minutes later, a gang officer brings in a chubby teenager. He was hanging out in front of an apartment in 11-Deuce territory. The gang officer, who is about 6 foot 4, 250 pounds, is a weight lifter and his biceps strain against his uniform. He glowers at the kid and tells him he better cooperate with the detectives if he does not want to get jacked up by police in the future.

"Who kicks it around there?" Winn asks.

"I don't 'bang," the chubby teenager says.

"If you want to keep this big SOB off your back," Razanskas says, pointing to the gang officer, "you better help us out."

The boy finally agrees to cooperate. He gives the detectives the names and descriptions of four 11-Deuce Crips with shaved heads. They are called G-Mac, J-Bone, E-Mac and G-Rag. He says he does not know their real names. Winn checks through the moniker file for them. But there are numerous G-Macs, J-Bones, E-Macs and G-Rags. She is going to need something more. As she and Razanskas leave the station, a young woman patrol officer approaches Winn.

"I wanted to tell you," she says, "that a few years ago, when I was starting out, my training officer said right off, 'If you want to be any kind of police officer, you better be like Marcella Winn.' I guess he worked with you a while back. . . . This guy wouldn't let me drive for seven months. He told me, 'The day you no longer screw up is the day you drive.' Then one day he threw the keys at me. . . . Well, now I finally get to meet you."

Winn is embarrassed by the attention, and Razanskas is more comfortable razzing someone than acknowledging a compliment. They hop into their car and drive off in silence. As they head up Broadway, into the early morning glare, the last of the hookers lingering in front of the motels are calling it a night.

"The guy's begging because he's got his boy with him," Razanskas says. "Begging. But that asshole doesn't fucking care. He's a cold-blooded motherfucker. He dumps him anyway. And for what? For ten bucks."

"A man getting shot in front of his little boy pisses me off," Winn says, smacking the dash in anger. "That's total bullshit. Let me tell you, I'm motivated on this one. I don't care what it takes. I want the little bastard who did this off the street."

Winn and Razanskas work all day on the Hernandez case, get home Wednesday night and are back in the bureau early Thursday morning. Winn gets a call from the coroner, and at midmorning she watches the autopsy of Hector Hernandez. The coroner points to the "through-and-through" wound below his left knee and the fatal wound—a reddish perfectly round circle above his left nipple. Hernandez's eyelids are half-closed, the eyes glittering under the fluorescent lights, lifeless, like marbles.

At the end of the autopsy, the pathologist balances Hernandez's heart in his hand and lifts it toward Winn. There is a jagged crimson hole right through the center.

When Winn returns to the bureau she tells Razanskas, "Now that I've been to a few autopsies, I've completely lost my taste for beef ribs. And I can't eat my steaks rare anymore, like I used to like them."

"Did you see it when they did that Benihana thing and sliced up the brain?"

She purses her lips and begins perusing the Hernandez murder book. Razanskas returns to his body dump case. He has had little time for the case and is no closer to solving it now than the morning the body was found. He has not even been able to locate any relatives to notify. Many of the addresses from the victim's arrest reports are out of date. Some are phony. It turns out that Elliot had given a number of bogus addresses and phone numbers to police when he was arrested. Razanskas calls Elliot's former parole officer, and he has no idea where Elliot's family lives.

He decides to check with the coroner investigator on the case. If someone has been missing a few weeks, family or friends often will file a missing person's report or call the coroner. But the investigator says no one has come forward on John Robert Elliot.

"We're shit out of luck," the investigator says. "He's got no job, and we can't find any wife, family, friends or kids."

"Well," Razanskas says, shrugging, "sometimes you get the bear. And sometimes the bear gets you."

Razanskas and Winn want to get another look at the Hernandez homicide scene in daylight. They drive over to South Broadway early Thursday afternoon, and Razanskas regales Winn with stories about cases he worked where people were killed for remarkably stupid reasons.

"Had one case at a nightclub on Manchester. A guy was sitting at a table, sipping a drink, minding his own business. Another guy walked over, didn't say a word and shot him in the head. Why? He was jealous because the guy was a better dancer and was getting all the chicks.

"Had another where a few Neighborhood Family Bloods were hanging out on a corner. A bunch of Crips rolled by, nice and slow. All the Bloods had enough sense to beat feet—except this one Blood. His attitude was like, 'If you're bad enough, go ahead and dump me.' So he opened up his overcoat and said, 'Take your best shot.'

"They do and he dies. And this clown wasn't even armed.

"Had another case where a guy got killed over a quarter. It was a biker bar and this one guy picked up a quarter. The guy who dropped it asked for it back and the other guy refused. So he yelled, 'Give it back or I'll kill you.'

"Now the guy who picked up the quarter said something so

crazy that everyone in the bar remembered it. He shouted, 'What is death?'

"He soon found out because the other guy went for his shit and shot him."

Razanskas is in a garrulous mood. He tells Winn an ethnic joke, and the punch line involves a Mexican. He laughs, but she stares straight ahead.

"I'll never forget the first time someone called me the N-word," she says softly. "I was thirteen and we'd just moved here from Texas. Me and my cousin and a few girlfriends were going to a movie theater on Wilshire. We were waiting for someone to pull out of a parking spot, and some skinny white guy with his wife and kids tried to cut in on us. But we beat him to the spot.

"He turned to us and yells, 'You niggers.'

"I stuck my head out the window and said, 'Your mother probably has more black blood than I have.' His wife and his kids all laughed at him."

Winn knows Razanskas has a Latino wife and she knows he is not a racist. But she wants to let him know she is not amused by ethnic jokes.

Razanskas listens to her story and nods his head somberly.

She is satisfied.

When Razanskas and Winn return to the office, he grabs the murder book on his four-year-old Oregon homicide. He picked up the suspect a few weeks ago and brought him back to Los Angeles. The preliminary hearing is fast approaching and Razanskas has to track down a few witnesses.

The murder stemmed from a loan that Adan Aguilar had made to Albert Salgado, a drug dealer everyone called the Pharmacist. One night, the two men and a few others were playing cards on the sidewalk when Aguilar mentioned the loan to Salgado and asked when he was going to pay him. The Pharmacist was outraged that Aguilar would "dis" him in front of his friends. He charged into his duplex, returned with a pistol and killed Aguilar. Salgado immediately packed a bag and disappeared. Razanskas tracked him for a while, lost the trail, but discovered he had a brother in Oregon. On a hunch, Razanskas sent a wanted flyer to the sheriff's department in the town where the brother lived.

For four years, Razanskas heard nothing. Then, a few weeks ago, he got a call from a sheriff's lieutenant in Oregon. One of the lieutenant's informants told him a man laying irrigation pipes at a ranch had been bragging about killing someone in Los Angeles a few years back. The lieutenant had a remarkable memory because he recalled the wanted flyer. He sifted through all his old flyers, located it and showed his informant the picture of Salgado. The informant identified him.

Razanskas first worked the case with Steve Watson, his detective trainee at the time. Now a supervising detective, Watson hooks up with Razanskas to see if they can locate the missing witnesses. But they have no luck. When they return to the office in the early afternoon, Razanskas confers with Winn about the next steps to take on the Hernandez homicide. Watson smokes a cigarette in the parking lot and recalls the days when Razanskas gave him *his* homicide training.

One of the first crime scenes they worked together was at a donut shop. A robber charged in with a toy gun. The owner pulled out a pistol and shot him. It was a through-and-through flesh wound and the robber was not badly hurt so he grabbed the portable cash register and ran out the door. At the corner he checked the register and realized the cash drawer had fallen out.

The robber was not a master criminal. He returned to the donut shop, still brandishing the toy gun, looking for the cash drawer. The donut shop owner shot him again. This time he blew his head off.

Razanskas and Watson arrived at the scene and were looking at a possible justifiable homicide. But they needed to track the path of the bullet to see if the trajectory was consistent with the owner's story.

Watson searched for the spent bullet, but he could not find a trace of it. Razanskas spotted a fiber on the floor of the donut shot, a tiny scrap of blue fabric that looked like lint. He found another fiber. And another. He ended up following the path of the fibers to the front of the store. Right by the last piece of fiber was the bullet, embedded in a cabinet. This was the through-and-through shot. The bullet had picked up tiny fibers from the man's sweatshirt. The fibers were like an arrow that led from the shot to the slug. But it was an arrow that only Razanskas could see.

Late Thursday afternoon, a day after the murder of Hector Hernandez, a homicide detective tells Winn one of his informants might know something about the murder. She asks the detective to have the snitch call her. When he calls, and Winn picks up the phone, he is surprised.

"Oh," he says. "You're a female."

"You got a *problem* with that?"

No, he tells her, he was just surprised. They chat briefly, but he does not tell her much. He says he will get back to her.

He calls back on Friday and tells her he talked to an LAPD sergeant who grew up in his neighborhood. "Winn is cool," the sergeant told him. Now he is ready to talk. They meet at a division station, and she takes him into an interview room. He is wearing shorts and a green T-shirt with a picture of Jesus emblazoned on the front.

"I'll try to make it plain and simple for you," he says. "When I get information, it's gold. But if I give you something, I got to get something in return."

He pulls a few bills out of his pocket and says, "It's all about this. You know what I'm sayin'?"

"I have no problem kicking some cash down to you," Winn says. "But I don't want no bullshit."

He nods. He tells her the killer was an 11-Deuce Broadway Crip. He does not know his name, but he knows how she can track him down. "The shooter is a little gangster. After the shooting went down, he dumped the gun with Joker. Joker called his homeboy and told him to move the gun. The homeboy's an 11-Deuce, too. He took the gun and hid it.

"Joker won't help you out. He's an O.G. from the neighborhood. He's a big gangster who'll do no talkin'. The homeboy's another story. You find him and you'll make your case."

He tells her the homeboy's name. They talk about the case for a few minutes and Winn pulls $10 out of her purse and hands it to the snitch. He frowns and says, "Ain't you a little light, sister?"

She throws down another five. He takes the cash and slides it into his sock.

"When I get that gun in my hot little hand," she says, "money will be no problem."

"Then just find the homeboy."

Winn leads him out through the back door, so he won't be seen leaving a police station. Before he leaves, he turns sanctimonious. "I have my own personal reasons for doing what I do. I'm against the crazy stuff. It's not good for our youngsters."

Winn cocks her head and flashes him a skeptical look as she lets him out the door.

She later approaches a patrol officer, Lyle Young, and tells him the name of the 11-Deuce who hid the gun. She asks Young to keep an eye out for him. Winn approaches Young because he is a street-smart veteran who patrols 11-Deuce territory and works the overnight shift. He knows the neighborhood gangbangers and where they hang out. He worked the Hector Hernandez homicide scene and was outraged that the father was killed in front of his little boy. She figures he, too, has a stake in the investigation.

If anyone comes across the suspect, she tells him, make sure they bring him into the station, and make sure to call her right away. She does not care how late it is. Just call.

Chapter 9
24 Hours

Sunday, August 7

Lyle Young and his partner are driving through an alley off South Broadway at about 3 A.M. when a woman flags them down.

"He has my keys," the woman yells to the officers. "Can you make him give me my keys back?"

"Who has your keys?" Young asks.

"Him," she says, pointing to a man scampering down the alley. She tells Young his name. He is the 11-Deuce Broadway Crip who hid the murder weapon, whom the snitch identified.

Young brings him to the Southeast station. He has a few outstanding warrants so Young is able to keep him in custody. He calls Winn and tells her he just picked up her suspect. Winn then calls Razanskas, and they meet at the station at about 9 A.M.

This is a critical interview for Winn. She knows the whole case is riding on the suspect. If she can turn him, she can get to the shooter. No one else is likely to talk. But if he dummies up, she probably will run out of leads, as she ran out of leads with her double-murder. She wants to put a stop to her losing streak right now.

She knows that pressuring people to talk is a delicate business. If you push too hard, they get angry and stubborn. If you do not push hard enough, they try to take advantage of you. If you promise them too much, they think you are lying. If you do not promise them enough, they have no incentive to talk.

This is a Sunday, so both Winn and Razanskas are wearing jeans. The suspect, who is waiting for them in the squad room, is wearing shorts, a T-shirt and a long Raiders jacket. They take him to a small interview cubicle, filled with stained, perforated insulation panels.

Winn asks him what he knows about the murder in the alley behind South Broadway. He shrugs and lifts his palms.

"Listen very carefully to what I'm saying," she says. "Some people think that only long-distance calls are logged. But we can dig up phone records and find out exactly who called who and when." She crosses her arms and pauses. "You know what I'm saying?"

"There's not much I can tell you."

She lowers her head and raises an eyebrow. "You know what accessory after the fact is? You can get five to eight years for that."

He strokes the stubble on his chin.

"I can take you down on that," Winn says. "Hard. So don't fuck with me."

He is nervous now. He taps a finger on the metal table. His calf muscles twitch.

"I'm not asking these questions because I'm pulling shit out of the wind," she says. "I know wha's up. I just want to see how you answer my questions."

He nods.

"What was it all about?"

"I heard it was territorial shit. Drug shit."

"Who was the shooter?"

"I can't really say for sure."

"Look. We got a bunch of warrants out for you. If you don't work with me, I'm going to make sure they nail you for every single one."

He taps his feet and she stares at him, listening to the drumming of his sneakers on the linoleum floor. She leans toward him and jabs a forefinger in his face. “Let me tell you what I don’t like about that damn murder. Y’all can shoot any fucker you want. But I won’t tolerate shooting a man in front of his little boy. That’s bullshit. That little boy is traumatized for life. I am very pissed off. If I have to get up at five o’clock every morning for the next year to find out who killed him, I will.

“I’m not going to ask you to testify before God and everyone else in court. I just want to know a few things. And if you don’t want to go down too, you best tell me.”

Winn, who is wearing a sleeveless denim blouse, crosses her arms, flexing her formidable biceps. She leans over and glares at him. She looks angry, menacing and moves toward him as he draws back in his chair.

“WHO IS THE SHOOTER?” she suddenly shouts.

He jerks back, wide-eyed with surprise. He massages a calf. “Lemme ask you something. If I co-op-er-ate,” he says, breaking at each syllable, “can you cut me loose?”

“It all depends on what you have to say.”

“OK. Word is J-Bone did the shooting.”

“You sure?”

“Yeah. Lot of people sayin’ it.”

“Where does J-Bone live?”

“I don’t know where he stay.”

“OK I’m going to ask you to take a wild guess. I mean a *wild* guess. Where do you think that gun was stashed?”

“In the ’hood.”

“Where in the ’hood?”

“Probably at some house.”

“Knowing J-Bone, what house do you think he stashed it at?”

“Could be a number of places.”

She leans back in her chair. “Listen to what I’m saying. I don’t give a shit about any flunky misdemeanor warrants. I work homicide.”

“You sayin’ if I find the gun I’m home free?”

“That’s what I’m sayin’.”

"I think I could find the gun."

Winn knows that the suspect knows where the gun is. Because he hid it. She also knows he will never cop to it. She decides to play along with the charade and let him go, so he can pretend to ask around and then, hopefully, tell her where the gun is.

"OK, homeboy. This is the deal. I'm going to cut you loose. But you have to call me back ASAP. With the location of that gun. But if you cross me on this, I'm going to do *you*. I'm going to do your *mama*. I'm going to do your *grand*mama. I'm going to do everyone and everything you hold dear. I'll be like a rabid dog on you."

He holds up a palm. "OK. OK. Like I said, I don't mind co-op-er-ating."

Winn goes into the squad room and returns with a Polaroid camera. He pats his hair.

"Fixing your 'do?" she asks, stifling a smile. She takes his picture and says, "If you screw me, I'll plaster this picture all over the division."

After they walk him out the back door, she grins. "He says he's sure J-Bone was the shooter," she says excitedly to Razanskas. "If he does his part, we're almost there."

While they're waiting for his call, they search through the computerized moniker file for J-Bone. But the system goes down, yet again. "You piece of shit!" Razanskas shouts at the computer. They wait 20 minutes. When the system is back on line they discover there is no J-Bone in the neighborhood. Razanskas is amused by one J-Bone in the system who is with a tagger (graffiti) crew, "Born To Jack."

"I'm embarrassed to be a cop," he says, shaking his head, "but he's proud to be a robber."

Since they can't find a J-Bone in the system who lives in the neighborhood, they know that the snitch is their only hope. If he skips town they are screwed. But an hour later he calls. He tells Winn someone moved the gun to a house on West 111th Place. It's in a metal box. The box is stashed in a backyard chicken coop. She hangs up, claps once and says, "We're in business."

But to get the gun, they need a search warrant. They do not want to wait until Monday and take the chance the gangsters will move the gun again. Winn sets up at a computer and begins writing the search warrant. Razanskas goes out for sandwiches. But when you get a sandwich for Winn, you just don't get any sandwich. She is an eater so picky that her nickname in vice used to be "Special Order" because every time she went out to eat she never merely ordered from the menu. Every dinner was an adventure replete with substitutions, additions and special requests. Now, instead of telling Razanskas what she wants, she writes it down on a piece of paper. She wants to make sure there is no confusion.

"Tuna on wheat," she writes. "With cheese. Grey Poupon mustard. Easy on the onions. Lettuce and tomatoes. Extra pickles. No oil and vinegar. No bell peppers. No mayonnaise on the bread."

He returns with the sandwiches and approaches Winn, a somber expression on his face. He tells Winn he brought her sandwich, but there is only one problem. The sandwich shop *forgot* the Grey Poupon mustard and *forgot* the cheese. And by mistake they *added* oil and vinegar, *added* bell pepper and *added* mayonnaise.

"WHAT?" she shouts.

"Just kidding," he says.

Winn eats at her desk while she completes the complicated search warrant form, which takes her several hours. When she is finished she has to wait another few hours for the LAPD helicopter to fly over the location and confirm that a chicken coop is there. When the helicopter confirms it, Winn takes the search warrant to the home of a judge, who signs it. The detectives are now ready.

Winn and Razanskas walk out to the station parking lot. They slip on bulletproof vests, thigh holsters and blue LAPD nylon jackets. They check their guns. They hop into their Caprice and, followed by a police car filled with uniformed officers, head out to the location on West 111th Place.

At dusk, they pull up in front of a lime green home with a neatly landscaped front yard and a backyard filled with fruit trees. Razanskas and a uniformed officer hustle to the backyard and, hand on their holsters, barge into the chicken coop. Winn and a few uniformed officers slowly approach two teenagers, who are leaning against a truck in the driveway. One, who has a shaved head, reaches into the truck.

"PUT YOUR HANDS WHERE I CAN SEE THEM!" Winn shouts.

He slowly moves away from the truck.

"WHAT'S YOUR NAME?"

He stares at his shoes.

"I'm not going to ask you your fucking name again."

"It's J."

"J what?"

"J-Bone."

CLICK. CLICK. In a split second she whips his hands behind his back and cuffs him.

The uniformed officers keep an eye on J-Bone. Winn finds Razanskas. She is so excited she has to share the news. "I got my shooter," she announces, breaking into a big smile.

Winn leaves Razanskas to search through the chicken shit and chicken feathers, and she returns to her prisoner. J-Bone slumps against a car in the driveway. He is wearing baggy blue pants, with a 40-inch waist, slung so low that half of his boxer shorts are visible. He complains that the cuffs are too tight. He asks Winn, "What's this all about?"

"A homicide."

"Ain't nothin' to it."

"If there ain't nothing to it, you don't have anything to worry about."

It is dark now, as Razanskas emerges from the chicken coop, feathers clinging to his arms. He is carrying a metal box. Inside is a Ruger revolver and a handful of shotgun shells.

"Lookin' good," Winn says.

"That J-Bone looked like he got caught with his hand in the cookie jar," Razanskas says.

"When he wouldn't look me in the eye," she says, "I knew he was dirty."

• • •

Back at the Southeast station they lead J-Bone to a holding tank.

"Why am I here?" he asks indignantly. "I don't understand this." Razanskas ignores him and takes a photograph of him for the six-pack photo display card. Winn briefly questions him and obtains his full name, his age, 17, his address and his arrest record. He tells her he was arrested once for car theft. She runs his name in the system and finds out he was arrested more than once. Within the past three years he has been arrested for possession of narcotics, possession of a firearm, armed robbery, two burglaries and numerous car thefts. He is currently on probation.

Razanskas sifts through a pile of booking photos. He is compiling several six-pack cards for the key witness in the case—the victim's girlfriend. "Avoid photos where people wear dark clothing," he tells Winn. "Witnesses always focus in on the dark clothing. . . . I'm going to bring the witness to the station to look at the six-packs. You can see a lot better under fluorescent lights than in some dim living room."

Razanskas studies the photo of a middle-aged Latino felon and shouts, "This is fantastic!" The felon looks exactly like Lieutenant Robleto. Razanskas pockets the picture. He has a practical joke in mind.

When he finishes compiling the six-packs, he picks up Trinidad (Hernandez's girlfriend) and a friend of hers, who goes along for support. Because Winn does not speak Spanish, she drives off to get them some dinner.

Trinidad sits next to Razanskas in the car. She looks like she still is in shock. She does not say a word; she just stares out the window, a thousand-yard stare. Her friend, however, is talkative and tells Razanskas that the rosary for Hector Hernandez was earlier in the day. She tells him that a group of gangbangers on the street warned Trinidad not to talk about what she saw. But Trinidad will not be intimidated. Razanskas tells her that if they have any more problems with gangbangers to let him know.

"You kind of old for a cop," the friend says to Razanskas.

"Yeah. I'm getting too old for this grind."

"You an O.G. [original gangster] cop," the woman says, laughing. She points at Razanskas' gun in his shoulder holster. "I didn't know homicide cops carried nines."

"Oh this thing," Razanskas says, tapping the barrel of his 9-millimeter. "This is for my wife."

"You must be married to a Mexican lady. We have bad tempers."

"As a matter of fact, I am."

"We don't take any shit from our men. Look at Lorena Bobbitt."

"She ain't Mexican. She's from Peru."

"Don't matter. She's a Hispanic lady."

When they reach the station, Razanskas tells the friend to wait in the squad room. He leads Trinidad to an interview cubicle and stacks up a sheaf of six-packs for her to look through. She is a tiny, birdlike young woman with short hair and wide frightened eyes.

He hands her the first six-pack. She holds it in both hands and scans the photographs. The moment she spots the picture in the top right corner—J-Bone's picture—she gasps loudly. Her eyes bulge and her jaw drops. Her body jerks and twitches. She throws down the six-pack. She pounds her fists on the table and sobs hysterically.

She cries and cries and is unable to talk for five minutes. Finally, between sobs, she lifts her head and tells Razanskas what he already knows.

"*Es claro.*" (It is clear.) "*Si. Es el.*" (Yes. It is him.)

Winn returns with fried chicken, and Razanskas tells her about the six-pack session. She is elated. He says they should now try to interview J-Bone and see if he'll cop to anything.

"That motherfucker can wait till I'm done eating," she says, grabbing a drumstick.

After dinner, they walk over to J-Bone's holding cell. He is sprawled out on a bunk, fast asleep. This proves one of his theories, Razanskas tells Winn. When innocent people are in custody, awaiting questioning, they are jumpy as hell. They pace their cells, chatter with the other prisoners, call out questions to the guards. But a guilty man always sleeps. He does not know exactly why. It is just something he has noticed over the years.

They escort J-Bone, who is handcuffed, to the squad room. Winn calls his mother and briefs her. The mother asks if she can speak to "Joseph." J-Bone does not look like a murder suspect now. He is just a scrawny teenager who is trying to placate his mother. "I don't know, Mom," he says, in answer to her many questions. "I just don't know . . . nothing . . . nothing. . . . They come over and handcuff me. They tell me I'm here for some murder. No. I didn't do anything."

Winn leads him to an interview cubicle. He sits down and begins sniffling, trying to hold back tears. "We seem to have lost our attitude," Winn says. "You and I are going to have a little chitchat." Razanskas reads him his rights. J-Bone agrees to talk to them without an attorney present.

"I don't understand all this whoop-de-do," J-Bone says.

"You need to speak English," she says. "This 'whoop-de-do' talk don't mean anything to me."

"I ain't killed nobody."

"You're not here because we think you look good," Winn says. "You're here because a witness identified you. She had no doubt it was you. If she hadn't picked you, you'd be on your way home now."

His chin drops, he slides down his chair and finally, surrendering to gravity, he falls to the floor and curls up in a ball.

"Sit up and act like a goddamn man," Razanskas says. "You're seventeen years old."

"Face up to what you did," she says.

"It's not like the shit fairy came down and picked on you," Razanskas says.

"Now is the chance to tell your side of the story," she says.

Razanskas gets up to leave. He stands over J-Bone and says, "This is the trademark of a fucking coward."

J-Bone stays curled up in a ball and does not respond.

Winn and Razanskas leave J-Bone in the cubicle and lock the

door. They write up the arrest reports, study his rap sheet and when they finish the paperwork, Razanskas returns to the interview room for J-Bone. He is sprawled out on the floor, dead asleep.

"Honey, I'm home," Razanskas calls out in a cheery voice. "It's time for booking." He rousts J-Bone and takes him to the station's jail, where he is fingerprinted, photographed again and booked for murder. J-Bone empties his pockets. He has $1.03 in one pocket. He pulls a single glove out of the other.

"He's got one glove," Razanskas quips. "O.J. has the other."

J-Bone pulls out of his back pocket a half-eaten Apple Stix, a pale green strip of sticky candy. He looks mournful, lost, as he holds on to it, reluctant to give up this last remnant of his childhood. A guard snatches it out of his hands and tosses him in a holding cell.

At 3 in the morning, Razanskas and Winn and J-Bone head for Los Padrinos Juvenile Hall in Downey. On their way to the freeway, they pass a woman in a tight dress climbing into a car.

"That's what you call a South End working girl," Winn says.

The detectives are in the front seat, joking, giddy from the high of clearing a case. J-Bone is curled up in the back seat.

"Is our little darling still asleep?" asks Razanskas, who is driving. She checks on him. He still is sound asleep. When they reach juvenile hall, Razanskas calls out, in a singsong voice, "Oh, J-Bone. Wake up. You're home."

The detectives escort J-Bone to the juvenile hall sally port. They hand his booking paperwork to a detention officer. In the office, a boxing match is blaring on the television.

"You *know* it's late," Razanskas says, "when you turn on the sports channel and see two *white* guys boxing."

When Razanskas and Winn finish up at juvenile hall, they drive back to the office. Winn still is energized, but the fatigue suddenly hits Razanskas. This night is not as much of a novelty for him; he has cleared a few cases in his time. He has been up about 24 hours now, running on adrenaline and coffee. His eyes are bloodshot, his lids are drooping and his hair, usually swept straight back, is splayed out over his forehead.

They return to South Bureau Homicide, Razanskas makes a pot of coffee and they finish writing evidence reports, juvenile arrest reports and a number of other required reports. When the first few detectives arrive early Monday morning, Razanskas gets his second wind. He returns to his desk and lays out a piece of white paper, tape, a felt-tip pen and the photo of the Latino suspect he lifted earlier in the morning. He tapes the photo to the paper, writes Lieutenant Robleto's name beneath it, and draws up a wanted poster with a variety of lurid crimes. He posts it on the wall near the front door, and when a detective walks in, Razanskas gleefully points out his handiwork.

Just after dawn—24 hours after Winn got the call from Lyle Young—she and Razanskas walk to the parking lot to retrieve some evidence from the car. Fluted columns of light stream through the underground lot. The morning already is warm; the day should be a scorcher. One case has been cleared, but on a day like this, it will not be long before there is another homicide, another victim, and another team of detectives beginning the search, all over again, for another killer.

Chapter 10
Two Mothers

Tuesday, August 9

Two days after Winn clears the Hector Hernandez case, Maria Rodriguez, the victim's former wife, comes to the station. She needs information on how to locate some of her ex-husband's belongings.

Winn asks Rodriguez how her son is handling his father's death. "Not well," Rodriguez says, shaking her head. "Not well at all. He misses his daddy. I never seen a child who loved his daddy so much."

The boy lives in a mobile home with his mother, 2-year-old brother and stepfather in Porterville, a small farming community in the San Joaquin Valley. After the shooting, Hector, Jr., kept asking his mother to take him to the hospital so he could see his father.

"How do you tell a five-year-old he will never see his father again?" she asks Winn. "I finally told him that his daddy is up in the sky, that he is a big star, and that he is watching us, whatever we do, wherever we go. Hector cried and cried. He idolized his father. His father was everything to him."

• • •

Hector Hernandez and his family moved from Guadalajara, Mexico, to Porterville when he was 14. He married at 16 and quit school to pick oranges with his father and brothers. On weekends, he worked construction jobs and learned about plumbing, carpentry and electrical wiring. He dreamed of owning his own small construction company.

After Hernandez and his wife separated last year, he moved to Los Angeles where two brothers and his father had found construction jobs. He did not want to leave his boys, but he could make much more money working construction in Los Angeles than picking fruit in Porterville. Hernandez called his two sons every night and visited almost every weekend. Five-year-old, Hector, Jr., was named after his father.

After work, Hernandez used to box at an L.A. gym to stay in shape. He was a promising welterweight who was offered $5,000 to turn professional. But he was not interested in a boxing career; he did not want anything to sidetrack him from his dream of starting his own construction business.

On the Saturday before his murder, his ex-wife had to go to Arizona for a funeral and took the 2-year-old with her. Hernandez picked up Hector, Jr., in Porterville and brought him to Los Angeles for a few days. Every morning, Hernandez took his son to the beach, and in the afternoon they wandered along the Latino shopping district on Broadway in downtown Los Angeles. Hernandez bought his son school clothes and a Teenage Mutant Ninja Turtle cup that he treasured.

Hector was having so much fun with his father that he did not want to return to Porterville, but Tuesday night he came down with the flu. His temperature was 102 degrees, he could not sleep, and Hernandez wanted to get him to a doctor. Hector was covered by his mother's medical insurance and the family doctor was in Porterville. Hernandez decided to leave early Wednesday morning and have Hector at his mother's house by daybreak.

Hernandez, his girlfriend Trinidad, and his son walked out to his 1986 Cadillac, parked by the alley. They chatted for a few minutes and were saying their good-bys, when J-Bone approached them and punched Hernandez in the face. If he had not been flashing a pistol, Hernandez, a boxer known for his fast hands, would have dropped a skinny kid like J-Bone in a heartbeat. But Hernandez kept his cool. He just wanted to protect his son.

Hector told his mother that the gunman wanted something from his father. But his father kept saying, "No, no, no. I don't have anything." The gunman shot a few times in the ground, Hector told his mother, like he was trying to scare his father. After that, he shot Hernandez in the heart.

At the funeral, Rodriguez finally understood the cryptic exchange between J-Bone and her former husband. Hernandez's brother came up to Rodriguez and said, crying, "It was my fault. That bullet was not meant for him. It was meant for me." The brother, who lived down the street, was selling crack. The 11-Deuce Broadways did not like the competition, the brother told Rodriguez. J-Bone was particularly angry because this was cutting into his own burgeoning crack enterprise. The day before the killing, J-Bone approached the brother by the alley. This was just a few hundred feet from where Hernandez was later killed. He asked him for drugs, but when the brother said he did not have any, J-Bone pulled out a pistol. The brother hopped a fence and hid behind a camper shell, as J-Bone capped off a few rounds.

Hernandez and his brother looked like twins. Even Rodriguez's parents confused the two. J-Bone mistook Hernandez for his brother and intended to hold him up for his drugs. When Hernandez could not provide drugs, J-Bone shot him. He grabbed the $10 bill from Hernandez's hand as an afterthought.

Hernandez's brother moved back to Mexico after the funeral. Trinidad left the state because J-Bone's homies continued to threaten her and warned her not to testify, but she told Razanskas she was willing to return to Los Angeles for the trial.

After the shooting, Hector, Jr., would not talk for several days. He used to a happy, animated little boy. Now he's always unhappy, always angry. He is gaunt—he lost five pounds after his father was killed—and has sad, haunted brown eyes.

He talks about his father all the time. He tells his mother he wants to be a boxer, just like his father; he wants to build houses, just like his father; he wants to wear cowboy boots and a straw cowboy hat, just like his father. And when he is sad, he mopes about, as his father moped about when he was sad, stuffing his hands in his pockets, hanging his head and stiffly shuffling about the mobile home like a penguin.

Hernandez used to call his sons at 8 o'clock sharp, every night. Now, every night at 8 o'clock, Hector glances at the silent phone and cries. After he saw the animated movie *The Land Before Time,* he broke down when the mother dinosaur died because it reminded him of his father's death. He has frequent nightmares, and Rodriguez often is awakened by his cries. He still is afraid to be apart from his mother, and when she goes shopping, he tells her friends, "Don't let anything happen to my mommy." Sometimes, she returns to find him crying hysterically. He tells her, "I thought you were never coming back."

In a cramped Los Angeles apartment, far from the orange groves and barley fields of Porterville, Patricia Wiley grieves for her 17-year-old son Joseph. His friends call him J-Bone.

Patricia Wiley was a junior in high school when she met J-Bone's father, Joseph, Sr. He was five years older than her, and she liked him immediately because he seemed more mature than the neighborhood boys who were running with the Bible Crips. He was a serious-looking man who did not seem the type to get into trouble.

Her intentions were good, but her instincts were poor. She became pregnant, dropped out of school, and three months after Joseph, Jr., was born, his father was arrested for murder. He and Wiley's brother were charged with breaking into a man's house, robbing him and killing him. Wiley's brother beat the charge. J-Bone's father left prints all over the apartment, was convicted of murder and sentenced to Soledad State Prison.

When J-Bone was 6 years old, his father was released from prison. He visited his son briefly. Wiley pulls out a yellowed Polaroid picture that she took when they met for the first time. J-

Bone is shirtless and wearing shorts, a lanky, grinning kid, all arms and legs. His father, who is wearing a powder blue fedora, has an arm around his son. The picture was about all J-Bone had to remember his father by because he rarely saw him after that visit.

Wiley, whose three brothers and sisters all have different fathers, knew how her son felt—she has never met her own father. After she had another son, J-Bone, became even more dejected. His stepfather lavished attention on his young son, but he ignored J-Bone.

"He saw how close they were and it make him real upset," Wiley recalls. "He be real quiet and to hisself all the time. You could see the hurt in him. It be like he have a thinking cap on, and all the time I know what he thinking. Sometime, he do all kind of things to get attention. He hurt hisself or fall down, just to get someone to pay attention to him."

J-Bone was raised in the small apartment where Wiley still lives. In a neighborhood of run-down apartment buildings, this apartment house stands out for its decrepitude. The pink stucco is falling down in chunks, the parking lot in front is covered with trash, and gang graffiti covers the sidewalk, the street, the telephone poles, the gutters. The apartment house has few amenities, but what it does offer is security. A six-foot-high metal fence surrounds the property. The front of the building is protected by a sliding steel gate, which is always kept closed. Every window is covered with thick metal bars; every screen door is made of heavy black steel.

Wiley's apartment is a tableau of disorder. Boxes and blankets and shoes and old newspapers and empty cookie boxes are strewn about. Dirty dishes spill out of the kitchen sink, onto counters and tables. The bedroom J-Bone shared with his brother and sister has no dresser. Instead, plastic garbage bags are filled with clothes. There are two worn and torn mattresses in the center of the room. In the living room, J-Bone's 10-year-old brother and 8-year-old sister are eating Kix out of plastic cottage cheese containers. They are watching *The Jenny Jones Show.* The topic is "Men Who Have Had Affairs With Their Wives' Best Friends."

Wiley flips off the television set, settles onto the sofa and provides a different portrait of life in the apartment. The two children snuggle up to her and she strokes their hair. Wiley proudly points to the living room wall, where she has taped their last report cards. The girl received almost all As, and the boy mostly Bs. Wiley does not worry about them now, but in a neighborhood like this, she knows that problems lie ahead during their adolescence.

Wiley cares about her children; she just seems tired and overwhelmed, as if the exigencies of daily life are too much for her. Now that J-Bone has been arrested for murder, Wiley knows the welfare office will deduct $120 a month from her check, because she has one less child to support. She does not know how she will be able to pay her bills.

Wiley, who is wearing a baggy denim coat and a gray rag wrapped around her head, sighs heavily when she talks about J-Bone. She says he did not have an easy life. When he was 13, Wiley became strung out on crack. For a few years he was saddled with the responsibility of taking care of his younger brother and sister. And his mother.

"He take good care of everyone, too," she says. "He make a real dinner. Chicken, rice, everything. That boy could *cook.* I come draggin' home and he try to make me eat. He heat up a plate and say, 'Here, Mama, eat. You got to eat.' "

After Wiley began having crack-induced seizures, she became frightened enough to kick her habit. She has stayed clean, she says, for the past few years.

When J-Bone was a teenager, the local gang, the West Side Geer Street Crips, pressured him to join. He refused. He was a quiet, sickly boy who had been diagnosed with sickle cell anemia and stayed close to home so he could take his medication and play video games. The action on the streets frightened him.

"He was a sweet chile," Wiley says. "But those boys give him a hard time. They say, 'You join, or you can't hang here. You join or you can't hang there. You can't do this. You can't do that.' Joseph not a bad boy. He jus' a boy wit' no confidence in hisself. I think he do a lot of what he do to try to belong. To prove hisself. A boy aroun' here try to prove hisself on the street. And the street no good for a boy like Joseph."

He never did join up with Geer Street. But a friend from school moved across town and became involved with the 11-Deuce Broadway Crips. J-Bone began visiting his friend. That is when he quit school, when his friends started calling him J-Bone, when his problems with the law began, when he began hanging out with the 11-Deuces and, eventually, when he was jumped into the gang.

J-Bone's gang, whose members are known for their drug dealing, holdups and drive-bys, bear little resemblance to the first gangs in the city, the Latino gangs of East Los Angeles, formed during the 1930s and 1940s. This first generation of gangbangers viewed themselves as warriors protecting their neighborhoods. Family membership in some East Los Angeles street gangs goes back generations.

The early black gangs were more ephemeral and did not engender the fierce neighborhood loyalty of the Latino gangs. During the 1950s, black youths in South Los Angeles, who formed gangs such as the Slausons and the Gladiators, had their rumbles. But they fought with their fists and occasionally chains or tire irons. Guns were a rarity.

Gang conflict subsided after the Watts riots when members found common enemies: the LAPD and the white political establishment. During the late 1960s, when the Black Power movement was gaining momentum, Alprentice "Bunchy" Carter, leader of the Slausons, was serving a robbery sentence at Soledad State Prison. He became a Muslim in prison and was influenced by Malcolm X and later the Black Panthers. He eventually returned to Los Angeles and founded the Southern California chapter of the Panthers. Other Slausons joined the Panthers, and a few former Gladiators joined US, another black militant group. The Panthers and US were bitter rivals, and their feud was exacerbated by the FBI, who spread misinformation in the hopes of inflaming tensions between the two groups. This was an operation of the FBI's Cointelpro, a covert program that sought to discredit and disrupt black militant and leftist groups.

In 1969, the rift between the two groups culminated in a shootout. US members killed two Panthers at UCLA, and these internecine killings presaged the gang warfare that was to come.

Black street gangs began to reemerge in the city to fill a void left after the demise of the Panthers and other black activist groups. Gang members imitated the Panthers' swagger and penchant for high-powered weaponry, but they ignored the group's history of political activism and neighborhood philanthropy, such as free breakfast programs.

The origin of the Crips can be traced to a Los Angeles high school student named Raymond Washington. He had been impressed by local Panthers who advocated black residents protecting and controlling their own neighborhoods. Washington's followers soon developed a reputation that quickly spread throughout South-Central. They were known as a gang that would not hesitate to kill. In 1971, a few members jumped and killed a pimp who was beating up a prostitute, and the next year they killed a 16-year-old boy when he would not hand over his leather jacket.

There are a number of theories about the origin of the name Crips. Some people said that a member had a bad leg and walked with a cane. Others said the members strolled along with a kind of rolling limp, like cripples, or crips, for short. A South-Central high-school teacher said he was told by one O.G. that Crip stood for Continuous Revolution In Progress.

The disintegrating family life in South-Central, the dearth of jobs and the widespread poverty created a breeding ground for new recruits and new Crip sets. Blue soon became the Crips color, because of the blue bandannas they wore over their faces when they rolled on rival gangs.

East of the Harbor Freeway, in Compton, a group of young men on Piru Street formed their own gang to protect themselves from the incursions of the Crips. They called themselves Pirus and, later, "Bloods," a term used in the black power movement and among black soldiers in Vietnam. Bloods took the color red.

The decimation of the city's black neighborhoods was soon accelerated by the confluence of two deadly forces—gangs and crack cocaine. Crack immediately raised the stakes—and the level of violence—for gangs. Drug wars broke out and homicide rates began to rise in every city where crack took hold.

Crack, however, was not the only reason for the escalating number of gang killings. There still were plenty of shootings over turf disputes and unsettled scores.

During the late 1980s, when almost two black or Latino youths were being killed every day in the county because of gang violence, residents of South-Central and East Los Angeles were outraged by the response to a single gang shooting in Westwood Village, an affluent neighborhood at the edge of UCLA. A young Asian-American woman, Karen Toshima, was strolling along a crowded Westwood street on a July night in 1988, when she was caught in the crossfire of a gang shooting and killed.

Los Angeles residents, who lived far from the ghettos and barrios, were inured to the carnage taking place there every day. Toshima's murder was different. The LAPD tripled patrols in Westwood. Thirty detectives were assigned to investigate Toshima's murder. Her death was a major news story. A Westwood merchant's association offered a $10,000 reward, and a city councilman requested that the city post a $25,000 reward. A week after the shooting, police arrested Toshima's killer.

Gang shootings, at one time, were personal. If a gang member wanted revenge against a rival gang member, he sought him out and tracked him down. But gangbangers soon sought more generic targets. A gangbanger seeking revenge against a rival would simply locate a group of the rival's homies and open fire—whether the offending gangbanger was there or not. This devolved into driving into a rival's territory, and calling out, "Where you from?" to young men on the street. If they called out the wrong gang name, or if their response of "Nowhere" did not sound convincing, they were shot. Now, many gang members seeking payback will not even bother calling out, "Where you from?" They simply drive to a rival neighborhood and spray bullets at all the young men on the street.

Crack simply added another volatile element to an already volatile mix. When federal authorities clamped down on south Florida, drug lords began smuggling more cocaine into Mexico and then on to southern California. Los Angeles replaced Miami as the nation's leading cocaine distribution center. But few of the gangbanger-drug dealers Razanskas and Winn see get rich from the sale of $20 rocks. Most of the major drug transactions, most of the real money, is made by outsiders who move the drug in bulk.

Crack created a new generation of gangbangers and addicts in Los Angeles. But during the nation's War On Drugs, drug treatment was derided as another failed government program. Punishment was the favored alternative. If you had a job and health insurance, you could check into a private treatment center. But in the big cities, there were long waiting lists for publicly funded residential drug programs. If you were unemployed, help was not available, so you stayed on the streets and, eventually, were locked up. During this time, Los Angeles area libraries, schools, youth programs and recreation facilities were deteriorating and scrapping for funds. But the county's jail system, overflowing with drug offenders, was undergoing a $500 million expansion program.

And while Governor George Deukmejian was vetoing funds for education, mental health, family planning, child care and local services, California was launching the largest prison construction program in the history of the United States. From 1984 to 1995, California built 19 new prisons. The annual prison budget had reached more than $3 billion a year, and about a quarter of all inmates were convicted of drug-related crimes. California now ranks near the bottom ten states in the nation in per capita spending on education and in the top ten in prison funding.

California's "three strikes" law, which went into effect in 1994, created even more of a demand for prison cells. The three strikes measure calls for a minimum of 25 years to life for anyone convicted of a felony after two "serious or violent" prior felonies. The problem is the measure is so broadly worded that a number of nonviolent offenses—from petty theft to drug possession—qualify as a third strike. Other states have passed a version of three strikes that reserves a life sentence for those who commit a third, violent offense. But in California almost three-quarters of state prison inmates incarcerated under the measure received their third strike for nonviolent offenses.

California officials now estimate the state will need 15 new prisons by the year 2000—and a prison budget that will drain even more funds from education and social programs. As a result, the next generation of impoverished youths in South-Central will be forced to endure even more crowded and dangerous schools, and have fewer opportunities for the kind of employment, job-training and other programs that might deter, even a few, from a path that could land them on a South Bureau Homicide suspect list.

Chapter 11

Love Is a Motherfucker

Tuesday, August 9

After Winn and Razanskas talk to Hector Hernandez's former wife, Maria Rodriguez, they hop into their car and head south on the Harbor Freeway. They are on their way to pick up Wizard, Razanskas' sole witness in a 14-month-old homicide. The case hinges on Wizard, but his homies have threatened to kill him if he testifies.

Razanskas has to keep Wizard alive, so he is planning to relocate him and his family. Razanskas has $1,865 in his pocket for first and last months' rent and moving costs. He will pick up Wizard, drive him to his new home, give the landlord the money and find out when Wizard can move in. Razanskas cannot turn the money over to Wizard and let him handle the arrangements himself because homicide detectives have been burned in the past. One detective turned over more than $1,500 to a witness, who quickly smoked up the rent money.

Last week, while Winn was investigating the Hector Hernandez murder, Razanskas had to drop everything to work the Wizard case because the preliminary hearing was coming up. Now, as Razanskas weaves through rush-hour traffic, he briefs Winn on the case. Four members of the Latino gang Eastside Torrance, including Wizard, were accused of stabbing a man during a fight. Wizard decided to roll over on his homies in order to save himself. He told Razanskas that he was on the street at the time, on his way to visit a buddy. He saw the stabbing, but he was not involved. His homies want to railroad him, he claims, because he stopped hanging with Eastside Torrance, because he left the gang scene.

Razanskas flips the volume up on the car radio and he and Winn listen to a news report of a police beating that reminds them of the Rodney King beating. A Compton police officer was about to arrest a 17-year-old boy when, according to a witness, the boy took a swing at the cop. While a neighbor was videotaping the arrest, the cop whacked the boy in the cheek with the butt of his baton and struck him repeatedly while he was on the ground.

"If he wants to fight, you got to give him a fight," Razanskas tells Winn. "You can't just walk away." He shrugs. "Did it look pretty? No. But he had to take him down. The kid took a swing at him."

Winn nods. "He challenged the officer, so he's going to lose. Back when I was a rookie I responded to a call from a bus driver who needed help. I'm on the bus, by myself, dealing with this big, buffed suspect. He refuses to pay his fare. He refuses to get off the bus. This guy has a *major* attitude. He sees a lone female and thinks he's got it easy. I try to cuff him and he pushes me out of the way. He's resisting and swinging and fighting with me. I notice this guy's got a cast on his leg, so I kicked that fucker right in the cast. And he went down. I mean *down.* He probably thought I was going to fight fair. Hell no. I ain't letting some cripple get the best of me."

"You can't let a suspect go off on you," Razanskas says.

"The kid in Compton tried to be all macho and he got his ass kicked."

"And now he's crying," he says.

They swap a few more yarns. Winn tells about the time she

was working a Rolling Stones concert at the Sports Arena. A riot broke out and a woman hit Winn's partner in the head with a bottle. "I kicked that bitch's ass," she says. "I gave her an ass whipping. Afterward another cop asked me, 'What she do, Marcella. Take your man?' I told him, 'No. She hit my partner.' "

Razanskas smiles. He likes having a partner who thinks like that. When cops tell war stories about fights with suspects, the conversation eventually, inevitably, drifts to Rodney King.

"Everyone knows," Winn says to Razanskas, choosing her words carefully, "if you run from police they'll be very pissed off. Especially if you don't obey their orders when they catch you. From what I understand, King made an aggressive move toward the police that wasn't on the tape. If he did, he should have been knocked on his ass and cuffed. But once he was down, that's it. It should have been stopped. That stomping on his head was bullshit."

She turns to Razanskas and asks, "What you think, Raz?"

"About what?" he says warily.

"Rodney King."

"He wanted to fight and he lost. That's what it comes down to. You know, I don't go to church anymore because of Rodney King. Last time I was at church, this priest was talking about all the brutal officers of the LAPD. I felt like saying, 'Hey, what about me? I'm not brutal. I avoid confrontation. I'd rather talk than fight.' But the priest went on and on about how bad we all are. That was it for me. I never went back."

In midafternoon, they arrive at Wizard's, a small, narrow house in a neighborhood surrounded by factories. He and his wife and two children share the house with his in-laws. Wizard, who is thickset and muscular from years of prison weight lifting, climbs into the car. He has been shot several times, and old bullet wounds—scarred tissue the size of dimes—cover his chest and forearms. Over his eyebrow and on his neck and arms he has Eastside Torrance tattoos.

As Razanskas pulls back onto the Harbor Freeway and heads north, Wizard says, "I'm twenty-seven years old now, too old for that gang shit. I got a good job on the loading dock and they just made me foreman. I got a wife and kids now. They made me realize there's more to life than bangin'. But my homies don't see it that way. They see me trying to move away from the set, so they say I'm not down for my 'hood."

Wizard and the two detectives get stuck in rush-hour traffic. It is hot and dusty and the air conditioner is whirring at full blast. The smog is so bad that the downtown skyline has disappeared behind a pale brown curtain. The only spot of blue is directly overhead, hovering over the city like an azure dome.

Wizard, who is in the back seat, is in a talkative mood. He tells the detectives his father was a *veterano* with the Harbor City Projects gang who thought it was funny to dress him, when he was 3, in the gang uniform of tan pants, baggy white T-Shirt and red bandanna around his forehead. "My dad was a junkie and he used to slam in front of me," Wizard says. "He gave me my first fix. I was lucky. I threw up. I didn't like it. . . . My mom was a little tramp. She had seven kids—all by different men. I was jumped into Eastside Torrance when I was ten. It was New Year's Eve and I was drunk as hell on Thunderbird. So it didn't hurt none.

"I been in a dozen foster homes. I lived with aunts and uncles and cousins. I been in boys' homes, juvenile hall and YA [California Youth Authority]. The only ones who were ever there for me were my homies. Yeah," he says, smiling ruefully. "They were there for me—in a bad way."

Razanskas and Winn nod knowingly.

"During my last bit in jail my second son was born. I thought I was hard core, but I cried, man. That was tough. That changed me.

"Ask the people who know me, ask my wife, my in-laws, my boss. They'll tell you I've straightened out. I been working steady, taking care of my family. I'm not banging no more. That's why this whole thing is such a joke. I wasn't involved in this killing. But those dudes want to pin it on me. They want me to take the fall because I don't bang with 'em no more.

"When those dudes threatened me, I didn't give a shit. If I was single, I wouldn't move. But I'm worried about my kids. . . . I was at a car show and about seven of them came up to me and said, 'Hey, ese. [dude] You a snitch. We going to kill you.' I said to 'em, 'Wha's up. I'm here.' I'm pretty decent with my hands, you know. They tell me, 'Later, ese. We going to do you.'

"I'm through with that shit. But I can never make a clean break if I'm still living in the barrio. This is my only way out."

At dusk, after a few hours of driving through heavy traffic, Razanskas pulls off the freeway. He cruises through the quiet, tree-shaded streets of Wizard's new neighborhood. This is a mostly white, middle-class development of shopping malls and three-bedroom tract homes with front yards, brick fences and two-car garages. People are walking their dogs in the twilight. Children are playing catch on their front lawns.

This is as far away from the barrio as Wizard has ever been. He tells the detectives that he is in paradise. "This is something I've always wanted," he says dreamily. "Man, you can park a car on a street like this and not have to worry about anyone messin' with it. You can have your kids outside and not have to worry about them getting shot."

Razanskas pulls up at the end of a cul-de-sac, in front of a ranch-style house with jasmine growing along a stone pathway that leads to the front door. They climb out of the car and Winn walks ahead. Wizard says to Razanskas, "Whoa. She's a good-sized lady."

"Yeah," Razanskas says, with a trace of pride. "She can probably kick your ass. If we get into a fight I'm just going to sit back and let her take care of it."

When the detectives tell Wizard that the landlord stood them up, he is crestfallen. He slides down the seat and his head falls against the window. But when Razanskas assures him he can still move into the house he perks up. The detectives will have to return another day to drop off the deposit and set up the move.

On the drive back to the city, Razanskas squirms in his seat. His back is beginning to ache. It is dark now and he has to take Wizard home and drive back to South-Central to drop off the squad car. He might not get home until midnight. He might not get to sleep until 1. Then it's up again at 4:20. He grumbles about the job for a few minutes, but when he turns to Wizard and launches into a monologue about his fall hunting trip, he forgets about how tired he is. As Wizard dozes off, Razanskas tells him about the smell of sage after the rain, the beauty of an eagle swooping down on a rabbit, the golden leaves of the aspen trees fluttering in the wind . . .

The next morning, a detective friend of Razanskas' strolls by his desk and tells him about a case he just cleared that he dubs "the small dick murder." A 15-year-old girl from the projects was heavily pursuing a 19-year-old, but he was not interested and he rejected her. The girl was so angry and vindictive that she lied and told the other girls in the projects that she had slept with the 19-year-old. But, she told them, he was so poorly endowed that she dumped him.

Still, she continued to pursue him and showed up at his apartment one night. By this time he had heard the rumors. He threw a head of lettuce at her and chased her out the door. She returned home, crying, and told her mother that a man had struck her. Her mother called her boyfriend and told him to head over to the projects right away and to bring his piece. The boyfriend confronted the 19-year-old and shot him four times.

"What a crew," the detective tells Razanskas, shaking his head. "When we got to the mother, we asked her where her boyfriend was when she called him on the phone. She says, 'Oh, he was at his *other* girlfriend's house.' After he agrees to grease this guy, our big, bad hit man can't even get to the projects because he doesn't have a car. The girl's mother had to pick him up."

Razanskas rummages through his desk drawer and says, "While we're on the subject of dicks and murder, I've got something for you." He pulls out an autopsy picture of one of his murder victims. In big block letters, right across the man's penis, is tattooed the name of his gang: WILMAS. "Now this guy," Razanskas says, "is what you call a hard-core fucking gangster."

Masuyama stops by Razanskas' desk and gives him an update on the Belizean body dump case. One of the victim's sisters spotted Alton, the suspect, driving the victim's 1970 Datsun. She chased Alton, but lost him and called Masuyama. He alerted patrol officers, but they could not track him down. Still, this news is important. After the victim was killed, his car disappeared; now, the car connects Alton to the murder. The detectives now know that Alton did not flee to Belize. If they can find Alton they probably will clear their case. Masuyama flies to Japan next week and will not be back at work until after Labor Day. He hopes Alton turns up this week.

Masuyama and Reyes search for Alton. Razanskas searches for Larry Charles Gary. But he gets more bad news. The producer from *America's Most Wanted* calls and tells Razanskas he has decided not to do a segment on the case because the murder would be too hard to recreate on television. The FBI's fugitive task force is Razanskas' last hope.

Winn has been preoccupied with keeping alive John Jones, her key witness in the Felipe Angeles Gonzales killing. A girl stopped by the apartment building that Jones manages and asked a resident to pass along this message: "Five-Deuce Hoover Crips orders John Jones to stay out of court. Or we going to shoot up him and the rest of his family." Jones does not want to move. So Winn spends a morning trying to arrange for some patrol officers to keep an eye on his apartment.

When she explains the situation to Razanskas, he angrily slams a murder book shut. "This really pisses me off. In the old days, if gang members were threatening a witness, we'd take them into an alley and give them some street justice. That would be the end of the witness intimidation shit."

In the afternoon, Winn and Razanskas drive back to the suburbs to meet Wizard's new landlord and hand over the deposit. She asks him for more detail on the case and he fills her in. The murder stemmed from a dis—a disrespectful remark. The dis led to a confrontation. The confrontation led to a homicide.

On a rainy spring night, the victim, Jose, his cousin Angel, and Angel's girlfriend decided to score some marijuana. They drove over to a neighborhood south of Watts where Angel knew the Eastside Torrance gangbangers who were street dealers. They found a few of them hanging out, smoking "primo"—a mixture of rock cocaine and pot—but their supply was low and they were not selling that day. Jose told Angel, as they were driving home, that one of the homeboys had made a crude comment about his girlfriend.

Angel drove back to the neighborhood and confronted the gang member who made the comment. While they were arguing, another gang member cold-cocked him. As Jose dragged Angel back to their truck, they were beaten and stabbed by a few other gangbangers. Angel survived, but Jose was pronounced dead at the hospital. Angel knew who had attacked them but he refused to give them up to Razanskas. Angel, a fatalist, told Razanskas he probably would end up in prison one of these days, and when he got there he did not want to be known as a snitch. He told the deputy district attorney handling the case, "Miss Prosecutor, if they had killed my kids it couldn't have hurt me more. But I ain't taking the stand. I don't want any paper on me. I don't want a snitch jacket."

Razanskas had to pursue the investigation without Angel. He eventually picked up a few leads, which led to the arrest of Wizard and three other Eastside gang members.

After Razanskas fills Winn in, he tells her that he is going to ask Wizard's new landlord if he ever has had a drive-by in the neighborhood. Razanskas laughs. "After he says no, I'll tell him, 'Well, you will now.' "

Winn is driving, they are listening to her favorite oldies station, and, after a news report, Razanskas, a staunch conservative and National Rifle Association member, makes a quip about President Clinton.

"I'm sick of hearing you and every other detective rip Clinton," Winn says. "He's our president and people better damn well get used to it. Bitch, bitch, bitch. That's all everyone does."

Razanskas takes a pinch of Skoal and spits into his cup. He hold up a palm, turns to Winn and says, "Whoa."

Winn pulls up in front of Wizard's new home. Razanskas gives the cash to the landlord and chats with him while Winn waits in the car. When he returns, she asks, "Did you get the keys?"

"Naw. Wizard can get them."

"That's a lot of cash to turn over," she says. "People get ripped off like that."

"Oh, they look like nice people."

She glares at him. "And what do *nice* people look like?"

"Oh no," he says angrily. "Don't start that shit with me. I'm not Masuyama," he says, referring to the argument about whether the body dump victim had black features. "You're not going to suck me in like that. What I was talking about was that these people had a *nice* house, and they just seemed like decent people. Period."

"Last week, *America's Most Wanted* featured a couple that sounds just like that. Now the FBI's lookin' for 'em."

Neither detective cares to continue the conversation. They return to the city in silence.

At the end of the week, it is time for Wizard's day in court, time for him to testify against his former homies. Before Razanskas leaves the bureau, he tells Winn, "This is turning out to be the case from hell."

Two days ago someone left a note for Wizard on the windshield of his father-in-law's car. It read: "Wizard you better not go to court. We have the green light to hit your pad." WIZARD was scrawled on the top of the note, in graffiti-style block letters, with the name crossed out. When a gangbanger Xs out a street name on a wall, it means the person has been targeted for a hit.

Wizard understood the note to mean that if Eastside Torrance could not get to him, they were going after his family, or his wife's family. He told the prosecutor he was backing out. He would not testify. Razanskas was irate. The days he spent setting up Wizard's move, the countless hours of investigation—all for nothing. Fortunately, the D.A. was able to calm Wizard down. He agreed, reluctantly, to appear in court. But now the prosecutor is spooked. She is worried about Eastside Torrance retaliating against Wizard's in-laws. She had planned to push for first-degree murder, but now she is prepared to cut a deal with the stabber's attorney. This will keep Wizard from testifying and will protect his in-laws.

Razanskas pulls up in front of Wizard's house, he climbs into the car and says, "You think I got any sleep last night? Hell no! I never been so nervous in my fucking life."

"How 'bout when you got married?" Razanskas asks.

"I was happy-scared then."

Last spring, on the day before Wizard was scheduled to get married, he told Razanskas that he had a problem. Earlier in the week, his old homies beat up his best man and told him they were going to kill Wizard at the wedding.

Razanskas had only 24 hours to set up security. He called a half-dozen specialized LAPD units, but none could spare the officers on such short notice. So Razanskas wandered through the squad room and gathered about a dozen homicide detectives. The next day they parked their squad cars in front of the church, to send a message to Wizard's homies, and wandered about in their bulletproof vests, thigh holsters and LAPD raid jackets.

"I don't know if I ever told you," Razanskas says to Wizard, holding the steering wheel in one hand, reaching for his cup with the other and spitting. "But your wedding was like something out of a goddamn movie for me. That church was the same church where I got married—the first time. Right before I went to 'Nam. Man, I had some serious flashbacks. I'm thinking, 'Oh shit! What am I doing here?'

"After the wedding. I didn't think you'd be safe at home. Remember what I told you?"

Wizard smiles and nods.

"I told you to go to a nice hotel, sit in a jacuzzi with your wife and drink some champagne while the bubbles were blowing up your ass."

"Yeah," Wizard says. "You even fronted me sixty bucks. I appreciate that."

When they arrive at the D.A.'s Hardcore Gang Unit in Compton, Deputy D.A. Linda Bushling tells Razanskas and Wizard her strategy on the case. Before the threats began against Wizard's family, she thought she had a good chance for a murder-one conviction. Now, she tells them, she has to compromise. Everything has changed. Bushling is five months pregnant, and she is highly agitated about the turn the case has taken. This is the last thing she needs now. She tells them it is not the threats to Wizard that have forced her to change her approach, but the threats to his in-laws. It is impossible to move everyone involved. Wizard's in-laws are middle-aged people who do not want to leave their neighborhood. This case, she tells them, is like walking a high wire. She is dealing with a killer. But she also is trying to protect Wizard's family. She has decided to err on the side of caution. She is going to try to cut a deal. But if the defense attorney won't agree to a long prison term, she will be forced to take the case to trial.

Bushling leaves the office for her meeting with the defense attorney. Wizard takes a deep breath and slowly exhales. "Man, I hope to God she can cut a deal," he says. "I do *not* want to get out there on that stand." Razanskas tries to keep him entertained, spinning yarns about his more sensational murder cases. But Wizard is too nervous to pay attention. About an hour passes before Bushling returns. She settles into a chair and smooths her maternity dress over her knees.

She turns to Wizard. "He pled."

"Man, I'm fucking relieved," Wizard says. "I was sweatin' this."

"He pled no contest to voluntary manslaughter and attempted murder," she says. "He pled to eleven years and he'll do sixty to eighty percent of it." She says to Razanskas, "I'm not going to ask you if you're happy. But can you live with that?"

He shrugs. "I guess I'll have to."

"I'm very disappointed myself," she says. "I feel like this is a victory for the gang and a loss for us. I feel like I let down the victim. This case should have gone to trial. I have no doubt he'd be convicted and would get life. But I couldn't put any more lives in danger. I'm not sure this is justice. But it's reality."

She and Razanskas are dejected. But Wizard is elated. He calls his wife and says, "Everything's cool. I didn't have to testify. I love you." He hugs Bushling. Before they leave, Bushling tells Razanskas that she plans to file charges against the gang members who threatened Wizard's life at the car show. She is going to nail them, she tells Razanskas, for making terrorist threats. This does not cheer him up much. He is in a glum mood as he drives Wizard home.

There is no better feeling for a detective than catching a killer. But after the initial burst of exhilaration, a gauntlet of frustrations often follows. The D.A. may tell the detective there is insufficient evidence and refuse to file murder charges. At the preliminary hearing a judge may refuse to hold the suspect over for trial. In the months leading up to trial, witnesses may become intimidated and refuse to testify. And on the eve of a trial, the D.A. may cut a deal with the defense lawyer.

It is so difficult to solve murders today that when a detective actually clears a case, he is embittered when the courts do not impose the maximum penalty or, in some cases, any penalty. An acquittal is a personal affront.

Razanskas pulls off the freeway, heads down the side streets and tells Wizard that is was misplaced machismo that got Jose killed. Jose died protecting the honor of his cousin Angel's girlfriend, he tells Wizard. But the girl, Razanskas discovered during his investigation, actually had a second boyfriend and was pregnant by a third boyfriend. Razanskas pulls in front of Wizard's house and parks.

"Getting killed over this girl," he tells Wizard, tapping the murder book with a forefinger, "proves one thing." Razanskas smiles, forgetting the frustration of the day for a moment, and says, "Love is a motherfucker."

Chapter 12
Back From the Dead

Sunday, August 14

Razanskas and Winn are back on the weekend rotation. They are third on the on-call list, but there is little doubt they will catch a case. This is the second weekend in August, the peak of the summer murder season, and a heat wave has enveloped the city.

August weather in Los Angeles is desert weather. The days bake under cloudless skies and the nights cool down with a dry breeze that blows powdery layers of dust across the city. August is a reminder that east of the ocean, past the city, beyond the urban sprawl of the smoggy suburbs, over the San Bernardino Mountains, looms the vast, broiling Mojave Desert. But this weekend Los Angeles feels like an alien place. The remains of Hurricane Ileana, lingering off the coast of Baja California, have cloaked the city in a humid haze, jacked up the temperatures and daubed the horizon with great billowy clouds. The steamy, sultry weather of the tropics has replaced the dry heat of the desert. Friday it was 104 degrees. Saturday was almost as hot. And the sticky nights bring little relief.

Early Sunday morning Razanskas and Winn get their call. It is still dark when they arrive at the 77th Street station. The station's air conditioner is not working and huge fans blow hot air through the room. A sergeant tells them that a man was driving home from a wedding with his brother and son when they got a flat tire. While changing the flat they were jumped by a group of Latino men, probably gangbangers. The driver was stabbed and beaten with a baseball bat. He died. His brother also was stabbed, but he survived and is now in the hospital. The son is at the station.

When the sergeant finishes briefing them, Razanskas tells Winn that one thing mystifies him. The wedding was in Pico Rivera and none of the victims lived near South-Central. Why were they changing a flat at 62nd and Hoover?

The victim's son is sitting at the watch commander's desk. He is 14 years old, has braces and stares off into the distance, mouth open, dazed. Razanskas, who is the primary on this one, wants to get a quick take on what happened, before hustling off to the crime scene. He knows he can talk to the boy again later in the morning. Razanskas puts a hand on the boy's shoulder and asks what happened.

"Me and my dad and uncle were riding around when we had a flat," the boy says. He speaks so softly that Razanskas asks him to speak up. "We stopped to fix the tire. A bunch of guys jumped us."

"Cholos?" Razanskas asks.

"Yeah. They came up to us and yelled, 'Get 'em.' "

"How many of them?" Razanskas asks.

"About six or eight?"

"The wedding was a long way from here. None of you live in South-Central. What were you doing around here?"

The boy picks at a cuticle. "I don't know where my dad was going."

"Did you fight any of those guys?" Razanskas asks.

"No."

Razanskas reaches over and taps the boy's right hand. The knuckles are scraped and bloody. "What's this?"

"I hit the telephone after I called for help."

"Okay, buddy. You write down everything that happened. I'll be back to talk to you some more when I finish up on the scene."

The detectives drive west on Florence and north on Hoover, through the dark, deserted streets. Razanskas tells Winn, "This kid is holding out on us. Big time. Maybe they were looking to buy dope. Maybe they were looking for whores. I don't know."

Winn nods. "He's not telling us the whole story."

At the homicide scene, Razanskas chats with a sergeant he knows. The cop has just returned from a street shooting. The victim, he tells Razanskas, just made the moron of the month club. He was a shirtless gangbanger with "BLOODS" tattooed across his chest in huge block letters. He made the mistake of wandering through a Crip neighborhood. It did not take long before someone took a pot shot at him for disrespecting the 'hood.

While Razanskas and the sergeant talk, Winn is growing increasingly impatient. When they arrive at crime scenes, Razanskas often encounters officers he once worked with and he chats with them. They catch up on LAPD gossip, swap stories or talk hunting. Winn likes to get right to work. This always is a source of contention between them. But this morning she sidles up to him and he breaks off the conversation without any prompting. They then walk over to the body together.

The victim is on the street, under a sheet, behind his new Ford Taurus. The rear windows have been smashed, and under the street lamps, the broken glass glitters on the asphalt like a handful of diamonds. Four white wedding carnations are scattered along the back seat. The car's emergency flashers are still blinking, and a jack and four lug nuts are lined up next to a front tire. Razanskas flicks on his heavy metal flashlight and studies the front tire, which is pressing against the curb.

"This guy was drunk," Razanskas tells Winn. "He didn't get a flat by hitting some nail. He busted the tire on the curb."

The night is clear, one of those rare nights when a panorama of stars shroud the skies. Fog or smog often obscures the night skies in Los Angeles, and it is rare when more than a few stars can be seen. But the oppressive heat has dissolved the fog and the miasma of haze that hovers over the city. Horizons usually obscured are now, briefly, unveiled. Even the crackheads and strawberries who wander by stop and gaze at the starry skies.

The detectives wander about the crime scene, illuminating their way with flashlights. Razanskas spots a single lug nut across the street from the car. "I figure one of the victims threw this at the shitheads," he tells Winn. "When you're fighting for your life, you'll pick up anything you can as a weapon." He studies a patch of dirt near the car and spots two sets of shoe prints—one fresh, probably made by a suspect, and the other a few days old. "I'm going to show you now that hunting isn't a total waste of time. Some of the shit you learn, like tracking, can come in handy." He lowers his flashlight a few inches from the shoe prints, and he shows her how to tell the difference between the old and the new shoe prints. The new prints are darker and the dirt around them is slightly sandy. The dirt around the old shoe prints is hard and brittle and covered with a film of dust.

He walks over to the body, lifts the sheet and takes a peek. The victim's head, which is a few inches from the curb, is surrounded by a nimbus of dried blood. He is still dressed in his tuxedo pants, suspenders and maroon dress shoes. His pleated tuxedo shirt is in the car. It was a hot night, so Razanskas figures the victim took it off before changing the tire. "I hate to make light," Razanskas says. "But the mortician's going to love this guy. Put that shirt back on him and he's ready for the funeral."

Winn rolls her eyes and turns to the police photographer and tells him what to shoot. Sweat streams down his face. He wipes his brow with a handkerchief and says, "I hope my next one is by the beach."

The pale radiance of dawn shows on the horizon and the stars begin to fade. It feels like sunrise in the tropics. The towering palms in the distance sway in the damp breeze. Huge lead-colored clouds hover over the Hollywood Hills, the purple escarpment sharply etched against the lightening sky. Streaks and smudges of pink and gold and orange begin to stipple the eastern horizon.

A street-level view of 62nd and Hoover offers a less aesthetically pleasing vista. The body is in front of a duplex surrounded by a sagging chain-link fence, with two battered, broken-down cars on the dead grass. The duplex is a pastiche of green and white splotches. It once was white, but it appears that someone decided to paint it green and then quit midway through the job. Across the street is a laundromat with malt liquor billboards overhead and an open-air recycling center, with a ragged tarpaulin covering the barrels and a sign that reads "Cash For Cans."

When the coroner investigator arrives, Razanskas points to a small, barely discernible scar on the victim's chest. "This guy's no cherry," Razanskas mutters. "He's been shot before." The victim has two stab wounds, small crimson slashes, one on his chest and one on his back. Along his sides and back are a few blotchy bruises, from the baseball bat. The investigator empties the victim's pockets, finds $120 in twenties and—Razanskas is thankful for this—a wallet. The victim's name is Ruben Gomez and he is 32 years old. The investigator cuts a small incision just above Gomez's belt and is about to insert a thermometer into the liver to estimate the time of death.

Razanskas points to a young woman, a student intern who is observing the homicide scene for a criminal justice class. "Give *her* the thermometer," he says to the investigator. "Let her do it."

She backs up and shakes her head nervously.

"There's nothing to it," Razanskas says. "You just give the thermometer a good push."

"No . . . No . . . I . . . I don't think . . . I can't . . . ," she sputters.

Razanskas winks to the investigator. The intern realizes Razanskas was kidding and she is greatly relieved.

The investigator thrusts the thermometer deep into the liver. The intern winces and turns her head. While the investigator is finishing up, Razanskas points to Hoover Street and says to Winn, "Had one there. A little further south. The suspect was a butcher. Guess how he killed his wife? That's right. With a butcher knife. Her body's in the apartment, and he makes it sound like it's self-defense. The guy tells a pretty good story. But we run his record and find out he did the same thing in Texas about seven or eight years earlier. With another wife. The first time the jury may have bought it. But not a second time."

He points to the laundromat across the street. "Had one there. Guy is taking his laundry back to his car and gets robbed. He doesn't have any money because he spent his last quarter on the washing machines. The shitheads are pissed off because he's got no money. So they shoot him. He crawls back into the laundromat and dies on the floor."

He points to a Mexican restaurant in a strip mall on the corner. "Had one there. The suspect is eating breakfast. In walk two guys who had been after him. They were all involved in a drug deal gone bad. The two guys who walk in spot the suspect and go for their shit. Now you don't want to fuck with his guy. He's a *pistolero,* an old pro who knows what he's doing. He turns around and runs. But not to run away. He heads for the kitchen so he can assume a defense position.

"I interviewed the guy after the shooting, and I asked him what he did next. He says, 'I grabbed my gun, twirled it on my finger and fired.' I can't believe what I'm hearing. It sounds like the fucking movies. I say: 'Whoa. You *twirled* the gun?' He says, 'Yeah. I twirled the gun. . . .'

"Anyone else tells me this, I think they're full of shit. But this guy, I believe. He's a bad dude. He's got a Colt .38 Super with a custom mother-of-pearl grip. Not factory engraving. Custom scrollwork. And that wasn't the first time he used that gun. This guy was cool as a cucumber. He was an old Mexican gunfighter who twirled the gun out of habit. He killed one guy and sent the other to the hospital. The D.A. called it justifiable homicide."

It is midmorning now and the temperature is rising quickly. Winn is hot and anxious to get out of the sun. When the driver of the coroner's van hauls the body away on a metal gurney, she motions to the car.

At the station, Razanskas and Winn take their witness—the victim's 14-year-old son, Ruben, Jr.—to a back office. His mother and stepfather, who have just arrived, join him. The mother, who is divorced from Ruben's father, tells Razanskas she is worried about her son. Will he have to appear in court? Will the killers come after him? Razanskas calms her down and tells her the LAPD will do everything it can to protect him.

1

Razanskas at his graduation from the LAPD academy with Chief Daryl Gates.

2

Winn at her graduation from the LAPD academy in 1987.

3

Razanskas getting his detective badge from Chief Gates.

4

Winn, a rookie officer, beside her patrol car.

5

Winn and Razanskas in front of a map of South Los Angeles.

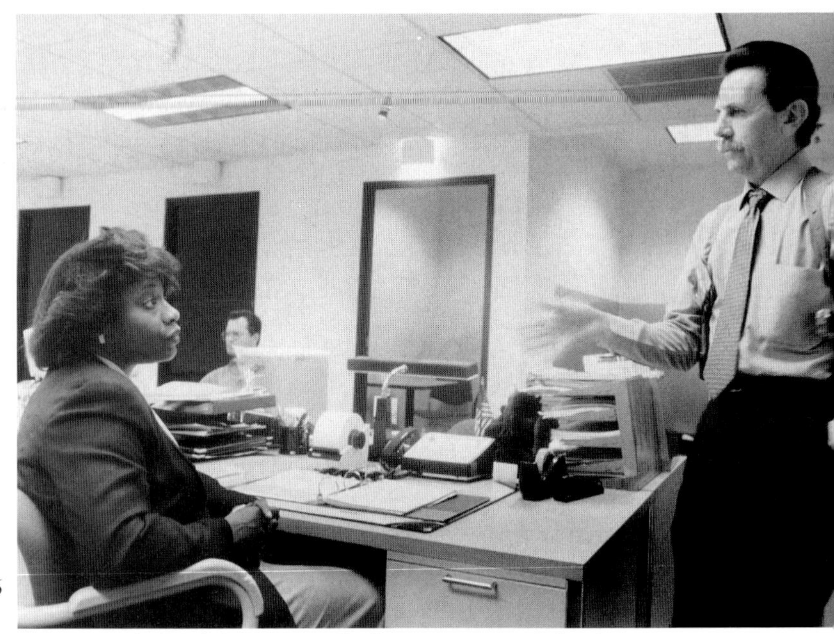
6

Razanskas and Winn off the streets and back at South Bureau Homicide.

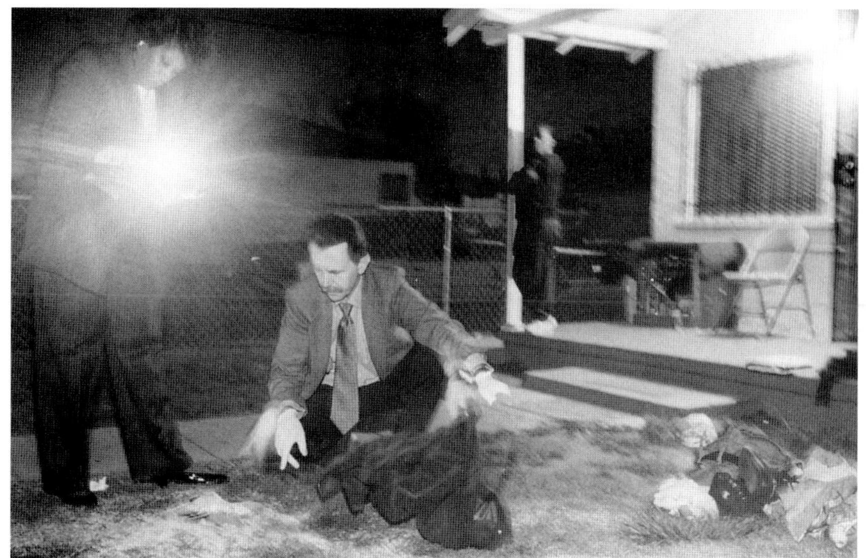

7

Razanskas and Winn examine the clothing of a victim who survived a gunshot wound to the head.

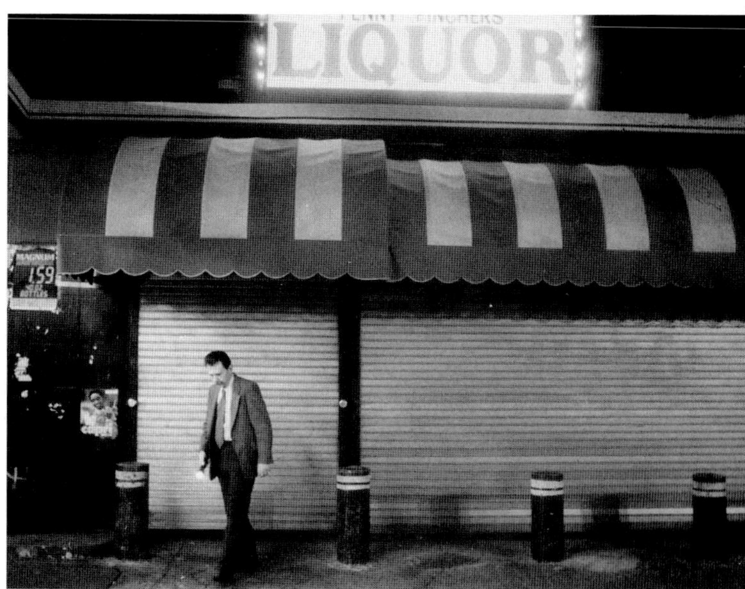

8

Razanskas searches for clues outside a liquor store where a man was shot.

Razanskas taking notes at a murder scene.

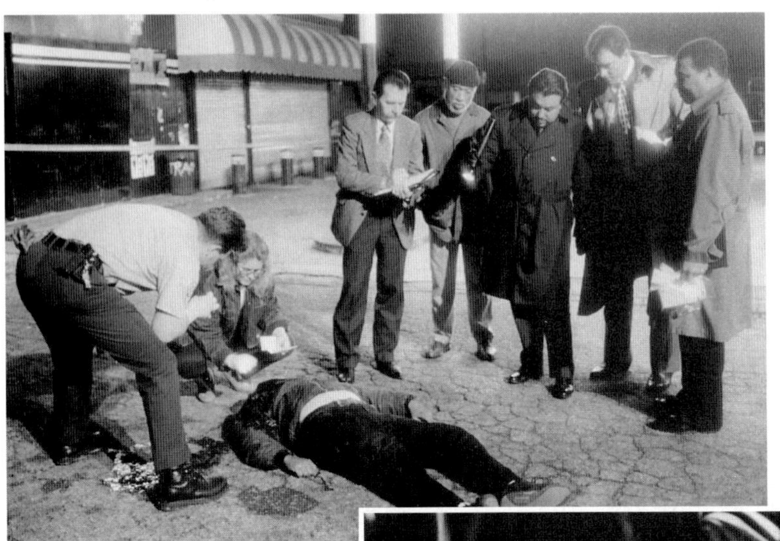

9

10

Razanskas examines the body of a murder victim.

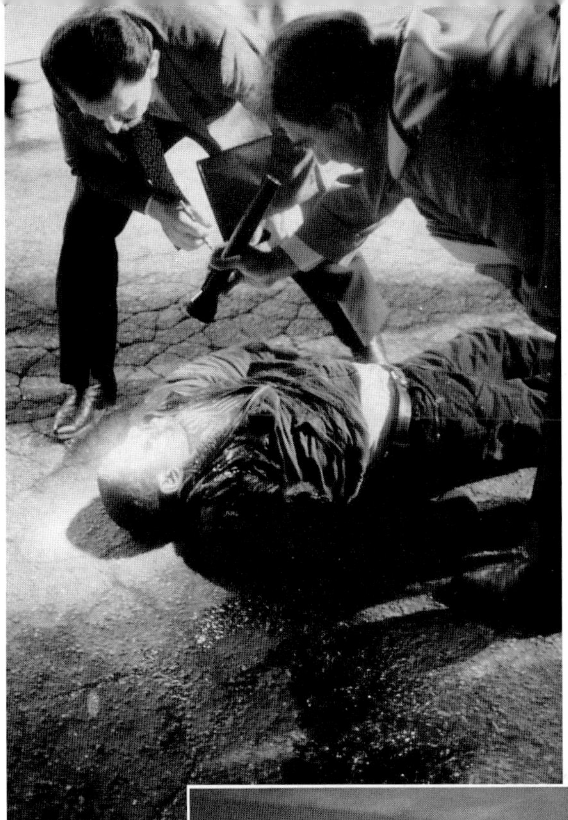

11

Razanskas and another detective hover over the body of a murder victim.

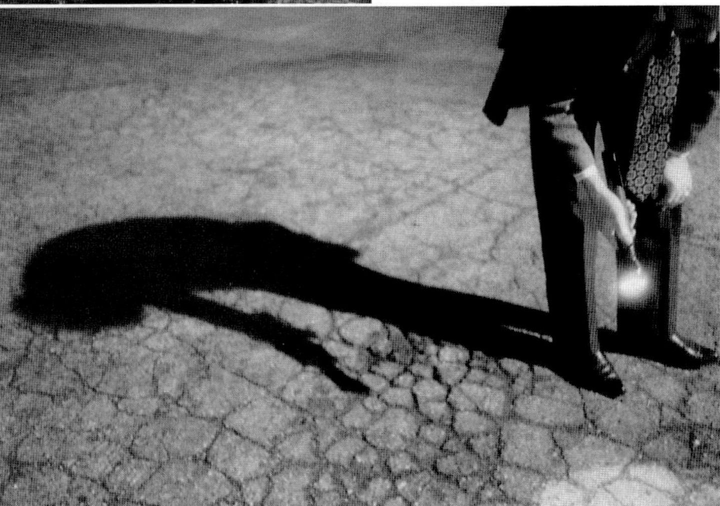

12

Razanskas searching for clues.

13

Razanskas and Winn studying the trajectory of a bullet in a street shooting.

14

Razanskas informs a man that his son has just been murdered.

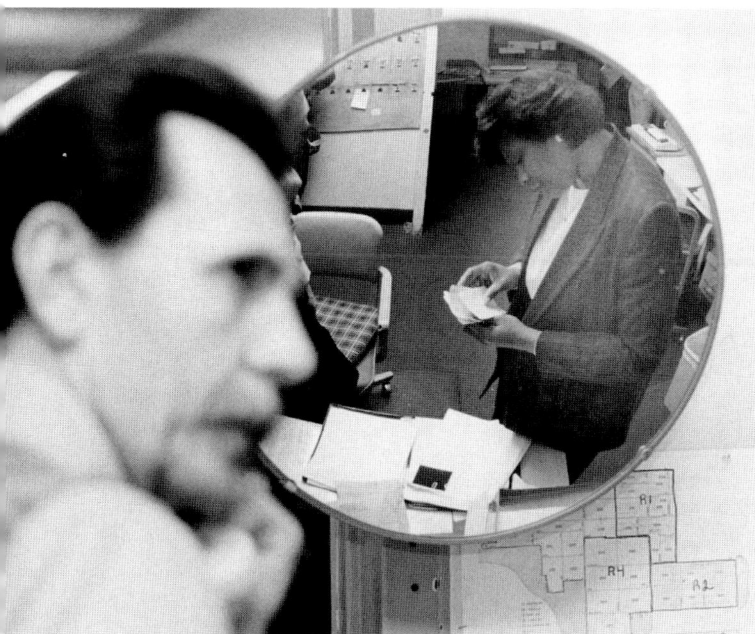

15

Winn sifts through field interview cards after a homicide.

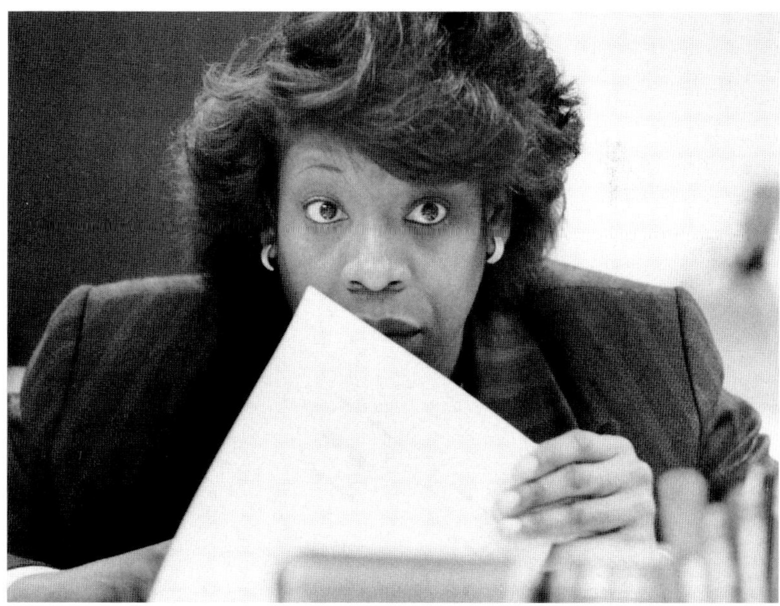

16

Winn studies a homicide report, searching for answers.

17

Razanskas plows through a stack of homicide reports.

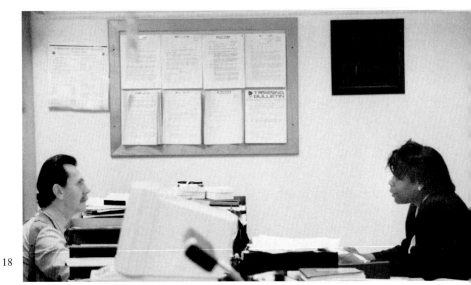

18

Razanskas and Winn head to head at the Bureau.

Ruben is wearing oversized green work pants and a white T-shirt. Razanskas figures he is a wanna-be gang member—not yet in a gang, but on the edge. Razanskas pulls his chair next to him and asks, "Why was your dad in that neighborhood?"

Ruben replies so softly Razanskas cannot understand him. Razanskas does not want to press him, but time is critical in a homicide investigation. He cannot wait a day or two until the boy calms down. He asks Ruben to speak louder.

"We just got off the freeway," Ruben says.

"For what reason?"

"For no reason."

"Were you looking for prostitutes?"

"No."

"Dope?"

"No."

"When your dad was driving home from the wedding, were you drunk or sleeping?"

"Whatever," he says, looking away.

Razanskas runs his fingers through his hair and stares at the ceiling for a moment. He tries to figure out how to reach the boy. "Let me explain something to you. I don't want to get you in trouble. I don't want to get your uncle in trouble. I just want to find out who killed your father. You'll be better off in the long run if you're up front with me. From the beginning."

He launches into an entreaty, one he has given many times before. "I need your help. I can be the best detective in the world, but without your help, I'm nothing. I can't do this on my own."

Ruben fingers his wispy adolescent mustache.

Winn extends her palms toward Ruben. "Look," she says, "this isn't just something you saw on the street. This is your father. We're trying to help you. But for us to do that you've got to tell us what you were doing in the neighborhood."

Ruben stares off into the distance.

Finally, his stepfather says, "They might have been looking for an after-hours club."

Ruben's mother adds, "Or they might have been looking for his sister's house. She lives around there."

"That late at night?" Razanskas asks.

The mother shrugs.

He turns to Ruben and asks, "What kind of weapons did they have?"

"One guy had a chain, another guy had a knife and another guy had a baseball bat."

"Were they dressed down?"

"Yeah. They looked like gangsters. They asked us, 'Where you from?' We said, 'Nowhere.' They said, 'Stop lying.' Then they started fighting us."

"Did you see your dad get stabbed?"

"Yeah," he says, dropping his chin to his chest.

"Did the guy with the bat hit your dad?"

"Yeah. In the back. My dad was fighting a few guys and my uncle was fighting a few of the others. My dad fell to the ground. A guy wearing shorts kicked him in the head."

"Were any of the homeboys injured?"

"One guy, I think. I saw my uncle stab one guy in the neck with a pen."

"What were you doing?"

"When those guys started coming toward us, my dad told me to run. I ran across the street. While he was fighting them he yelled to me, 'Run.' "

The story is confusing is many ways, but one thing is clear to Razanskas: Ruben's father's last act was to save his son. He and his brother fought off a half-dozen men long enough for Ruben to get away.

"I ran across the street," Ruben says. "I looked back and they were still beating my dad. I found a phone and was going to call the police. Finally, one of them said, 'That's enough.' And they all ran and drove away."

"What kind of car?"

"A Jeep."

"Color?"

"White."

Razanskas leans toward Ruben and says, "This is very important. Can you remember any bits and pieces of the license plate?"

"It was 'OG ROB.' "

Razanskas freezes and stares at the boy. "That was the whole plate?"

"Yeah."

"You sure."

"Yeah."

Winn bolts upright in her chair. She and Razanskas exchange a glance. They cannot believe this. The boy has virtually cleared the case for them.

Winn looks at the mother for a moment to gauge her reaction and then turns to Ruben. "How did you get such a good look at the plate?"

"When they ran to the Jeep and drove away. That's when I saw the plate."

The detectives ask Ruben a few more questions, but they cannot get much more out of him. Razanskas walks the family out the door and tells them he will keep them apprised. Back inside he tells Winn, "This is my lucky fucking day." He has had a string of tough cases. He feels he was due for a break.

Razanskas does not doubt that Ruben was able to memorize the license plate number. It was an easy plate to remember. A streetwise kid, Razanskas figures, would assume OG meant original gangster and ROB meant rip-off. But he tells Winn that one thing bothers him. Ruben was lying about *how* he spotted the plate. Ruben told them he ran across the street, was trying to call police from the phone booth and memorized the Jeep's plate as the suspects drove off. But from the phone booth, Razanskas tells Winn, it would have been impossible for Ruben to have seen the Jeep's license plate. That is something he plans to pursue the next time he interviews Ruben.

His plan of action now, he tells her, is to delay arresting the owner of the Jeep. Instead, he plans to contact patrol and the LAPD gang unit in the area and tell them to watch out for the Jeep. When they spot it—and hopefully the driver will have a few passengers—they will bring everyone into the station and call him.

"I don't want just the driver," Razanskas tells Winn. "I want them all. If I only have one guy, he'll tell me to fly a kite. If I can pick up two or three, I can play one against the other and bring everyone down."

"I say you run the plate and jam the owner right now," Winn says angrily. She shakes her head and crosses her arms. "I don't like this waiting around."

"If I jam the owner, maybe he'll lay everyone else out. But I doubt it. My odds are much better if I can scoop up more than one of them at the same time. I have a better chance to get the guy with a knife that way."

"Arrest the owner *now* and you still might be able to get the guy with the knife later."

"Let's use some patience and do the job right. I want more than the driver. I want all of 'em."

"I want all of 'em, too. I just don't like letting murder suspects wander around here, free as birds."

They argue for a few more minutes. But Winn finally gives up. She went through this with Razanskas once before with the Larry Charles Gary case. She wanted to arrest him right away; he wanted to wait. She learned then that although Razanskas will listen to her opinion, he is, in the end, immovable.

"Since there's nothing more for me to do now," she says with a trace of irritation, "I'm going home."

He decides to return to the crime scene and pick up the pen Ruben's uncle used to stab one of the suspects. Razanskas recalls spotting the pen near the curb. He is embarrassed now that he did not make the connection at the time.

He pulls up at 62nd and Hoover, climbs out of the car and spots a bent pen with ink dripping from the tip. He deposits the pen in an evidence envelope. It is sweltering now, inching toward 100 degrees. He climbs back into his car, veers over to Broadway and heads south, to the Southeast Division station, where he often parks his truck. He crosses 82nd Street and, for the next two miles, drives past almost 40 storefront churches. There are a few traditional churches on this stretch of Broadway, but most are ragtag operations, single rooms with doors open to the street and only a few worshipers inside. As Razanskas drives down Broadway, the voices of the preachers—warning against the wages of sin, shouting biblical homilies, bellowing in the grips of divine inspiration—echo out into the street. Their voices mingle with the faint trace of an organ, an amen chorus hollering, "Praise the Lord!" and a single voice wailing a spiritual. The preachers make up for the modest surroundings by granting their churches lofty and mellifluous names. Razanskas drives past Miracle of Faith Apostolic House of Prayer Incorporated, past Triumph The Church And Kingdom Of God In Christ, past Whosoever Will–Prayer Temple of True Holiness, past I Am That I Am's Church of Eternal Salvation, which Razanskas calls the Popeye church.

Razanskas parks his squad car in the lot and places his 9-millimeter on the passenger seat of his truck—within easy reach in case he should encounter trouble on the way to the freeway.

He just bought a new Austrian spotting scope for his fall hunting trip, and at dusk tonight, if it cools off enough, he plans to spend the waning daylight hours in his backyard, testing it again, studying the movement of ants 60 feet away. Dreaming of those cool autumn mornings in southern Wyoming is keeping him going.

In Pico Rivera, a few freeway interchanges east of South-Central, a mother sits in the living room of her small apartment, crowded with friends and relatives, and cries with her children. Mary Gomez has nine children, and Ruben, her oldest, was the most accomplished. How, she wonders, did he end up stabbed to death at the corner of 62nd and Hoover? Had Ruben been murdered ten years ago, she would not have been surprised. But not now, not after he went back to school, found a good job and became an executive.

Ruben had come so far. When he was 11 his father died, and the family struggled without his meager earnings as a gardener. Ruben was a rowdy teenager, in and out of juvenile hall. During one stint in custody he met a member of White Fence, a notorious East L.A. gang. When Ruben was released from juvenile hall he began hanging out with his new friend, and he soon became involved with a White Fence girl known as Li'l Sleepy. Ruben was jumped into the gang when he was 15.

Soon he was known throughout East L.A. as Poison, a hard-core gangbanger who was down for his set. If White Fence had to retaliate against another gang, he was always among the first to volunteer. If he was walking down the street and caught a rival looking at him, he would scream, "What you looking at?" and pummel him. He carried a razor-sharp Buck knife, which he dabbed with furniture polish. He told his homies that if the stab wound did not kill his enemy, the furniture polish *would,* because it was poison. He now had a street name.

Ruben was a high school dropout with a rap sheet, but he was different from his homies. He liked to read and would spend hours in his mother's garage, reading crime novels, history books, science fiction. He may have acted like a psycho, but Ruben was bright. He could fix anything. He would repair his homies' cars, refrigerators, stereos and televisions.

Everyone knew Ruben had potential, but his attitude was: *Fuck it.* He was destined for the penitentiary and he did not care. But one Halloween night he had an epiphany. It inalterably changed his life and turned him away, forever, from the gang life.

He was at a party, and both White Fence and King Cobras, who had called a truce, were there. A fight broke out anyway and the truce was shattered. Bullets flew. Ruben was right in the middle of it and was shot three times and stabbed three times. His heart stopped during surgery. The doctors were doubtful he would survive. A priest was called into the intensive care unit to administer the last rites. But after a week in intensive care, Ruben finally began to improve.

When his family visited him, he told them that during surgery he could actually see his life slipping away. He felt himself hovering above the operating room, and in the distance he saw a door. Behind the door he saw a man. Behind the man he saw a bright blinding light. He did not know if he should pass through the door and into the light or stay on the operating table. But the man behind the door told him, "It's not time. Go back." When Ruben recuperated from surgery, he talked constantly of his vision. He told his family that God had given him another chance, that God had instructed him to change his life.

While recovering, Ruben read about Mexican history and the

Chicano political movement. He married Li'l Sleepy. They had a son, Ruben, Jr. He avoided his homies and stopped dressing down in khakis, white undershirts and wraparound sunglasses. He enrolled in a technical institute and worked his way through school repairing televisions. When he graduated, Ruben was offered technician jobs by a number of firms, including IBM and Kodak. Ruben took a job with GTECH, a firm that manufactures and installs lottery systems, because it offered the most money.

GTECH had just been awarded the contract for the California lottery, and Ruben was hired as a technician to service the lottery's terminals. Within a year he was promoted to lead communications technician. His supervisors were impressed with how hard he worked, how quickly he grasped new technology, how everyone he worked with seemed to like him.

The next year, GTECH, which had a number of contracts in Mexico and South America, was considering Ruben for a managerial position in its Latin American division. He was bilingual, he knew the technical aspects of the business, and he had a charismatic personality. During a job interview, he talked frankly with the executives about his past. They knew he had an arrest record, and he told them about his years as a gang member. After the interview they concluded that he had made mistakes, but was not likely to make them again. They offered him the job.

Ruben moved to Mexico and helped set up the communications network for the national lottery. He was known in the office as "the gadgets guy," because his office was always filled with equipment he tested and took apart. He spent all his free time reading scientific journals and learning about computer technology and satellite communication. Although he attended trade school instead of college, and was rebuilding the engines of Chevy lowriders while his contemporaries were studying engineering, he soon developed a reputation for technical innovation and expertise.

After two years in Mexico, he transferred to Puerto Rico and after about six months there was sent to Argentina and Chile and then Trinidad. He was promoted frequently and developed a reputation for being able to tackle difficult jobs. If a location presented technological challenges, GTECH would send Ruben. In Trinidad, Ruben was made a project manager. He no longer was in charge of just the technical aspects of the job; he supervised every aspect of the operation. Now he was an executive who had a few dozen people working for him.

By now he was divorced from Li'l Sleepy and did not get a chance to see much of his son. Ruben, Jr., treasured the letters from his father and showed his friends the postcards his father sent him from the Caribbean and South America. His father soon began helping out the entire extended family. If his brothers and sisters had trouble paying an electric bill or their car registration, or needed a washing machine or school clothes for their kids, they would write Ruben. He never turned them down.

He was working in Barbados, setting up the national lottery, when his sister told him she was getting married. She wanted him to give her away. He flew to Los Angeles and rented a white Ford Taurus. He paid for his sister's wedding, walked her down the aisle, and gave her $500 as a wedding present. After the wedding, Ruben, his brother and Ruben, Jr., hopped into the rented Taurus. Ruben's mother, Mary Gomez, sent another son to tell Ruben not to stay out long. Ever since he was stabbed and shot at the Halloween party, she worried when he went out at night in Los Angeles. But by the time her other son went looking for Ruben, he already was gone. A few hours later Ruben was dead.

She still does not know why Ruben was killed. She does not know how someone who has come so far, who lived through gunshots and stab wounds, who almost died on the operating table, who transformed himself from a gang member to an executive, could have been murdered while changing a flat.

Chapter 13
Miami

Monday, August 15

The day after Ruben Gomez's murder, Razanskas and Winn are back in the squad room. He tells her that he called the gang unit and asked them to watch for the Jeep with the license plate OG ROB. But their disagreement over when to arrest the owner is soon moot because Razanskas gets a call from the FBI's fugitive task force. They have nabbed Charles—Larry Charles Gary—at his brother's house in Miami. As soon as the detectives get their travel plans approved and finalized, they will fly off to Miami and bring him back.

Razanskas is elated. The D.A. had filed charges against Charles, but Razanskas did not get credit for a cleared case because the suspect was not in custody. He had been particularly worried about this one. Charles had been on the lam for a few months and Razanskas did not want to wait four years for him to surface, like the suspect in his Oregon case. He also hopes that now the second-guessing by Winn will end. And Razanskas is particularly pleased that Charles was arrested in a beautiful seaside city like Miami. Razanskas has visions of spending a day at the beach, napping in a lounge chair, before picking up Charles and bringing him home.

Early Wednesday morning the detectives board a flight to Miami. When they arrive they wait in line for a rental car and hear a man shouting, "Help! Help! Someone call the police!" The detectives jog toward the man. He has a video camera and is whirling around, taping the airport security officers as they attempt to take him into custody. It turns out that the man had attempted to rent a car, but the rental company ran a check on his credit card and rejected it.

"The only reason they won't accept my card is because I'm white," he shouts. "Anybody touches me . . . I'm going to sue."

"Give me a baton," Razanskas calls out to Winn. "I know what to do. I'm with the LAPD. We have experience with batons and videos."

Razanskas and Winn burst out laughing. Even in Miami, they cannot escape reminders of Rodney King.

They drive from the airport to their hotel in Miami Beach, following the route where several tourists have been ambushed and killed. But they are not worried. Anyone who tries to carjack these two will be in for big surprise. Both have their Berettas within easy reach.

It is a sultry, sticky day, with brilliant turquoise skies and great billowing clouds. When Razanskas spots the Miami skyline, he studies it for a few minutes, lost in a reverie.

"It looks a lot different from the last time I saw it," he tells Winn. "They didn't have that skyline when I was here in 'sixty-three."

"I didn't know you'd been to Miami before."

"Yeah. We'd just emigrated from Venezuela."

"Why'd you leave?"

"I was walking home from school one day and I had to pass through a political demonstration. My dad was sick of me coming home from school with tears in my eyes from the tear gas. That time was the final straw for him. He took a look at me and said, 'That's it. We're going.' He went to the U.S. embassy and applied for a visa.

"We took the boat from Caracas to Miami. My dad bought a Chevy station wagon and we drove cross-country to L.A. You know why we ended up in L.A.? . . . My dad had always heard about what a good school UCLA was when he was in Venezuela. So he figured he would move to California so his sons could go to UCLA." He laughs. "Me and my brother never did make it there."

The family ended up in Torrance, a suburb of Los Angeles, because steel plants there were hiring. His father found a job as an electrician and eventually became president of his union local.

"You're not going to believe this," he says. "My dad is a Democrat."

They both laugh, because Razanskas, the staunch Republican, has made so many diatribes against Democratic politicians.

The detectives check into their beachfront Holiday Inn, where they get a government rate. Winn is wearing a canary yellow linen suit and a short-sleeved silk blouse, and she fits in with the other vacationers wandering about the lobby. But Razanskas, who is wearing a gray tweed sports coat, gray wool slacks and black cowboy boots, looks out of place amid the men in their shorts and swimming trunks and the women in their pastel sun dresses.

They meet in Winn's room to plan their schedule. Today is already shot because of the travel time and the three hours they lost traversing time zones. Tomorrow they will make contact with the FBI and interview Charles' brother in the morning. They can spend the afternoon at the beach or by the pool. Friday they will bring Charles back to Los Angeles. It is evening now, and they drive off to a restaurant overlooking Biscayne Bay. Sitting at a table by the water, watching the sunset, sipping drinks, Razanskas and Winn relax for the first time in months. They are worn down after two months of summer, with the steadily increasing body count, the pressure of juggling cases, the mountain of paperwork, the long hours, the sleepless nights. He always has breakfast at Pepy's, his only meal of the day, and she skips breakfast and has lunch later in the morning, so they rarely eat together. Most of their time together is spent working cases, and most of their discussions center around cases. But now, free of the pressures of the job, at least for the evening, they can relax and talk about other things than murder.

She tells him about growing up in Robstown, Texas. And although she frequently complains about his spitting, she makes an admission to him. "My grandma back in Robstown has some countrified habits," she says, smiling. "I hate to admit it, but she chews Days Work tobacco every now and then."

He points at her and says, "You'll be chewing, too, before I get through with you."

They both order baked grouper and then he makes an admission to her. His real first name is not Pete. That is his middle name. His real first name is Rytis, he tells her.

"Rytis?" she asks, struggling with the pronunciation.

"Yeah," he says. "He was some Lithuanian knight."

He is grateful she does not kid him about the name, like a few of his previous partners. When they finish their dinner, he tells her about Vietnam.

"I still don't carry family pictures in my wallet because of 'Nam. It seemed like every fucking time I talked to someone and they showed me pictures of their family, they'd get blown up by a rocket or something. Fuck that. It's like a jinx.

"I had enough close calls over there that I don't sweat the small stuff anymore. A lot of things on the job, a lot of the frustrations that get people all bent out of shape, don't bother me.

"I'll tell you about one close call I had. I went to the NCO club one night. I walked to the bar. I ordered a drink. I took two steps. Right then a big overhead fan crashed to the floor. Right where I'd been standing."

He laughs. Razanskas rarely talks about Vietnam. That is one of the few stories he is comfortable telling.

They finish their Key lime pie and return to the hotel, happy that instead of having to wake up at about 4 o'clock tomorrow morning—their usual schedule—they can enjoy the luxury of sleeping until 6.

• • •

The next morning they drive to the Miami FBI office, a tan, anonymous-looking building at the edge of a residential neighborhood. They talk to the agents in the Violent Crimes/Fugitive Task Force, a unit where FBI agents and local law enforcement agencies team up to track down fugitives. The agents brief Razanskas and Winn and tell them they located Charles after he made a few calls to Los Angeles from his brother's house in Miami. Before they drive out to interview the brother, an agent says to Winn, "Let me take a look at that big LAPD badge. I've seen it on *Dragnet* all these years." He fingers her badge, compares it to his own, which is much smaller. "You don't need a vest," he says, "when you got that thing with you."

Razanskas and Winn follow two members of the task force to Charles' brother's house. The brother, George, rents a room in a tract home, across from a strip mall, about 45 minutes from downtown Miami. George is 6 foot 8 inches tall and skinny, an ex-college basketball player who now works for a Miami youth organization. George tells the detectives that Charles arrived in Miami in late April. The double murder was May 4, so the detectives figure George and Charles concocted the late April date to provide him with an alibi.

"What day did he arrive?" Razanskas asks him.

"I'm not sure of the exact date. I just know it was sometime in late April."

"Did he say anything to you about why he decided, all of a sudden, to come to Florida?"

"He wanted to get away from the gang atmosphere. That's why I find this whole murder thing very hard to believe. That's not his mind-set. He's no killer."

"How did he get to Florida?"

"Maybe the bus, but I'm not sure. He just called me one day and said, 'I'm in Liberty City. Pick me up.' "

He tells Razanskas that Charles became involved with a woman named Christy shortly after he arrived in Miami. She, too, can testify that Charles arrived in late April. The detectives get her work number and set up an interview with Christy for the afternoon. Razanskas had planned to spend the day at the beach, lounging by the surf, sipping a tropical drink with an umbrella in it. Instead, he and Winn drive about an hour south of Miami to a housing project where Charles' girlfriend runs a teen center.

The case is virtually cleared, Razanskas tells Winn, and the preliminary hearing should be no problem. But he is not satisfied. He wants to bolster the case for trial and ensure that Charles is convicted. He figures that Charles persuaded George and Christy to lie and say he was in Miami weeks before the murder. Razanskas is not concerned about George. Because he is Charles' brother, a jury will find his testimony suspect. So Christy remains Charles' key alibi witness. If they can persuade Christy to tell the truth, and his alibi is shattered, Charles is screwed.

Christy is almost the twin of Charles' Los Angeles girlfriend whom the detectives interviewed earlier in the summer. Both are about 200 pounds and have an ingenuous, trusting manner. Razanskas figures Winn might be better able to establish a rapport with Christy, so he lets her take the lead. Christy is sitting behind a desk in her small office at the edge of the housing project. There is no air conditioning in the office, just a small rotating fan that does not help much on an August afternoon in Miami. Christy is dressed in a peasant skirt and a tan blouse and her hair is pulled back and tied with a brown scarf. She has the demeanor and the precise speaking manner of a schoolteacher.

"When did you first meet Charles?" Winn asks.

"The latter part of April."

"Did he tell you why he moved to Florida?"

"He said he wanted to get out of the gang life and away from those people. I thought he was quite interesting. He told me he was an ex-gang member and he had served time in prison."

"Do you remember the exact date you met him?"

"No. I just remember it was late April."

Winn frowns and taps a pen on her palm. "I didn't come all the way to Miami for a bunch of bullshit. You're the second female we've talked to who's in love with this guy. I guess he must be a charmer. I don't understand it myself. But whatever you tell us isn't going to prevent us from taking him back to California."

"I *know* why you're here," Christy says indignantly. "Charles told me that he knows nothing about those murders. I feel the two of us are honest with each other. We have a good relationship."

Winn nods knowingly. "Every female I talk to says the same thing. They all think they have a good relationship with this guy."

"Did he have a job?" Razanskas asks her.

"No."

"How'd he get his money?" he asks.

"His brother would give him money. I'd give him twenty or thirty dollars sometimes."

"You fit his profile," he says. "He likes women who are older than him, who have jobs, who will support him. The last woman we talked to bought a car for him. I gotta be honest with you. He's looking for a meal ticket."

Christy looks hurt. So Winn says to her, "He's not saying that to insult you. He's just being honest. I don't think you really know as much about this guy as you think you do."

"He's wanted for more than questioning," Razanskas says.

"We wouldn't come three thousand miles," Winn says, "if we weren't pretty sure that he killed two people."

Christy is starting to weaken. "I want this to be over with," Christy says, wringing her hands. "I can't see him doing anything like that."

"The family of that sixty-eight-year-old lady he killed couldn't see it either," Winn says. "But it's real."

"You saying he killed a sixty-eight-year-old woman?" Christy asks. Winn nods. Christy closes her eyes briefly.

The detectives see they have found a sensitive spot and decide to exploit it.

"Imagine being the daughter of that sixty-eight-year-old woman and having to bury her," Winn says.

"That's right," Razanskas says. "We're not talking about a drive-by. We're talking about killing an old lady in cold blood."

Christy massages her temples and says softly, "I can't believe this is happening."

"Charles is a big dude," Razanskas says. "How can a frail old lady be a threat to a guy like that?"

"Especially when she invited him into her house," Winn says. "She knew Charles. He lived in the neighborhood. He's a friend of her son's."

"Oh, Lord Jesus," Christy murmurs.

Winn leans toward her and says, "I don't believe that you met him in April. We got reports of him being in L.A. in May. You know, we talked to his L.A. girlfriend and she loved him so much. She told me, 'I'll talk to Charles,' Winn says, mimicking the girlfriend's high voice. 'I'll tell him to turn himself in. He loves me so much, he'll do it for me.' Well, you can see how much power *she* had over him."

"He used her," Razanskas says. "The same way he's using you."

"WHEN DID YOU FIRST MEET CHARLES?" Winn shouts.

Christy flinches and says weakly, "Late April."

"I wouldn't advise lying about this in court," Razanskas says. "Judges take perjury very seriously."

"He ain't worth it," Winn says. "No man's worth lyin' for."

Christy begins sniffling and tries to keep herself from crying.

"You know how we tracked down Charles?" Winn asks her. "He made all these phone calls back to L.A. And a lot of them were to his girlfriend." Winn mimics the girlfriend again. " 'Charles is so sweet. He even takes the food out of the freezer sometimes.' "

"The guy's a bullshit artist," Razanskas says.

"If you want to be concerned, don't be concerned about Charles," Winn says. "Be concerned about that sixty-eight-year-old lady. She didn't have a diseased bone in her body. She could have lived twenty more years. I couldn't live with myself knowing I'd killed a five foot two, hundred-pound woman."

Christy wipes her eyes with the back of a hand and says, "He seemed like such a different person than the person you're telling me about."

Winn stands up, walks over to Christy and asks, "Is it *possible* you met him in mid-May?"

"I don't know," she says weakly.

"So now you don't know," Winn says, nodding.

"Let me tell you something, Christy," Razanskas says. "I'm an old guy. I been around. I been married a few times. Every one of my wives could tell me the exact day we met, where it was, what I was wearing. I don't remember jack. But women are different. They remember. So I don't buy that you don't remember when you met."

Christy stares out the window and says dreamily, "It all seems so unreal. . . . When I met him I was struck by the fact that he had three first names. . . . He'd buy me roses now and then. . . . He seemed so sweet."

Razanskas looks disgusted. "You're talking about a guy with a tattoo on his arm that says, 'FUCK A SNAKE BITCH.' That don't sound so sweet to me."

Christy closes her eyes and holds her palms together, as if she is praying.

"If we bring you to court," Winn says, "and you keep saying you met him in late April, I'll hook you up myself for perjury. That's a felony. You can get five years for that."

Christy stares out the window, tears streaming down her face. The detectives back off and let Christy think about her predicament. It is quiet in the room now, just the whirring of the fan and an occasional sniffle from Christy.

"Now tell us the truth," Winn says. "When did you meet Charles?"

"I can't remember," Christy says. She sifts through a desk drawer, finds a Kleenex and dabs her eyes.

Razanskas motions Winn to meet him outside. He tells her they might have better luck if she talks to Christy by herself—woman to woman. He walks off to the car and Winn returns to Christy's office.

"You seem like a nice person," Winn says. "You deserve someone better than Charles. You're young. Why ruin your life for a murdering fool like him?"

Christy says to Winn, in a confidential tone, "I asked God three weeks ago, 'If this isn't good for me, take him away.' " She emits a sob, a quick intake of breath. "I just didn't know God would answer me like this."

Winn, as a young girl, spent every Sunday morning at the Pilgrim Missionary Baptist Church, so she knows how to talk to a witness who invokes God. "Remember, with His help, all things are possible," Winn tells her. "I pray to the Lord that he'll reveal my enemies to me. And he always does."

"People just want to *take* from you," Christy whispers.

"Remember Isaiah, chapter 54, verse 17," Winn tells her. " 'No weapon that is fashioned against you shall prosper.' "

"I thought he was the one for me," Christy says, sobbing.

"It's not a crime to be by yourself," Winn says. "If more women thought like that, they wouldn't fall for someone like Charles."

"I don't believe it," Christy says, covering her mouth with a fist.

"Believe it. I'll tell you how real it is. I went to that old woman's autopsy the day before Mother's Day. For her to die like that was a crime and a sin. I don't understand how someone can take the life of a sixty-eight-year-old woman. But like my mama says, 'What I don't understand would make a whole new world.' "

Christy covers her eyes with her palms and cries.

"I'm not here to upset you," Winn says softly. "In my line of business I see a lot of senseless killing. I'm trying to do something about that. I'm not here to arrest an innocent person. I'm here to protect other potential victims." She hands Christy a Kleenex and says, "Let's be honest."

Christy sits up and dries her eyes.

"I want you to tell me when you first met Charles?" Winn says solicitously.

Christy sighs and shakes her head. She does not have the energy to resist. Eyes glazed, she pulls out her appointment book. She leafs through the pages. She circles a date with her forefinger.

"What's the date?" Winn asks.

Christy tries to speak, but she is too weak to utter the words. She taps the date on the appointment book.

"CHRISTY . . . WHAT . . . IS . . . THE . . . DATE?" Winn asks in a commanding tone.

"May 11," she mutters.

Winn wants to make sure Charles did not arrive in Miami until after the murders, so she asks, "How do you know he wasn't here before May 4?"

"Because . . . because . . . ," Christy stutters, lips trembling, "he wasn't here for . . . Mother's Day." She throws her head on the desk and bursts into tears, her body racked with deep sobs.

Winn puts an arm around Christy's shoulder and says, "I'm sorry you had to find out this way. But you'll find someone else, Christy. Someone who's honest with you, who's not full of lies and deceit." Winn comforts her and sits with her for a few minutes. Christy, eyes red and swollen, tears streaming down her face, signs a witnesses statement form that summarizes the interview. Winn gives her a card and tells her to call if she needs anything.

Back at the car she tells Razanskas his strategy paid off. "She laid Charles out."

"This woman had it bad for him," Razanskas says.

Winn shakes her head with disgust. "This gangbanging, hip-hugging, tattoo-wearing motherfucker . . . he must have a gold tip down there. This is the second woman we talked to who's all starry-eyed over him."

"Now that Christy gave him up, he's screwed," Razanskas says. "For a circumstantial case, something like this is very important."

"We're breaking down his defense," Winn says.

"There goes his alibi," Razanskas says. "We're giving the D.A. a case that's tied up in a nice, neat little package."

The detectives drive off. Razanskas, staring straight ahead, says, "We worked well together on that one."

"Sure did," Winn says, looking down, embarrassed.

Good partners quickly pick up the rhythm of an interview and intuitively understand where the other one is taking a witness. Good partners ask questions that will not break, but enhance the mood their partner is trying to set. During interviews, at least, Razanskas and Winn are beginning to develop that kind of teamwork.

They recount the interview now, laughing, giddy from their

success, as they drive into a tropical sunset, on their way to South Beach for dinner, their past arguments about when to arrest Charles, the acrimony over the case, now forgotten.

The next morning the detectives pick up Charles at the Miami jail. Six-foot-six and slender, Charles towers over the other prisoners in the holding cell. He is wearing a sweatshirt and black jeans with a sharp crease, which indicates he has some experience behind bars and knows how to curry favor with the jail laundry.

Razanskas introduces himself and Winn and says, "If you act like a gentleman, I'll treat you like a gentleman."

"That's the way I was raised," Charles says. "Can I ask you what's this all about?"

"When we get back to L.A., we'll talk," Razanskas says.

"I got nothing to tell," Charles says. "But I got plenty to ask."

Before they leave the jail, Razanskas gets on his knees and places a leather and metal brace on Charles' right leg, a device used to prevent a suspect from running. Charles takes a deep breath. "Lord Jesus, help your son," Charles whispers. "I got my life in the good hands of the Lord, and I'm going to let Him lead me."

On the way to the airport, Charles closes his eyes and sings along with a song on the radio, "It's going to take a miracle . . . to make me love someone new . . . 'cause I'm waiting for you. . . . It's going to take a miracle . . ." Winn and Razanskas exchange a glance when Charles sings the refrain. Yes, they think, after what Christy told them, it *is* going to take a miracle for Charles.

At the airport, Charles has to limp through the terminal, flanked by the detectives, with his leg in a brace and his hands cuffed. He mutters, "Shit. This is embarrassing. Being tied down like a damn dog."

While they wait to board the plane, Charles says to Razanskas, "Just like you, I'm in a recognized gang." He smiles slyly. "I'm a Crip. You an LAPD."

"How old are you?" Razanskas asks.

"Twenty-one."

"I been a cop longer than you've been alive."

"Let me ask you something," Charles says. "Did you talk to Christy yesterday?"

"Why?"

"I called her from jail and she wouldn't take my call."

Razanskas smiles and waves a forefinger at Charles. "I've got your number, buddy. I know exactly what you're looking for in a woman. She has to be older than you, have a nice place to live and have a good job. Am I right?"

Charles flashes a rakish grin at Razanskas. "Let me ask you something?" Charles says. "You talk to any more ladies I know?"

"How many more you got?" They both laugh and chat amiably for a few minutes.

"You take this brace and these cuffs off," Charles says, "and you and me could go down to the Keys and have us a fine ol' time. We can forget about this shit here."

It is time to board now, and the detectives escort Charles to the back of the plane and sit on either side of him. He no longer seems like the giant, menacing, double-murder suspect on the lam. He acts like a big kid on his first airplane trip, craning his head to look out the window, flirting with the flight attendants, joking with the detectives, launching into one monologue after the other. He does not seem to comprehend what is facing him in Los Angeles. He does not seem to realize that he is a good candidate for the death penalty.

"You know," Charles tells the detectives, "If I be some big fugitive, I done a piss poor job of it, with all those calls I made back to California."

The detectives chuckle. Charles keeps talking. He talks not because he is nervous, but because he seems desperate for the detectives' approval, wants them to like him, wants to prove to them that he is not a thug. "I can talk about other things than street shit," he tells them. "I feel pretty good about that."

Razanskas removes Charles' handcuffs so he can eat his airline lunch. "You know why I joined a gang," Charles tells them. "That's love a brother looking for. Did I find it? Yes and no. I been gangbangin' damn near eleven years, but I never did a drive-by," he says proudly. "Whenever they was fixin' to do one, I be MIA. . . . I had to leave that bangin' behind 'cause the kind of woman I like don' go for that bangin' shit. You know Kim. She the first woman I ever loved. I got out of YA [California Youth Authority] on a Wednesday, met her at a party and that night moved right in with her."

"If you loved Kim, why were you running around with Christy?" Winn asks.

"OK, I admit I may not have been completely honest with Christy. But I gave her a feeling of confidence. I made her feel like a complete woman."

Winn rolls her eyes.

"Now Kim was a beautiful person. She was from Gardena. Not like a lot of those women from South-Central."

"Hey," Winn yells. "You don't like people stereotyping you. Don't stereotype women from South-Central."

Charles, who can turn on an ingratiating charm, says, "I'm very sorry. I surely didn't mean any offense." When a man in front flips his seat too far back, Charles says, "Excuse me, sir, can you move your seat up a touch." When the flight attendant serves him his lunch, he says, with a cheery lilt, "Thank you ma'am and have a nice day." And he says to the detectives, near the end of the flight, "Even though this has been a sticky situation, it's been a pleasure speaking with you."

The plane begins its descent into the smog and Charles turns on the charm with Winn. He tells her she looks like an angel. "If things go my way on this, I want you to visit me in Miami. I'll cook you the best enchilada dinner you ever had. And for dessert I'll serve you up a white chocolate cake or a peach pie." He winks at her. "I can bake, too."

Winn gives him a suspicious look out of one eye and says, "Hmm."

Charles turns to Razanskas and says, "When a sister say, 'Hmm,' you know she mean, 'No.' "

They all chuckle.

On the way back to the Southeast station, Charles sings again, "It's going to take a miracle . . ."

"That's what Christy was saying yesterday," Winn tells him. "It's going to take a miracle for her to love someone else."

"She can't accept life for what it really is," Charles says. "When I get out of this and go back to Miami, she's going to be riding my jack more than ever. I don't believe in nonbelievers. If she love her man, why she half-step? Why she let the PO-lice terrify her? Now she half-steppin' for me."

They take Charles to an interview room at the station and Razanskas gets him a cigarette. He takes a deep drag, nervously looks around the tiny interview room and mutters, "I don't believe this shit." For the first time he seems to understand the gravity of his position. His eyes are wide with fear and he jiggles his foot. Thinking ahead is something Charles seems to have a problem with. He has a childlike capacity to become lost in the present. When he left Miami, he was enjoying the novelty of an airplane trip and was preoccupied with charming the detectives. Los Angeles seemed a long way off. Now he is here; now he begins to worry.

Charles narrows his eyes and stares at Razanskas. "Do you really care? Honestly?"

"Hey, I could retire right now if I wanted to," Razanskas says. "See all those blue-suiters in the station. They work seven to three and never get called out at night, on weekends, on holidays. For me, it's not a job, it's an adventure."

"For you, it's an adventure. For me, it's my life." He takes a last drag, smashes his cigarette in the ashtray and snarls, "I don't give a fuck anymore."

Razanskas reads him his rights, and Charles agrees to talk without an attorney present.

"Do you know Anthony and Virginia Baker," Razanskas asks him, "the two people you're accused of murdering during the course of a robbery?"

"Not really."

"Well, they knew you well."

"They knew me from buying marijuana from their place. I done smoked with him a few times."

"Ever been to their house?"

"Yeah. I'd buy a five-dollar bag and split. Yeah I knew him. Yeah I bought weed from him. So what. I ain't the only person named Charles in that neighborhood."

"You buy weed on May 3?"

"No."

"May 4?"

"No."

"How can you be sure?"

" 'Cause I was in Miami."

"How'd you get there," Winn asks.

"Greyhound."

"To what station?"

"Started with an L."

"Liberty City?"

"That's it."

"How much was your ticket?"

"I don't know. Maybe sixty, seventy bucks."

"When did you leave L.A."

"April 13 or 14."

Winn leaves the room and Razanskas continues to question him. When she returns she tells Charles, "You shouldn't lie about things that are verifiable. I just contacted Greyhound. They don't stop in Liberty City."

He shrugs.

"Exactly how much did you pay for the ticket?"

"No more than a hundred bucks."

Razanskas stares at Charles. "First you say you paid about sixty or seventy bucks. Now you say no more than a hundred. First you say you didn't know Anthony Baker. Then you say you smoked weed with him. First you tell us you took the bus to Liberty City. Then the bus company tells us it doesn't have a stop there." Razanskas spits in a trash can and looks up at Charles. "Why don't you level with us. It'll be better for you in the long run."

Charles nervously licks his lips. "I'm out of gas. That's all I know, bro. I'm through with this until I get a lawyer."

Razanskas writes up on a statement sheet what Charles has

told them and asks him to read it and sign it. Charles reads it and angrily throws it on the table. "That shit don't sound right to me. You playin' wit' me. You tryin' to do me."

They argue for a few minutes, Razanskas makes a few minor changes and Charles signs the statement. They escort him to the station's jail for booking. The booking clerk looks up at Charles and asks, "Ever play any ball?"

"Just baseball," Charles says. "I don't like any unnecessary physical shit."

He turns over his belongings to the booking clerk and reluctantly parts with his sandals. He has forgotten about his plight and worries only about his $125 Stacy Adams sandals. He asks Winn if they will be safe. Winn shakes her head and tells him he has bigger problems ahead than the theft of his sandals.

After he is fingerprinted, Winn asks to see his famous FUCK A SNAKE BITCH tattoo. He sheepishly shows her the inside of his right forearm.

"Damn," Winn says. "What's that mean?"

"A bitch is someone who just tryin' to work you," he says. "Like a gopher snake that wanna bite you. That why it be there, mama."

"I'm nobody's motherfucking mama."

"I didn't mean no disrespect, sweetheart," Charles says.

"Hey!" Razanskas shouts. "Don't call my partner 'sweetheart.' "

Charles throws up his hands in frustration.

Before the detectives book Charles, they ask him some questions for the booking form. He gives them his mother's name and address. Razanskas asks where his father lives.

"I have no idea."

"What does he do for a living?"

"I have no idea. If you find him, let me know."

Winn recalls her conversation with Charles' older brother, George, in Miami, who told her about Charles' childhood. Maybe he confided in her because he felt that, as a black woman,

Winn would have compassion for Charles, and, as a detective, she would have the power to help him.

He told her that he and Charles have the same mother but different fathers. George grew up on the East Coast, with his father's family. Charles was raised by his mother in Los Angeles with his brother and sister. Charles' father, an alcoholic, was long gone; his mother worked at a bottling plant. Without a father, Charles craved attention and affection from his mother, but his mother always was tired from working long shifts and overtime and had little time for Charles. This is the kind of mother Charles had, George told Winn. "I'm her first son and she hasn't spoken to me since I was three," he said, still hurt by the memory. "She's never even made an attempt to talk to me . . . not even a call on Christmas or Thanksgiving."

Charles was a promising baseball player on a city league team. He told George he was hurt because all the other parents watched their sons play, but his mother never showed up. Charles became interested in music and showed a flair for the drums. He scrounged up a few dollars to buy a snare drum and used to practice after school. But his mother told him that after working all day she could not stand the racket and did not want him playing the drums in the house. This, George told Winn, was just another positive outlet denied Charles, another detour that led him to the gang life.

He had a few juvenile convictions, with no crimes of violence, and eventually was sent to the California Youth Authority, to a facility known as a gladiator school, a place where Charles fought constantly. When he was released after a few years, he was angry and hardened. His eyes, which always had been so expressive and full of fun, were now flat, impassive. He bought a .380 semiautomatic pistol and began robbing people on the street so he could buy food. Charles, who never worked a day, had found a profession. "I got to eat," he would tell friends. "So I got to do what I got to do."

When Charles arrived in Miami, he may have looked like a gangster, but he still acted like a child hungry for affection. Every morning he would wake George, hug him, kiss him on the cheek and say, "I love you, bro." He was happy in Miami because, living with his brother, he felt like he was part of a family for the first time. When George finished telling Winn about his brother's life, he gave her a nylon gym bag filled with a few things he had just bought for Charles. The bag was filled with a box of crackers, a jar of peanut butter, shaving cream, a razor, some underwear and a jacket. George wanted Charles to know that when he went to jail, at least one person still cared about him.

Right before an officer takes Charles to his holding cell, Winn says to him, "Save yourself."

"What you mean?"

"I ain't saying you were there or weren't there. But if you were there, and you didn't do it, and someone else did, then save yourself. You know what I'm saying? It's not about snitching. It's about telling the truth. I hate to see a young brother, twenty-one years old, handsome and intelligent, rotting behind bars."

He nods and considers what she said. "Do I still have a chance?"

"Yes. But you got all the cards, not me." She hands him her business card. "If you want to talk, with or without your lawyer, call me."

As he walks down the dim hallway toward his cell, she calls out, "Good luck, homeboy."

He waves and says, "I won't forget you."

It is dark as Razanskas and Winn drive to the homicide bureau to complete their extradition paperwork. "A lot of kids like Charles have to grow up on their own these days," Winn says, staring out the window. "When I was on patrol I'd always be going to houses where I'd find six- and seven-year-old-kids all alone in these filthy apartments, roaches scurrying all over, no parents anywhere in sight. When these kids would see me they'd be embarrassed. They'd try to clean up real quick and apologize for the mess." She shakes her head. "This is a lost generation of kids. I don't think Charles is downright evil. It's not like he was born a bad seed. Environment has got a lot to do with it. It's sad. Twenty-one years old and his life is over."

Razanskas spits into his cup. "I'm not interested in Charles' poor, pitiful, boohoo childhood. This guy never once tried to do anything with his life. All he does is take advantage of everyone around him. I don't feel sorry for him. I feel sorry for his victims."

When they arrive at the squad room, the detectives have a surprise waiting for them—two suspects from the Sunday night murder of Ruben Gomez. Before they can even sit down at their desks, Armando Reyes walks over and briefs them.

Earlier in the day, patrol picked up a call about a residential burglary in progress. When they arrived, the suspects had already disappeared. But one of the officers, who had heard a white Jeep had been involved in a murder Sunday night, spotted one parked out in back with the plates missing. Later, four men who lived down the street gathered in front of the house to see what the commotion was about. The officer questioned the men, discovered that one of them owned the Jeep, arrested them and called South Bureau Homicide. Because Razanskas and Winn were out of town, Reyes took over. He photographed the suspects and showed six-packs to Ruben, Jr., and his uncle, who had survived the attack. They picked out the owner of the Jeep and his younger brother.

At first the older brother was "lyin' and denyin'," Reyes tells Razanskas. But eventually he talked. Reyes has a rare rapport with young suspects. He is so easygoing, so quick to smile, that suspects relax around him. He seems more like a big brother than a cop to them. They trust him. They think if they are honest and confide in him, before talking to an attorney, their honesty will be rewarded. They are wrong.

In 1966, the Miranda decision guaranteed a suspect the right to an attorney during police interrogation. Still, a surprising number of South Bureau murder suspects agree to talk to police without an attorney. They end up sealing their convictions. Even suspects who have been arrested many times, who should know better, have not figured out the system. Talk to any homicide detective, and he will tell you if he ever is arrested for murder he will never—*ever, under any circumstance*—say a word without an attorney at his side. But some suspects think detectives will assume they are guilty if they ask for an attorney. Others let detectives talk them into waiving their rights.

Detectives trick murder suspects in many ways. They will falsely tell a suspect that the blood found at the murder scene matches his blood, or that a witness spotted him at the murder scene, or that the fingerprints on the gun match his fingerprints, or that his partner confessed and implicated him. Later, suspects are outraged. Convicts always complain that they were framed because police lied to them. But detectives are well within their legal rights to deceive suspects in order to get to the truth. The courts have upheld the use of deception by police as long as their tactics are not so egregious that they could force an innocent person to confess. Detectives can use a variety of ruses. What they cannot do is use is physical violence to obtain a confession, refuse to "Mirandize" a suspect, or employ outrageous tactics such as posing as a public defender or a minister.

A few hours before Razanskas and Winn returned from Miami, a suspect in the Ruben Gomez murder, the older brother, asked Reyes, "What should I do? I'm scared."

"Tell the truth," Reyes told him.

Because the suspect did not have an attorney present, he was acting under a number of misconceptions. And Reyes certainly was not going to disabuse him of these misconceptions. The suspect thought that because he did not actually stab the victim he would not face serious charges. So he cooperated with Reyes and then expected to be released. Instead, he now is facing a murder charge. The suspect's ready cooperation, his willingness to speak without an attorney present, are irrelevant. By the time he confers with an attorney, it will be too late. He already has told detectives his version of events and signed his statement sheet.

Razanskas reads the statement sheet and tells Reyes he wants to talk to the suspect himself and get a feel for him and his story. The suspect, Ramon Roberto Sanchez, is waiting in an interview room, nervously crossing and uncrossing his legs. Sanchez is one of the more unusual suspects Razanskas has encountered. He is not some trash-talking, gangbanging, tattooed killer with a long rap sheet. Sanchez is a 20-year-old junior at California State University, Los Angeles, who is majoring in business administration, with a minor in criminal justice. He is articulate, polite and cooperative. He is wearing a button-down paisley shirt, his hair is neatly parted and he looks like a preppie. He never has been arrested. No one in his family ever has been arrested.

He tells Razanskas that on the night Ruben Gomez was murdered, he and some friends had been cruising for girls in Whittier. Later, they stopped for gas in Pico Rivera and began talking to a few girls at the gas station. While they were talking to them, three men in a white Taurus pulled up and tried to horn in on the girls. They began arguing with Sanchez and his friends. One of the passengers in the Taurus threw something at the Jeep and another passenger flashed gang signs. Sanchez tells Razanskas he got scared and took off, but the white Taurus followed him. He headed east on the Pomona Freeway, north on the San Gabriel River Freeway, east on the Santa Monica Freeway, south on the Harbor Freeway. But he could not shake the white Taurus. The driver kept tailing them, pulling up beside them, his passengers yelling and flashing gang signs.

When he reached South-Central, where he lives, he eventually lost the Taurus. But he was angry. He spotted a few acquaintances from his neighborhood and told them that some guys in a white Taurus had been tailing and threatening him. Once he had some backup, he and the others began looking for the Taurus. They finally spotted it at the corner of 62nd and Hoover. The driver had his shirt off and, with the help of his two passengers, was changing a tire. Sanchez tells Razanskas he just wanted to beat them up for chasing him. He ended up throwing a few punches and kicking the victim in the face, while he was down. He did not know that the men in the other car, his backup, had a knife and a baseball bat.

"My intention was to just kick their ass." He sighs and shakes his head. "I had no intention of killing anyone."

He tells Razanskas that he can give him first names of the men who used the knife and the baseball bat. He knows they live in the neighborhood, but does not know their last names, nor their addresses. He claims that his 14-year-old brother, who is in another interview room, was not with him that night. He has no idea why the victims picked his brother out of the six-pack.

Razanskas knows that patrol officers discovered a baseball bat in the back seat of the Jeep, so he suspects that Sanchez used more than his fists during the attack. But while he questions elements of Sanchez's statement, he believes the thrust of his story. His version of events makes a lot more sense than Ruben, Jr.'s dubious scenario. Sanchez acknowledged that, at one point, he lost the Taurus, but because he was angry he went back and searched for the car. These statements have doomed him because they show premeditation and now he cannot claim self-defense.

Razanskas' interview with Sanchez answered many questions. Now he knows how Ruben, Jr., memorized the license plate—because he had a clear view of the rear plate during the chase. Now he knows how the white Taurus ended up in South-Central. Now he knows why they were attacked. And now he knows what the license plate OG ROB stands for. The OG, Sanchez says, is an abbreviation for "original." Rob is his middle name, what his friends call him. Original Rob.

But it still is a mystery to Razanskas why the victim, Ruben Gomez, an executive, a man who had so much to lose, would chase a bunch of kids from Pico Rivera all the way to South-Central. The coroner's test results have just come in, and Razanskas learns that Ruben's blood alcohol level was .18, more than double the legal limit. Since he was drunk, Razanskas figures, a little bit of the White Fence in him, which had been dormant for so long, might have emerged for a few hours.

The missing pieces now are falling into place. Razanskas still wants to find the suspect with the knife and the baseball bat, and he wants to interview Ruben, Jr., again. But because he already has a confession, the case, for the record, is as good as cleared.

Razanskas tells Winn about the interview. They return to their paperwork and, after an hour, call it a night. Razanskas had hoped that during the sojourn to Miami he would be able to catch up on his sleep, pick up a tan, relax and return home refreshed. But like most plans he makes during the summer, they soon are dashed by the exigencies of the job. It is about midnight now—3 A.M. Miami time—when he and Winn finally walk out to the parking lot. It has been a 21-hour day, and Winn is exhausted. But Razanskas is in a great mood. This has been a productive night. He has cleared two cases—cases in which he was the primary—in a few hours.

Chapter 14
A Faustian Agreement

Monday, August 22

Razanskas and Winn get a little extra time to recuperate from their Miami trip. They do not have to be at work on Monday until 3 in the afternoon, because this week they are assigned the P.M. or night watch shift, a shift that rotates among the detectives. Each team has to pull a few night watch shifts a year, including one during the summer.

Razanskas and Winn will work seven days straight—3 P.M. to 11 P.M. on the weekdays, 4 P.M. to 1 A.M. on the weekends. Their job is to wait at the office, respond to all homicides in South Bureau, and work the crime scene while the investigating detectives are on their way. When the investigating detectives arrive, the night watch detectives usually help interview witnesses, locate evidence and assist them during the initial stage of the investigation.

While the detectives wait for a homicide, they usually interview witnesses from their own cases at the bureau or catch up with paperwork. Razanskas has worked enough night watch shifts, he tells Winn, to know that it is best to eat early. Because if you wait, things could get so busy you may never get the chance. So for this week, at least, they will eat together every afternoon. Like typical partners.

Razanskas and Winn decide to begin Monday's shift with a big meal at a Mexican restaurant, around the corner from Winn's former high school. Before they leave, he makes a few calls on the Ruben Gomez case. He wants to reconcile the suspect's and the witnesses' conflicting stories. He sets up a 6 P.M. interview with the victim's brother, who was with him the night he was killed.

At the restaurant, Razanskas tells Winn about one of the bureau's most bizarre cases. He was called in as a translator on a case where a man was beheaded with a machete because he touched his friend's stereo. Instead of trying to keep a low profile, the killer drew attention to his crime in a most graphic manner. A case like this, Razanskas tells Winn, keeps detectives from becoming complacent, from assuming that for every action on the street there is an equal and opposite reaction, a reaction that can explicate a murder. Sometime the madness on the streets simply cannot be explained.

A Guatemalan immigrant by the name of Humberto Amaya strolled into his neighborhood market on a Sunday morning, bought a beer and bragged to the employees that he had just killed someone. But he was known around the market as a drinker and they all thought he was kidding.

Amaya was so incensed no one believed him that he returned to his apartment, chopped off his victim's head and tossed it into a roasting pan. He marched back to the market and dropped the roasting pan beside the pastry case. When Amaya had silenced all his doubters, he deposited the head in one of the market's yellow plastic bags and dumped it in a trash can.

Razanskas shakes his head. "You know what really gets me. No one at the market called the cops. They all see the head, but no one wants to lay this guy out. Finally, though, one of the employees tells a customer about the head. The customer calls us."

When Razanskas and Winn return to the bureau, he pulls out the murder book on the case. He tells Winn that the lead detectives tracked down the killer at his job, where he worked as a tailor. At first, the killer claimed that he was walking down the street, a robber tried to mug him and he killed the man in self-defense.

"The guy eventually copped out," Razanskas says. "He was at his apartment, drinking with his buddy. He dozed off, and when he woke up he saw his buddy touching his stereo."

Razanskas shows Winn the transcript of the interview with the suspect.

"How did you kill him?" a detective asked.

"With a machete," the suspect said.

"Why?"

"Because he wanted to steal my stereo."

"Who was he . . . a friend of yours?

"Just for nipping, that's all."

"Nipping?"

"Drinking."

"And how long had you known him?"

"Not a long time. A month."

"And why did he want to steal your stereo?"

"I don't know. I was very drunk."

"OK. And so you attacked him with the machete?"

"Yes."

"He wasn't armed?"

"No."

"How many times did you hit him with the machete before you cut his head off?"

"Two times."

"Why did you take the head [to the neighborhood market]?"

"Craziness. . . . My mind is a bit off."

Razanskas shuts the murder book and puts it back in a dusty filing cabinet. Winn mutters, "Sick."

After the man was booked for murder, he tells her, South Bureau detectives coined a catchphrase, a mantra that was repeated anytime someone wanted to borrow a stapler, a pencil, a flashlight, an eraser.

"You touch my stereo, I chop off your head."

• • •

At 6:30, Ruben Gomez's brother, Gilbert, stops by the bureau. While Ruben left the gang scene, went to school and became an executive, his brother looks like he is still banging. Gilbert is wearing baggy denim shorts, knee-high socks and sneakers and has QVC (Quiet Valley Chicos, his gang's name) tattooed on his forearm. Quiet Valley is an Eastside gang, and Gilbert is not familiar with South-Central.

"I want to get something clear straight off," Razanskas tells him. "I want you to be up front with me. When we go to court, if you're not telling the truth, it'll be obvious to the jury. If the jury believes you're holding out, they'll kick these suspects loose. So I want the truth. Understand?"

Gilbert nods.

"How did this whole thing get started?"

"I have no idea. I passed out from all the drinking I did at the wedding. I woke up when we hit the curb and got the flat."

Razanskas jabs a finger at Gilbert and says, "Right now you're giving me the biggest line of shit I've ever heard in my life." He shouts, "IT'S NOT MY BROTHER WHO WAS KILLED. IT'S YOUR BROTHER. If those guys walk, don't blame me or my partner. It'll be on your head."

"It doesn't matter that you were following them," Winn chimes in. "It doesn't matter that you had an argument with them. What matters is your brother got killed."

"We're not out to get you," Razanskas says. "We just want you to do the right thing. I don't care if you stabbed someone in the neck with a pen. That's legal. That's self-defense. I just gotta find out how this whole thing started."

Gilbert thinks for a few minutes, nervously jiggling his keys. Finally, he says, "OK. We were following them." He tells them that his brother followed a group of girls to a gas station. The guys in the Jeep also were trying to pick up the girls, and his brother had words with them. They threw something at his brother's car. His brother became enraged and ended up chasing the Jeep from Pico Rivera to South-Central. His story is essentially the same as the suspect's.

"My brother died in my arms," Gilbert says. He takes a deep

breath and slowly exhales. "He was trying to breathe, his eyes were fluttering. I lifted his head and so much blood was streaming into the curb it was like someone had tipped a glass over. His eyes fluttered again and he stopped moving. That was it."

He closes his eyes for a moment. "My sister got married that night and we were all so happy." He pauses and stares at his shoes. "You know, my mom said to me, 'Why did he have to die? Why didn't you die instead?' Everyone in the family was saying it. They were all saying it should have been me who died." He shakes his head. "That hurt me real bad. Only one person in my family would visit me in the hospital—one of my sisters. That's fucked up."

Winn feels sorry for him and says, "Don't let all that get to you. Prove 'em all wrong." She talks with Gilbert for a few minutes, consoles him, and walks him out the door.

For the next few hours the streets are calm, but a few minutes before 11—when their shift ends—they pick up a report of a security guard who is "circling the drain" at a nearby hospital. A few men tried to steal the guard's gun, and the struggle ended up in a shootout. One suspect was wounded and arrested a block away. The guard was shot in the chest, a watch commander tells Razanskas. But the guard takes a turn for the better at the hospital, and instead of a homicide, police are left with an attempted murder. Razanskas and Winn head home.

The next day, Razanskas discovers he was not the only one who had a fugitive picked up by the FBI. Alton, the suspect in Masuyama's Belizean body dump case, has been picked up in Pennsylvania. An FBI agent was told by his snitch that a man who was wanted for a murder in L.A. was ready to hop a bus from New York to Pittsburgh. The FBI arrested Alton in Pittsburgh. Reyes and Masuyama will pick up Alton next week, when Masuyama returns from Japan.

On Tuesday night, Ruben Gomez's son, Ruben, Jr., comes to the bureau with his mother and stepfather. Razanskas says to them, "To be honest with you, our suspect is being more honest than Ruben, Jr. We know what happened that night. We just need Ruben, Jr. to tell us his version of the events."

"We know he has not been entirely honest with you," the stepfather acknowledges. "He tells us he'll feel more comfortable talking to you if we're not with him."

Razanskas nods and takes Ruben, Jr. into the interview room. He tells Razanskas that the men in the Jeep made "smart remarks" to his father and threw some things at their car. His father began chasing the Jeep and shouting, "I'm going to kick their ass." The rest of his story is the same as Gilbert's.

"Why didn't you tell me all this before?" Razanskas asks.

He shrugs. "I guess I was scared and nervous."

Razanskas studies Ruben, Jr.'s jeans, which are sliding down his hips, and asks him the size. The boys shrugs, embarrassed.

"What do they call you in the neighborhood?" Razanskas asks him

"Looney."

Razanskas nods knowingly. He puts his hand on the boy's shoulder and says, "You're a wannabe right now. It's not too late for you. If you want to save your mom a lot of aggravation, you got to get out of that scene. The gang life is going to lead you to one place—prison. How do you think your mom's going to feel when people ask her, 'Where's your son?' And she has to tell them you're in the fucking joint. You may think that's cute. Like, 'Hey, I'm big and bad.' But it's going to bite you in the ass for the rest of your life. There's no fucking way out of the gang life. You either end up shanked in the joint or shot in the street. I just had an OG, a hard-core *veterano,* who tried to get out. His homies laid him out and tried to stick him with a murder. I had to move him and his family out of the neighborhood."

He pats Ruben, Jr. on the back. "That's the last fucking lecture you'll get from me. So cut this shit out."

Razanskas updates the mother and stepfather on the progress of the investigation. The next step for him is to find the stabber and some of the other suspects. But that will have to wait until next week, because while he is working the night watch shift, he has to stay close to the office.

He tells the mother about the lecture he just gave her son. She nods and throws her hands in the air in frustration. She knows all about the gang life. After all, when she met Ruben, Jr.'s father she was a White Fence girl known as Li'l Sleepy. Now she is 31, conservatively dressed and matronly. She wears a watch to cover the Lil' Sleepy tattoo on her wrist.

"I tell him I know how it is because I been through it," she says. "I tell him I don't want him to make the same mistakes I made. Sometimes he listens. Sometimes he doesn't." She looks at her son, studies him for a moment and says with a wan smile, "He's getting the same attitude his father once had."

Razanskas walks over to an evidence locker and gives Ruben, Jr. a plastic bag filled with his father's belongings. Ruben, Jr. walks across the squad room and into the underground lot, head down, despondent, carrying the plastic bag with his father's tuxedo shirt, jeans, belt and sunglasses.

His stepfather asks him why he did not tell detectives the truth earlier. He shrugs and tells him he does not trust the LAPD.

"They're always trying to screw us over," Ruben says.

"Where'd you learn that?" the stepfather asks.

"From my dad."

There is a long history of enmity between the LAPD and the city's minority communities. And the source of this enmity, in part, is the legacy of William H. Parker, who headed the department from 1950 to 1966.

Before Parker became chief, the LAPD had been beset by corruption and embarrassed by a number of highly publicized scandals. In 1950, after a retired Marine Corps general briefly took over the department and began instituting changes, Parker was named chief. Parker continued reforming the department and eventually "converted the LAPD in the early 1950s from an inefficient and unreliable organization into a national model of a professional police department," wrote Martin J. Schiesl in *20th Century Los Angeles*.

Parker, a decorated Army captain during World War II, created an aggressive, efficient, militaristic organization. He rooted out corruption, emphasized technology, and set up a division to analyze crime patterns. But what he gained in efficiency he lost in community relations. Parker was reviled in black and Latino neighborhoods because of the style of policing he devised for the LAPD. This was an era when many police departments assigned officers to walk beats in minority neighborhoods so they could get to know residents and merchants. This is known today as community-based policing and is recognized as a good way to fight crime and defuse tension in the inner city. Parker did not believe in this approach. He wanted his officers to regularly rotate assignments so they would not get too familiar with the people they were policing or each other. This would, in his view, reduce the likelihood of corruption. Parker wanted his men off the street and into squad cars, where they could be mobile, aggressive and make more arrests. Parker felt it was important to discourage criminal activity before it happened. He called this "proactive policing."

Daryl Gates, Parker's driver who later headed the department himself and perpetuated the proactive approach, explained this type of policing in his autobiography, *Chief:* "If a man was suspected of a burglary, we put him under surveillance. If someone looked out of place in a neighborhood, we had a little chat with him. If a description of a thief could be obtained, we stopped everyone fitting that description, even if it meant angering dozens of innocent citizens. . . . Using these proactive tactics, LAPD would become the most aggressive police department in the country."

While Gates and Parker regarded this style of policing as aggressive, residents in black and Latino neighborhoods, who bore the brunt of "proactive policing," considered it harassment. When minorities entered white neighborhoods, they were routinely tailed, stopped and searched. In their own neighborhoods they complained that, without provocation, they often were bullied and intimidated and beaten.

Police felt they had the authority to stop anyone, at any time, for any reason. Black and Latino residents soon began complaining that LAPD patrol officers, who were predominately white, acted as if *they* were the occupying army and *you* were the occupied.

All the outrage over the police, the poverty, the neglect, the hopelessness and frustration ignited the 1965 Watts riots. In the aftermath, the LAPD proved that it had learned little from the six days of rioting. Chief Parker was asked what had touched off the unrest and he replied, "One person threw a rock, and then, like monkeys in a zoo, others started throwing rocks."

Parker died in office in 1966 and was replaced the next year by Tom Reddin. Reddin attempted to improve relations with minority residents. He assigned an inspector general to assess citizen complaints. He mandated that officers wear name tags and encouraged patrol officers not to give tickets and make arrests for petty violations—which had been a constant complaint in South-Central—but to instead issue warnings. He was moving the department in the right direction, but he lasted only two years. He retired from the department when he failed a treadmill test.

Ed Davis replaced Reddin and headed the department through much of the 1970s. He, too, attempted to soften the image of the imperious LAPD patrol officer. Davis halted the practice of frequently rotating patrol assignments, because he wanted officers to get to know the people they were policing. He initiated several community policing programs, and ordered officers to meet regularly with neighborhood groups and listen to their concerns. In the city's barrios and ghettos, however, residents felt Davis did not do enough, did not address the excessive force complaints, the police shootings—the issues that had been festering for so long.

Still, Davis had made progress. But after he retired from the department in 1978, much of this progress was halted by Daryl Gates, his successor. William Parker's protege, Gates deemphasized or dismantled many of Davis' neighborhood programs and promulgated a paramilitary approach. As a result, during the 1980s, the reputation of the LAPD in minority communities continued to deteriorate.

Gates pushed proactive policing—with a vengeance. He approved battering rams mounted on armored military vehicles and neighborhood barricades. Even the names of the operations he promoted connoted confrontation. He created the acronym for the department's SWAT (Special Weapons and Tactics) team. He initiated a program called CRASH—Community Resources Against Street Hoodlums. He approved Operation Hammer, antigang sweeps that resulted in the arrest of tens of thousands of young black and Latino men, many of whom were released with no charges filed.

During Gates's years as chief, lawsuits against the LAPD continued to rise. In 1980, the city paid $891,000 in all LAPD-related litigation. In 1990, the city paid $9.1 million and the next year $14.7 million. Los Angeles was among the nation's leaders in settling excessive-force lawsuits.

The LAPD assiduously rooted out officers who stole money, took bribes or used drugs. As a result, the department was not beset by the corruption scandals that have plagued a number of Midwestern and East Coast police departments. But the LAPD traditionally has been lenient on officers who used excessive force.

LAPD officers had to be aggressive, Gates claimed, because his officers were outmanned. The LAPD had the lowest ratio of officers to residents of the nation's six largest cities, according to a Police Foundation study based on 1986 statistics. Overwhelmed and overworked LAPD officers had to patrol a vast, sprawling city with a swelling crime rate and the worst gang problems in the country. Suspects were more violent, more unpredictable, more likely to be high on drugs or armed when arrested. Police faced a greater danger on the streets than ever before. Assaults against officers across the country were at a record high, according to FBI statistics. The number of officers killed probably would have been at a record high too if not for the advent of bulletproof vests. Hundreds of cops wearing vests survived shootings that probably would have been fatal.

The Police Foundation study of the six largest cities in the nation found that LAPD officers had the highest number of recorded violent crime and property crime arrests per officer. It also revealed that LAPD officers killed or wounded by gunfire more civilians per officer than any of the nation's other five largest cities.

For decades, Los Angeles residents, who had rejected several bond measures that would have increased police funding, had a Faustian agreement with the LAPD: the department would keep order in the city, in its own way, at a bargain price, and residents and politicians would not ask too many questions about how they did it.

Many LAPD officers, in the model of their chief, paid little heed to the concerns expressed, continually and vociferously, by blacks and Latinos. Big-city police departments throughout the country are accused of brutal, racist behavior. But in Los Angeles the relationship between police and minority residents was exacerbated by the hyperaggressive, proactive policing ethos.

During the 1980s and early 1990s, young black men continued to complain about being stopped for trumped-up reasons, proned out on the sidewalk, sworn at, humiliated. Sometimes their wives were proned out with them. Sometimes guns were put to their head if they did not move fast enough. And sometimes they were beaten.

On a March night in 1991, two LAPD officers pounded Rodney King 55 times with their aluminum batons—while their sergeant and a group of more than 20 other officers looked on.

The officer who struck the majority of blows, Lawrence Powell, had been accused of brutality in three previous incidents. Sergeant Stacey Koon had been suspended for five days for kicking a robbery suspect after a chase in South-Central and failing to report it. Theodore Briseno, who stomped once on King's neck, had been suspended for 66 days for kicking a handcuffed prisoner and hitting him with his baton. Timothy Wind, who kicked and struck King a number of times, was a rookie officer.

In the LAPD, a department that emphasized conflict over conciliation, a department where proactive policing could be interpreted by officers in many ways, a department where officers who used excessive force were not assiduously tracked and disciplined, a debacle like the Rodney King beating probably was inevitable.

People across the nation were shocked when they saw the beating, videotaped by a neighbor, replayed repeatedly on television. But not in South-Central. Everyone knew of a Rodney King in their neighborhood.

A 1991 commission headed by prominent Los Angeles attorney Warren Christopher, who would later become Secretary of State, was formed to investigate the LAPD in response to the King beating. When the commission issued its highly critical report, the reputation of the LAPD was further tarnished.

The report concluded the department was out of touch with minority communities and tolerated racially motivated brutality. It sharply criticized the LAPD for its laxity when it came to disciplining officers guilty of excessive force. Officers involved in brutality claims were promoted, the report found, even after being cited numerous times. Complaints sometimes were left out of their personnel files.

"The failure to control these problem officers . . . ," the report stated, "is a management issue that we see as the heart of the problem of excessive force." Still, it was almost impossible for city officials to discipline or fire Daryl Gates. At the time, the Los Angeles police chief—unlike the chiefs in many major cities—had civil service tenure.

The officers who had fractured Rodney King's cheekbone, cracked his right eye socket, broken 11 bones at the base of his skull, broken his ankle and struck him with such force they knocked several fillings out of his teeth were acquitted by a Simi Valley jury. This was the final fillip for South-Central residents, and it set off the nation's most deadly urban insurrection of the century. Fifty-one people died and about $1 billion in property was destroyed. The LAPD once again was denounced, this time for its disorganized and poorly prepared response to the unrest. Although police knew since 1 P.M. that a verdict would be coming that afternoon, hundreds of officers were allowed to go home at the end of their afternoon shifts. A dozen LAPD patrol captains were attending a training seminar in Oxnard, 61 miles north of Los Angeles. And as buildings burned, Daryl Gates left police headquarters to attend a fund-raising party in Brentwood.

Unlike Watts, this riot was not confined to the city's black neighborhoods. This riot was a microcosm of Los Angeles, itself—sprawling, amorphous, both urban and suburban, multiethnic. There was rioting in the Valley. There was rioting in Pasadena. There were buildings burned on the edge of the Westside. There was massive destruction in the largely Central-American Pico Union area. In fact, about half of those arrested during the riots were Latino. Still, much of the damage was concentrated in South-Central, the riot's epicenter.

Now people throughout the world knew about South-Central and its problems. But South-Central meant different things to different people. After the 1992 riots every black neighborhood south of downtown was called South-Central by outsiders. The boundaries of South-Central are still disputed, because it is not a single neighborhood but an amorphous conglomeration of neighborhoods. While no one can set the exact dimensions of South-Central, everyone agrees that the patrol parameters of the 77th Street station—the area where Razanskas and Winn investigate murders—is the epicenter of South-Central.

It was here where, after the Rodney King beating and, later, the riots, police officers faced the greatest hostility. Snipers began firing on patrol cars. Walls were covered with antipolice graffiti such as, "Kill LAPD," and "Police 187"—California Penal Code for murder.

In the past, homicide detectives had not faced the same enmity as patrol officers. They did not prone out motorists or jam suspects on street corners. They obtained information in a far different fashion, relying on subtlety and guile. But after the Rodney King beating, people began turning on detectives, too. Information always was tough to obtain, but now it was tougher. People always viewed detectives with some reserve. Now it was outright hostility.

Homicide detectives were shot at while working crime scenes. Witnesses would not only refuse to talk to detectives, but would angrily throw them off their property. In the aftermath of the riots, LAPD officers thought the reputation of the department could not sink any lower.

Then the O. J. Simpson trial began. People throughout the country watched as defense attorneys accused LAPD detectives of being so racist and corrupt, of planting so much evidence and blood, that they had pulled off the conspiracy of the century.

The detectives *had* made a number of significant blunders, but they were the result of maladroit, not malicious police work. Much of the criticism was merely the strategic posturing of lawyers scrambling for a defense. Still, few had sympathy for the LAPD after Detective Mark Fuhrman was exposed as a liar and a racist.

During the early 1980s, when Fuhrman applied for workers' compensation benefits and, later, a stress disability pension, he told psychiatrists of his hatred for blacks and Latinos and his penchant for violence. During his last six months in the Marine Corps, he told a psychiatrist, he "got tired of having a bunch of Mexicans and niggers that should be in prison telling [me] they weren't going to do something." Fuhrman told another psychiatrist, "I answer everything with violence."

One psychiatrist concluded that he was unsuitable for police work. Another recommended that Fuhrman not be allowed to carry a gun.

His statements, however, did not hinder his career at the LAPD. Fuhrman, who has been sued unsuccessfully several times by people who claimed he used excessive force, was named a training officer five years after his disability pension was denied. In 1989 he was promoted to detective. When Fuhrman's past was revealed at the Simpson trial, many wondered how the LAPD could have promoted and rewarded a man so bigoted and unsuitable for police work. The department never provided a sufficient answer.

As the years pass since the Rodney King beating, the riots and the Simpson trial, since Daryl Gates has been replaced, since LAPD leaders have attempted to improve relations with minority communities, homicide detectives are regaining the respect of the residents.

Even in South-Central, people value the homicide detectives. Because, unlike other police officers, they pursue a single, worthy, unambiguous goal: the apprehension of murderers.

Chapter 15
Night Watch

Tuesday, August 23

After Razanskas' and Winn's night watch shift ends, the first murder of the week goes down. Patrol officers found the decomposed, badly beaten body of a 38-year-old woman near the intersection of the Harbor and the Century freeways. The woman was a street person who had been arrested a few times for prostitution.

It is another body dump. But it is a body dump with a twist. The victim has not been killed and dumped; she has not been dumped and killed. She was killed about three days ago, her body had been stored and preserved, and then she was dumped. The criminalist was able to determine this because of the bloating of the body and the lack of "environmental activity"—which means there were no insects infesting the corpse. Two South Bureau detectives, who know the chances of solving the murder are slim, reluctantly take over the investigation.

Wednesday afternoon Razanskas and Winn have dinner at the Sizzler down the street from the bureau. An hour after they eat, they get their first homicide call of the week. They hop into

South Bureau's crime scene van and pull up to a car wash where paramedics have just given up trying to revive the victim, who is lying beside his car with a single bullet wound in his chest. Razanskas and Winn crouch beside the body and study a neat black circle surrounding the bullet wound. It looks like a bull's-eye surrounded by a target ring. The circle is a powder burn, which means the shooter's gun was just inches from the victim.

The detectives talk to paramedics and a few car wash employees and piece together a rough scenario of the shooting. The victim, a 23-year-old man named Charlo Davis, was vacuuming his car when a teenager ran up and shot him in the chest. Razanskas and Winn interview a few bystanders and a patrol officer, who used to play basketball with the victim in a church league.

"He was a decent dude," the officer says. "No dope. No problems. And he could play some serious ball."

Razanskas speculates Charlo probably was killed for one of three reasons. He had just purchased his powder blue 1989 Thunderbird from a man who some people on the street say was a drug dealer. Although Charlo was not involved with drugs, this could have been a case of mistaken identity. It could have been a bungled carjacking. Charlo had a pair of expensive Dayton wire wheel rims for his car, "killer rims," cops call them because several people have been killed this year by carjackers who wanted the rims. But the most likely explanation, Razanskas figures, is Charlo was killed over his gold chain. Witnesses said the suspect grabbed Charlo's gold chain with one hand and shot him with the other. The chain's clasp and a few links are scattered near the body.

The two lead detectives on the case, who were called at home, finally make it to the scene, located at a busy intersection. On one corner there is a motel, its parking lot protected by an eight-foot fence topped by razor wire, the type of fence at state prisons. On another corner there is a taco stand covered by the graffiti of a half-dozen gangs, using a half-dozen different spray paint colors. A run-down strip mall is across the street, and behind the car wash there is a large apartment complex where residents are peering through their windows, watching the detectives.

It is rush hour now, the streets jammed with cars and buses. A truck occasionally rumbles by, the driver grinding his gears as he slows down to check out the action. A pack of mangy dogs scamper into the street and the blast of car horns adds to the cacophony.

News of the shooting quickly spreads through the neighborhood and dozens of people, most wearing shorts and thongs, line up behind the yellow tape. Charlo's mother arrives at the scene and faints. A few bystanders help her into a patrol car, where she stares out the window, sobbing. Charlo's fiancee, who is wearing a sun dress and sandals, runs up, crying and clutching a picture of Charlo in a wooden frame. A few tall young men, who were Charlo's high-school basketball teammates, gather in front of the car wash. One, who is about 6 foot 6 and 250 pounds, falls to the curb and wipes his eyes with his palms.

When the coroner arrives, Charlo's mother climbs out of the patrol car, strains against the crime scene tape and shouts, "Oh, Lord, don't take him from me. This is my child, Lord. Please don't let him die. Please don't take my baby." She collapses into the arms of a friend. Detectives call Reverend Ferroll Robins, a volunteer at the 77th Street station, and ask her to help with the family. She takes Charlo's mother into the patrol car and tells her that her son is dead.

"Why anyone want to kill my baby?" the woman shouts. "He don't bother nobody. He went to school. He found the Lord. He was getting married next month. Why? Why? Why?"

Robins places her arm around the woman's shoulder. A few minutes later, Lieutenant Robleto walks over to the mother, crouches, so they are at eye level, and holds her hand. "I just wanted to tell you how sorry I am," he says. "I promise you I will do everything I can to find out who did this."

She wipes her eyes and says, "I want to see my son."

"I'll do my best," he says.

The body is on a metal gurney and is about to be wheeled into the coroner's van. Robleto checks with the coroner investigator and gives the OK sign to Reverend Robins, who escorts Charlo's mother under the crime scene tape, through the car wash parking lot, to the body. Robins lifts the white sheet and Charlo's mother lightly pats her son's cheek. It is bright and breezy, and the wind rustles the sheet like a sail. The car wash is surrounded by more than 100 people now, lining the sidewalk three and four deep. But everyone is quiet as they watch Charlo's mother. The only sounds that can be heard are the rumble of traffic and the idling of the coroner's van.

Charlo's mother smooths her son's brow and closes his eyes. She takes a last look, tilts her head slightly, tears streaming down her face. Robins leads her across the parking lot, back under the crime scene tape and to the car of a friend, who takes her home.

Razanskas and Winn return to the office. He hopes the rest of the evening is calm because he has a lot of paperwork to catch up on. He is in South Bureau's doghouse again because a few of his 60-day reports are long overdue. His supervisors have told him they cannot let him slide any longer. They want those overdue reports this week.

Razanskas opens the murder book on an unsolved case, pulls out a few pencils and begins writing one of his long-awaited 60-dayers. While Winn types out reports on her laptop and prints them out on her desktop printer, Razanskas' method is much more time-consuming. He scrawls a report on a legal pad, turns it over to a secretary, corrects her copy and has her retype it before he turns it in.

He hunkers down at his desk, writing furiously, when he tilts his head back and sneezes. "Damn," he shouts. He slowly wriggles in his chair. He tentatively tries to lift himself up. He grabs his desk for support. He tries to stand. But he is bent like a question mark.

His back is out.

The long commutes to and from work, the endless hours in the squad car, the sleepless nights, the overtime, the nine straight months of work without a vacation, the long hours during the Miami trip . . . have all caught up with him tonight. The first thing he thinks of is his hunting trip. In about a month he will leave for Wyoming. He worries that he will not recover in time.

The rest of the night he limps around the office, winces through an hour or two of paperwork and shuffles off to the parking lot at the end of the shift, taking a few minutes to slowly contort his body so he can fit into his truck without too much pain.

Razanskas spends the next morning at the chiropractor's office and limps into the office in the late afternoon. During the past few days South Bureau has been thrumming with activity. The lieutenants spent hours huddled in an office. Supervisors gathered in the conference room. Teams of detectives crowded over piles of search warrants and maps. Early Thursday morning, dozens of South Bureau detectives, deployed throughout the county, served 20 search warrants, recovered six guns and arrested five gang members for murder.

This was the culmination of an almost two-month investigation launched after the Mexican Mafia murders at the beginning of the summer. Two gang members associated with the Mexican Mafia were attempting to collect drug-dealing taxes from the home of a Harpy gang member. He was fed up with the taxes, killed both of them and disappeared. Three nights later, the Mexican Mafia exacted their revenge and gunned down a Harpy and his 17-year-old niece. At the end of July there was another murder connected to the feud. Detectives were concerned that this was the beginning of a full-blown gang war. Fortunately, there was a standoff between the two gangs for a few weeks, but detectives felt it was just a matter of time before the gang war resumed. Now, however, those involved in murders are either under arrest or on the run, with warrants out for their arrest. Detectives figure this will alter the dynamics of the gang war by getting the most violent members off the street.

Because Razanskas and Winn are on the night watch shift, they do not take part in the bust. It is just as well, because Razanskas would not have been much help.

All week, Razanskas and Winn have been talking about the Key lime pie topped with meringue that they had one night in Miami.

"That's a pie that'll kick your ass," Razanskas tells Winn.

"That meringue had it going *on,*" she says.

Winn has called all over town, but she cannot find a Key lime pie with meringue topping in Los Angeles. She settles for a lemon meringue pie and brings it in on Thursday night. She and Razanskas have a few pieces, reminisce about the Miami trip and laugh at some of the humorous things Charles said on the plane.

"He was sweet on you," Razanskas says.

Winn looks embarrassed.

"Oh yeah. He said when he got out of jail he was going to make you an enchilada dinner."

"By the time he gets out of the joint, I'll probably be dead."

Razanskas chuckles, tries to stand up but is so sore he drops back into his chair. Fortunately, it is quiet Thursday night in South Bureau; there are no murders and Razanskas muddles through the rest of the shift.

Since their trip to Miami, Razanskas and Winn are more comfortable around each other. The three days in Miami were a milestone in their partnership, a make or break trip. If they had not gotten along, their partnership would not have had much of a future. But they worked well together. They let down their guard and were able to truly relax around each other for the first time. And while working the night watch shift, they have eaten all their meals together and have been alone in the squad room every night. It seems now, for the first time, they have the ease, the trust of true partners.

Although Razanskas does not tell Winn, he is impressed with her work. He likes her tenacity and her instincts on cases. He likes her street smarts, her ability to establish a rapport with witnesses. He likes her aggressiveness, her drive. When she is not around he'll tell another detective, "She's a keeper," or "She's going to make a damn good homicide detective."

Razanskas gives Winn advice, but he also gives her considerable freedom. He treats her more like a partner than a trainee. Although she would never tell him, she appreciates him as a supervisor.

Some of the detective trainees, however, are unhappy with their supervisors. A few are overbearing and scrutinize every move the trainees make, or are so condescending the trainees find the relationship degrading. Several trainees and supervisors have just split up.

Now, because of the shake-up, Winn is concerned she may get stuck with another supervisor. On Friday afternoon, Winn asks Razanskas if she can talk to him. In private. They enter one of the soundproof interview cubicles.

"I want to make sure you'll be my partner for a while," she says.

"I haven't heard anything about you and me splitting up."

"I just don't want to get stuck with a total asshole."

"Don't worry about it. I ain't giving you up so easy."

Late Friday night Razanskas and Winn pick up the first murder of the weekend. He shifts in the van, wincing each time Winn drives over a pothole or a bump. She pulls up near the corner of 87th and Main, in front of a stately Catholic church, built in the 1950s when the neighborhood was more affluent. The mission-style church has a red tile roof, graceful bell tower and small stained glass windows.

The church is directly beneath the LAX flight pattern and the jets roar low overhead, as if they are preparing to land a few blocks away. It is a balmy night with a warm breeze carrying the smell—sometimes sweet, sometimes acrid—of jasmine and exhaust fumes.

The uniformed officers tell them that the victim was at a *quebradita* dance at the church. *Quebradita* is a fad among young Latinos in Los Angeles. They dress in cowboy boots and western clothing, listen to Mexican *banda* music and dance the *quebradita,* a blend of country-western, lambada, polka and flamenco-style dancing.

The victim and a friend left the dance, and as they were about to drive away, a cholo walked by, stuck a .22 rifle in the car and shot both of them. The friend survived the shooting and is at the hospital.

The uniformed officers have detained a witness, a 16-year-old dressed down in baggy khaki pants and white undershirt who was on the street during the shooting. Razanskas slowly climbs out of the car and hobbles behind Winn. She interviews the witness, who is wide-eyed and jumpy.

"What were you doing out on the street?" she asks.

"I was just standing by this blue car," he says, swiveling his head around. He looks like he is afraid someone is going to ambush him. "I heard shots and ducked. Then a lot of people came out from the church to see what was happening. They thought *I* had something to do with it. They started mad-dogging me and beating on me. Someone tried to stab me."

"Exactly what did you see?" Winn asks.

"Nothing."

Winn scrutinizes him for a moment. She points to the church parking lot, where hundreds of people from the dance are still wandering about. "I'm ready to throw you back over there if you don't start telling me the truth."

She questions him for a few more minutes, but he sticks to his story. She and Razanskas talk to the church custodian, a few more patrol officers and some people who were outside during the shooting. The detectives determine that the victim and the survivor were not gang members, just two teenagers out for a night of dancing. A gangbanger approached the car and asked, "Where you from?" The victim mumbled something, and the gangbanger yelled to three friends, "Get the machine." They handed him a .22 rifle. He fired a few shots and shouted "18th Street"—the name of his gang. He was very casual, a witness told the detectives. After the shooting, he chatted with his friends for a minute or two and then hopped on a Moped and drove off.

The lead detectives arrive and Winn briefs them as Razanskas leans against a patrol car for support. Winn and the lead detectives diagram the area, study the shell casings and search for evidence. Razanskas is in so much pain he has to return to the van and stretch out. A half hour later, Winn returns to the van. She is worried about Razanskas.

"How you doin'?" she asks.

He sits ups and mutters, "Not much better."

"Look, I'll take you back to your truck so you can get out of here early tonight."

"Naw. I'll stick it out. I just got to catch my breath. I'll be with you in a few."

As she walks away he tries to stand up, winces and mutters, "I feel like a goddamn old man."

On Saturday night a member of the Hardtime Hustlers is shot in a video store parking lot. He dies at the hospital a few hours later. No one at the scene will say much, but at 3 A.M. the victim's friend shows up at the hospital with a bullet wound in his foot. He was with the victim when he was shot and he was shot too. He knows the nickname of the shooter, a member of a rival Crip set, but he will not cooperate with detectives. He will only say, "I'm going to take care of this. Myself. For my friend."

Sunday morning, hours before Razanskas' and Winn's shift begins, a gas station attendant who is counting money in his back office is stabbed to death and robbed. The station has surveillance cameras inside. But the killer knew what he was doing because he removed the videotape before he disappeared.

In the afternoon, Razanskas and Winn are sent to a crime scene where the victim was shot four times and survived. This is a false alarm, because homicide detectives are only supposed to be called out when there is a death, not a near-death. Someone screwed up, and Razanskas is angry. He does not want to go through all the agony of limping across the squad room, climbing into the van and suffering during the trip to a crime scene, if there is no homicide.

Sunday night, the last night of the detectives' P.M. shift, is quiet. But Razanskas has been in so much pain he has not been able to finish up his overdue 60-dayers. He just hopes to get through the night without a murder and get home early. Because he has worked seven days straight, he has Monday and Tuesday off. He plans to spend a lot of time at the chiropractor's office.

It is 10:30 now, just 30 minutes to go before his shift ends. He is filing away his paperwork and getting ready to head home. Then he gets the call he has been dreading. A watch commander calls and tells him, "Male Hispanic. Shot to death in front of a liquor store. West Florence Avenue . . ." Razanskas grabs his sport coat and limps out the door.

At the scene, a sergeant, embarrassed about the afternoon's false alarm, tells Razanskas, "I'll guarantee you *this* guy's dead. He took three in the head."

The liquor store manager, who has both a cigarette and a toothpick in his mouth, stands out in front. He is so nervous he paces, smokes and chews on his toothpick at the same time. He tells Winn the victim had pulled up in front of the liquor store. A man with a gun held him up. The victim yelled, "No. No. No."

"The dude didn't pull his wallet out fast enough, so the guy just fired. *Pop. Pop.*" He grimaces. "It was bad, man. I saw the blood gushing from the holes in his temple and his jaw." He takes a quick drag from his cigarette and chews on his toothpick as he exhales. "It had been such a beautiful Sunday. I was watching James Bond on the tube. I was clownin' around. Then this."

The liquor store is at the edge of a strip mall that houses a Mexican bakery and a Chinese restaurant. The strip mall is on a busy, industrial stretch of Florence Avenue, dotted with body shops, auto parts stores, machine shops and a few apartment buildings with plastic signs hanging from the side: "*Se Renta Apartmento.*" Down the street from the liquor store is a market with a wooden sign on the sidewalk advertising the soul food specialty—"Hand Cleaned Chitterlings"—known as chitlins, which are sections of pig intestines, usually served fried.

A sergeant walks over to Razanskas and say, "Another black suspect. Another Mexican victim. I feel a race war brewing."

Traditionally, there have been few problems in Los Angeles between black and Latino gangs. But there have been several shootings between black and Latino gangs in Venice over the summer. And in the county jails there is now constant warfare between blacks and Latinos. Most cops fear that these conflicts will spill out into the streets.

"If they go at each other in South-Central—stand by," Razanskas tells the sergeant. "It'll make what we've had so far seem like nothin'. When that happens, it'll be time for me to retire."

The lead detectives arrive and they interview patrons of a bar across the street. At the time of the shooting, a security guard was outside the bar and a number of people were milling about in front. But now the guard and the patrons tell detectives that everyone was *inside* the bar during the shooting. No one saw a thing. In order to refresh the security guard's memory, detectives close down the bar and herd all the patrons outside. This has been a busy night and the bar owner stands to lose a lot of money. The owner talks to the guard and some of the patrons. Their memories begin to improve.

Razanskas and Winn finish up at the homicide scene and return to the station at 2 A.M. It has been a long week for Razanskas, seven straight night shifts, the last five with his back out. Because they worked seven days straight, they will take Monday and Tuesday off.

"Take some extra time off next week," she says, as they walk to the parking lot.

"I should be OK by Wednesday."

"Don't be a hero. If you need more time, take it."

Razanskas nods, waves good-by and limps across the parking lot to his car, one shoulder a good six inches lower than the other, listing and rolling like a ship at sea.

Chapter 16
Losing a Child

Wednesday, August 31

Razanskas shuffles into the office, his back a little straighter, his step a little surer. He feels better, he tells Winn. But more important, he feels confident he will recover in time for his hunting trip.

This is going to be a short week. A few days of work and then Labor Day weekend, which both detectives have off. Winn plans to visit relatives in Texas. Razanskas will continue his back therapy.

During this abbreviated week they try to find others who were part of the mob that killed Ruben Gomez. They are particularly interested in the stabber. They talk to the family of the suspects and pick up a few leads, but the week is over before they have a chance to make much headway.

In some areas of the country, Labor Day signifies the end of summer. But in Los Angeles the subtle fall still is a ways off. At the end of September or early October, the Santa Ana winds usually kick up one final heat wave, a few days when the temperatures hover above 100 degrees, when the days bake and the nights are unbearable. At the end of this final heat wave, the temperatures drop to the 90s, then the 80s, then the 70s. There might be other hot days and Santa Ana nights during the fall, but that last extended heat wave is the true end of summer in southern California. People know that fall has begun.

While Labor Day does not mean the homicide detectives' season is over, detectives can sense that the season is, at least, nearing an end. But for the *families* of homicide victims, Labor Day represents the inauguration of *their* season, the first holiday in a string of painful holidays, culminating in Christmas. The families endure a visceral *frisson* on Labor Day, a warning that they best brace themselves because the upcoming months are going to be the most painful months of the year.

On a Saturday morning in early September, Charlo's mother, Virginia Davis, decides to seek help. She is inconsolable, and neither her friends, nor her relatives, nor her pastor can help her.

After Davis' son was murdered at a car wash, and a friend arrived to take her home, Winn told the friend that Davis needed help, and recommended a counseling center in South-Central, Loved Ones of Homicide Victims. The center offers therapy free of charge, and the counselors specialize in helping people whose children have been murdered. The therapists are from the neighborhood, Winn said. They understand.

So on this Saturday morning, Davis drives over to the Baptist church where Loved Ones holds its meetings. The center is located in a few cramped, cluttered offices and classrooms behind the church. The carpeting is frayed and held together with silver duct tape, the ceilings are water-stained, and the paint is peeling from the walls. The focus of the center is the hundreds of funeral programs tacked to an enormous bulletin board near the entrance.

The programs include lists of pallbearers, hymns, poems, pictures, accomplishments. The brief eulogies create poignant portraits of lives lost too young: "As our beautiful angel passes on . . ." "Charles, we love you and always will . . ." "Robert, when tears come to our eyes, we must remember you were never too busy or sad to smile . . ." "Ernie, we miss you. You were our everything and we will always love you . . ."

The Saturday morning support group is composed of about 20 people, mostly middle-aged women, who are gathered in a circle. The therapist who heads the group, Robert Bennett, turns to Davis and says, "This is your first time here. Can you tell us what happened?"

"On August 24, someone shot my son. He was only twenty-three years old."

She tells the group Charlo had been a basketball star at Manual Arts High School, the year the team won the state championship. He received a scholarship to California State University, Sacramento and was a semester away from graduating. He was planning to take the LAPD qualifying exam the week he was killed.

"He was a young man in his prime," Bennett says, nodding. "I'm very sorry."

"I don't want to get up in the morning," Davis says, staring at the ground. "I don't want to sleep. I don't want to do anything. I haven't eaten in the last three or four days. My heart feels heavy every day. I want to cry. Scream. I want to know why? Why he have to take my son's life? Why he have to kill him? My son was a good kid. A college student. A basketball player."

"You feel numb all the time, don't you?" Bennett asks.

She nods. "I'm having a real rough time," she says, covering her mouth with a fist. "Every time I close my eyes, all I see is my child lying there with the sheet over him." She cries and a woman hands her a tissue. "I lost three other family members. But there's nothing like losing a child."

"Who would like to tell her something?" Bennett asks the group.

"My nephew was killed in a drive-by January 27," a woman says. "Your answers will come, but it will take time. In time you'll find peace within you. Because your son still lives inside of you. He hasn't left you. He's just gone to a better place."

Davis dabs her eyes with a tissue and says, "I can't even be around people because I cry so much. So I just stay at home. I feel like someone just cut my heart out. I could understand it better if he'd been sick. Or if it had been an accident . . ." Her voice trails off.

"My child was shot over fifteen times," a woman says. She walks across the room and holds Davis' hand. "I couldn't eat or drink and I couldn't stop crying. I, too, felt like someone reached in and snatched the heart out of my chest."

Bennett turns to another woman and says, "Tell her about your son. Tell her if you ever found peace."

"I cried for over a year," the woman tells Davis. Every . . . single . . . day. People think after a few months you should be getting over it. It doesn't work like that. Give yourself time. Don't put too much pressure on yourself. Being a mother is a different kind of bond. Ain't nothing worse than losing your child."

Bennett turns to a young woman who lost two brothers in May and asks, "What would you tell her?"

"It would be good for you to get away. It helped me to get away."

"I'd like to get away," Davis says.

"Where would you go?" Bennett asks.

"I have a sister in the Bay Area. I could visit her. I need to leave L.A. for a while. Every time I walk down the street and I see a tall black kid, I see my son's face. Every time I sleep, he comes to me in my dreams. He say, 'Hey, girl, what you doin'?' Or 'Hey, mama, I'm home.' "

"I know what you saying," a woman shouts. "Every time I see a guy with a shaved head, I think of my son. Every time I see a stocky, bald kid, my eyes flash."

"My cousin was killed in Inglewood," a woman calls out, "and for the longest time I couldn't go to Inglewood anymore."

"I can't drive down the street where he was killed," Davis says. "I don't go anywhere near that car wash."

A woman named Frankie walks across the room and hands Davis a box of tissues. "Let me tell you, babe," she says softly. "I understand your feelings. I felt like all I wanted to do was kill myself. My son was murdered more than three years ago, and every day it feels like it happened yesterday. I remember everything about that day. It was cold and it was raining a little. I ran out of the house when I heard. But there was no place to run. . . ."

Davis nods and says, "A girl came to my door. I heard my sister scream. I jumped out of bed. I ran out into the street. By the time I got to the car wash, they already putting the sheet on him."

Frankie says to Davis, "I waited two years for him to come home. Every holiday I'd wait for him to take his first piece of pecan pie. There were many nights I'd lie awake at two o'clock in the morning and think, 'I'm going to get me a thirty-eight, go to the corner of Main and Avalon, and I don't care who I shoot.' For so long, I didn't know how I'd make it." She puts an arm around Davis and says, "But I *did* made it. And I know you will make it. You *will* find some peace."

Bennett asks the group, "How does she find this peace?"

"Only through God," a woman calls out. "Peace has to come from above. No need to look for it here."

"If I wasn't going to church," Davis says, "I'd be over the edge right now."

"God will make it easier," Frankie tells her. "In His time. Not your time. I know there is a God. And I know God is good. Don't get me wrong. I'm still grieving. But I survived. It was God who helped me survive. And it'll be God who helps you survive."

At the end of the session, everyone holds hands, closes their eyes and a group member leads a prayer. After the prayer, they hug and gather outside the classroom. They tell Davis that they all have been through what she is going through, that she cannot survive it alone, that she needs to come to meetings and ask for their help, that the pain will never entirely go away but, gradually, it will begin to lessen. A woman named Maxine gives Davis her phone number and asks her to call when she needs to talk. "I know what you're going through," Maxine tells her. "I've been there."

Saundrea Young recognized the need for a South-Central counseling center when she was a social work administrator at a hospital near Watts. She was stunned by the endless parade of people who passed through the emergency room, people whose relatives had just been murdered. She and her staff of social workers would take the families into a small office and briefly counsel them. And that was all they could do. This was the mid-1980s, and there was no place she could refer them to where they could get the psychological counseling they would need in the weeks, months and years to come. Most of the grieving family members did not have the money—or the health insurance—to afford their own therapists.

Young met a woman named Norma Johnson, a city employee who worked with crime victims and had formed a support group where victims met weekly. Because no one else would help them, they helped themselves and each other. Young suggested they combine forces. Johnson had the trust of the victims' families. Young had access to the therapists. They called their organization Loved Ones of Homicide Victims.

Young and another volunteer therapist counseled the first victims themselves. She later convinced other therapists to donate their time. Word spread and Loved Ones soon began offering individual and family therapy sessions and holding weekly support groups.

Before Loved Ones was founded, most people who sought therapy after family members were murdered had to leave South-Central for help. The therapists they saw usually were white and had little experience working with minority clients. They told Young they felt uncomfortable and alienated by the experience. So Young and Johnson adopted a mission statement, a guiding principle to underscore everything their center would stand for: *Healing Begins Within Our Community.*

Everyone knew about black-on-black crime. Young and Johnson, however, wanted to create a place for black-on-black healing. They sought out black therapists and black volunteers. They rented offices in a Baptist church, where black clients would feel at ease. Robert Bennett, a clinical social worker for the state, volunteered to counsel clients and lead support groups. When he was in school, the psychological literature was geared to middle-class white clients. When he began working in South-Central, he felt he had to create his own way of communicating with black clients. So he and Saundrea Young began emphasizing faith and spirituality in their group sessions. They knew this would not be effective with suburban clients. But for virtually all of their clients, religion was a central part of their upbringing. Many of them, or their parents, were raised in the South, where there was a strong emphasis on the church. Bennett and Young believed their clients' faith would help them heal. They discovered that despite all the death and despair in their clients' lives, they still believed. Preachers had often told them, "God won't give you more than you can bear." Most people in the group, despite their losses, still held this belief. Faith became the core of their shared survival.

Bennett never forced religion on his clients. The clients introduced it to the sessions, spontaneously, and he simply recognized it as a powerful force, a common denominator, and employed it as a therapeutic tool.

Everyone who has lost a loved one to violent death feels a profound anger. But for Bennett's clients, the anger often is more acute, directed at more specific targets, and is more difficult to treat. Many of his clients, who have endured a lifetime of discrimination, often feel the police do not care about their loss. The criminal justice system does not care. White people do not care. Many feel that the prevailing attitude is: *Just another dead black in the ghetto*. They are angry because they feel that, like rape victims, people blame the murder victims. Every young black man killed in South-Central, they feel, is assumed to be a gangbanger or a drug dealer.

Bennett volunteered his services for a year and a half before there was enough funding to pay him. He continued to work for free because he felt the need was so great. One of Bennett's first clients was a woman whose teenage son had been shot to death in front of their apartment. He had been dead three months, but she still refused to believe that her son was gone. She was so distraught, she paid the mortuary to dig up her son's coffin. It was only then that she could accept that he was dead.

As South-Central changed and the Latino population multiplied, the center changed with it. Spanish-speaking therapists were hired and Latino support groups were added. Now the center is funded by a variety of grants and private donations and has ten paid therapists and four paid staff members. More than 300 people a month take part in individual therapy and group sessions, including groups for children and teenagers. Some of the younger clients want revenge. Others are filled with anger and anguish. They are at a critical age, and the therapists know how important it is to reach them now, before they repeat the cycle of violence.

When the state of California made funds available for crime victims and their families, a number of therapists from Westside clinics contacted Loved Ones, requesting referrals. But Young told the therapists the clients would be better off at her center. "Healing," she told them, "has to begin within our community."

Since Virginia Davis is the newest member of Loved Ones' Saturday support group, her loss is the most recent, her grief the most immediate.

Others in the group have lost children months ago, some years ago. This summer, some have undergone transformations. Others have found redemption. They tell their stories to Davis in the hope that she, too, will find the strength to go on.

At the beginning of the summer, Vanessa Money told the group she had decided to move to Memphis because she could no longer live in the city where her 21-year-old son, Garland, was murdered.

Garland had only been home for a month after his discharge from the Air Force. He was out one night with two high-school friends, one of whom had recently witnessed a gang shooting. The shooter killed the witness—and he killed Garland and the other friend for good measure.

When Garland was killed, Money felt she was mourning two deaths. The death of her son. And the death of Los Angeles. Her family moved to Los Angeles from St. Louis when she was a young girl, and she was enchanted by the city. She had always loved the balmy weather and the proximity to the mountains and the ocean. She loved spending her days at the beach and her evenings at the jazz clubs by the water.

Money grew up in a clapboard house at 52nd and Van Ness, shaded by a big avocado tree in the backyard. She knew about the gangs and the crime, but she felt she knew what gang turf to avoid. Because Garland was a good student and a high-school football player, and was not involved with gangs, she assumed he would be safe, too. When her son was murdered, she felt deceived, violated, as if she had been deluded all these years. Now she detested Los Angeles and was counting the days until she could leave. It was only on Saturday mornings, at Loved Ones meetings, that she would talk about her son's death. She was just trying to get through the summer, living from Saturday to Saturday, from meeting to meeting.

At the beginning of the summer, Money cleaned out her bank account and wired her sister the money to use as a down payment for a house they would build in Memphis. She planned to move in with her mother, her sister and her sister's children, and leave Los Angeles, and all the terrible memories, forever.

One afternoon in August, at her job as a credit union representative, she could not concentrate and could not work. She was as depressed as she had ever been. That afternoon she called the police station for Garland's case number. She was applying for funds from a state victim's assistance program to pay for his funeral. After the call, she felt as if she were about to have a nervous breakdown. But at that moment, she could feel her son's embrace and could hear him say to her, "Mamacita, it's all right. I'm here."

That afternoon she realized that although Garland was gone, physically, he was still with her, spiritually. She could still commune with him. She began visiting her son's grave and talking to him. After work, she would wander about the house and tell him how her day went, how she was feeling, how much she missed him.

After Garland died, Money was on the verge of losing her faith. But now she began praying again. She read more than fifty books about death and spirituality and overcoming grief. At the Saturday morning meetings, she began telling the others what she was learning.

By Labor Day, she told the group she had come to a decision. She no longer felt the need to run away. She lost her son. But she did not want to lose all her friends. She did not want to lose the support group. And she did not want to lose Los Angeles. She decided not to move to Memphis. She felt that now, for the first time, she had the strength to stay.

Frankie Armstead's 29-year-old son, Tyrone, was shot in the back and killed three years ago. After his death Armstead was stunned by the response of her neighbors. Tyrone, a machinist who lived at home, was killed right out on the street in the early evening, just a few doors from home. Armstead knew people were out on the street when her son was killed, knew people had seen what happened. But not a single neighbor would cooperate with police.

Armstead has lived in a small tan house on East 99th Street for 34 years. In the summers, at lunchtime, she used to make tacos for all the children on the block. Her husband, a construction foreman, used to take the fatherless boys horseback riding. He invited them to his backyard barbecues and gave them part-time jobs. Now, when she needed something from her neighbors, they turned their backs on her.

After Tyrone, her only child, was killed, she would not go to counseling. She did not want to talk. She even withdrew from her best friend, Magdalene May. May lived down the street and their sons had been best friends. But after Tyrone was killed, Armstead made it clear to May that she was no longer welcome to stop by every morning for coffee. She made it clear to May that their friendship was over.

Armstead's only reason for living, she felt, was her husband. She could not abandon him.

It took another murder on East 99th Street to force her out of her shell. Two years after Tyrone was killed, Magdalene

May's son was murdered. Every Saturday morning, May attended the Loved Ones support group. A few times, she asked Armstead to join her. But Armstead refused. Finally, after May asked her yet again, Armstead decided to pray to see whether she should go. She received an answer. She felt that Tyrone wanted her to go.

She attended her first support group meeting in July, and she did not miss a meeting the rest of the summer. After Tyrone died, she became angry when people told her, "I understand how you feel." She would snap at them, "Until you've seen your only child lying dead on the sidewalk, you will *never* understand how I feel." At the support group she met a group of people who she felt truly did understand.

One Saturday afternoon, after a meeting, she said to Magdalene May, "Let's tell the truth and shame that ol' Devil. . . . Sometimes a person can feel a need to be distant. But that can change."

"I'm just where you left me," May told her.

Now, Armstead and May drive to the support group every Saturday morning. Together.

Maxine Douglas' son was robbed and murdered three years ago. Last year she felt as if she had endured a second death. The suspect, who she is convinced is guilty, was acquitted at trial.

Douglas was a single mother who had no other children. The last time she saw her son was on a Wednesday morning, a bright spring day without a hint of smog. Robert, a high-school sophomore, was leaving for school. She watched him climb down the steps of their apartment house and walk down the street. He turned around, flashed a radiant smile and walked off, disappearing into a canopy of trees on the horizon. That afternoon, after school, he was killed. He was, she makes a point of saying, 15 years, 10 months, and 3 days old.

Douglas sits in her small apartment, surrounded by Robert's belongings. She has his blue Boy Scout shirt and his red vest filled with merit badges. She keeps his favorite shirt—a Los Angeles Raider's jersey—in a plastic zippered bag. She has his Cub Scout pictures, his kindergarten graduation pictures, his certificates of achievement from school. Her shelves are filled with Robert's football and basketball trophies. Robert was already 6 foot 3, 235 pounds, quick and coordinated, a promising high-school football player who dreamed of a college scholarship. He was a bright boy and a good student. She had so many dreams for him.

After his death she could not sleep, eat or talk. A friend took her to a Santa Monica hospital. The psychologist could not help her. Her friend took her to a hospital in Inglewood. The psychologist there could not help her. She thought she was losing her mind. She had decided to commit suicide when she discovered Loved Ones. She believes the center saved her life.

After one meeting, she thought, "If I'm going to have to live in this mean, vicious world, I'm going to make a commitment to God. I'm going to make a commitment to help other people who have lost children." She began offering an occasional, tentative comment to the new group members. People seemed to respond to what she said; her insights and experiences seemed to help them. During the sessions, therapist Robert Bennett began calling upon her more frequently to share her experiences, to put new members at ease. Now, after the sessions, she often is the first one to approach a new group member—as she did with Virginia Davis—to give support and offer her phone number.

She has found a purpose for her life. Now she tries to help others find their own reasons to go on.

Not everyone who passed through the center this summer was helped. Some found the group sessions intrusive. Others saw therapists a few times and disappeared. Some had spiritual questions the support group could not answer.

Erlinda Acuna has spent the summer trying to find out who killed her 17-year-old son, Ernie, who was shot to death four years ago. Since then, Acuna—who has tattooed on her left wrist "ERNIE R.I.P."—has been a regular at the Saturday morning sessions at Loved Ones. During the week she has to stay strong for her other children. Saturday mornings are her time.

After her son was killed, homicide detectives arrested a 19-year-old gang member, Jerry "Gizmo" Johnson. Acuna was grateful that police had caught her son's killer and that the jury convicted him. But in June, she received a letter from Gizmo that made her question everything. All summer she has been tormented by doubt. Has Gizmo, she wonders, been convicted of a murder he did not commit? Is the real murderer free?

"Dear Mrs. Erlinda," Gizmo wrote. "I'm writing to you this letter in reguards of what happen to your son Ernie. I know in your mind you believe I'm the person who took your son Ernie life. But with all my respect to you and your family, I'm not guilty for taking your son Ernie life. And I just pray that you would believe me in your heart of what I'm telling you in this letter. . . . So Mrs. Erlinda I just hope and pray that you would take this letter and understand my feelings in reguards of your son Ernie."

Gizmo wrote that the key witness to Ernie's murder had lied. The witness was Donna, Ernie's cousin, and her testimony sealed Gizmo's conviction.

"Your niece Donna really knows in her heart that I didn't take your son Ernie life. Cause your niece Donna knows in her heart that Im not guilty. Cause I have spoken to Donna before about your son Ernie when I was being charge for taking his life. Mrs. Erlinda I know if you speak to Donna and ask her for the honest truth . . . Donna will tell you the truth and tell you Im not guilty."

When Acuna first received the letter, she ignored it. Gizmo's trial had been a traumatic time for her. His conviction was a relief. But over the course of the summer the letter began to torment her with doubts. She called the deputy D.A. and the detective who handled the case. They both assured her that Gizmo was just trying to manipulate her. He was appealing his case, they told her, and he knew he could improve his odds if he could get her support.

But she could not put the case out of her mind. Finally, she contacted a priest whom Gizmo mentioned in his letter. Acuna told the priest to ask Gizmo, "If you didn't do it, who did?" Gizmo was a member of the 29th Street gang, and people in Acuna's neighborhood knew that 29th Street was behind Ernie's murder. If Gizmo was innocent, Acuna was convinced he knew which one of his homies killed Ernie.

In August, Gizmo wrote her again. "I don't want you to hate me," he wrote. "I just want you to know I had nothing to do with what I was blame for. Your niece Donna will tell you the truth. And I know how you feel every day about your son Ernie. I really wish he could be with you. So he could tell you I had nothing to do with what I was blame for. So if you are willing to help me Im willing to help you. . . . So if you would like to write me back, I will give you a address where you could write me at. Remember I would like to talk with you."

Gizmo suggested in the second letter that he would tell her who killed her son. But he was not willing to do it through a third party. She would have to see him herself.

Acuna wished she never had heard from Gizmo, never allowed herself to become ensnared in doubt. She told the others at the Saturday support group about her ambivalence. They told her to ignore Gizmo, that her search would only cause her more pain, that she might never know for sure. But now that she had communicated with Gizmo—through the priest—she felt she had crossed a line. She could not rest until she knew for certain who had killed her son.

She had not talked with Donna since the trial. Donna had moved away from the neighborhood, did not have a telephone, and her side of the family was not close with Acuna's. All summer Acuna could not make up her mind whether to contact Donna. She was afraid Donna's answer would make her more confused. But after Gizmo's second letter, Acuna decided if she was ever going to learn the truth, she would have to do two things. She would have to talk to Donna. And she would have to visit Gizmo in prison.

Now, on Labor Day weekend, she decides she will contact Donna before the end of the summer. She will ask her to recount, once again, what happened the night Ernie was killed. She will ask her if she is absolutely certain she saw Gizmo pull the trigger.

Then Acuna will make arrangements to visit Gizmo in prison. She will ask him if he killed Ernie. She will look into his eyes for the answer.

Chapter 17
Polygraph

Tuesday, September 6

The morning after Labor Day, Winn and Razanskas are back in the bureau. Winn has just returned from visiting relatives in Texas. Razanskas spent the long weekend at the chiropractor's office and preparing for his hunting trip.

He tells Winn that during the past few days he has sharpened his knives and bought ammunition. He spent an afternoon at the range with a hunting buddy, sighting his guns.

"I just got to get through September," he says. "Then Raz is in the mountains, away from all this, killing Bambi."

Winn ignores him. She is still rattled by an encounter she had earlier in the morning. It is the first time this summer that Winn has shown fear.

When she arrived in the squad room, a detective who sits near her announced that he had found some mouse droppings on his desk. Now she is unable to work, unable to concentrate. She nervously glances under her desk every few minutes and flinches when she thinks she spots a mouse scurrying by. Winn is afraid to put her feet under her desk and her chair now is a good three feet away. She leans down and sneaks yet another glance beneath her desk as Detective Armando Reyes slips behind her and lightly walks his fingers along her back. She yelps and jumps out of her chair.

Reyes and Razanskas roar with laughter.

A few minutes later, Paul Masuyama wanders by. This is his first day back from a month vacation in Japan. Razanskas and Winn are curious to know if he was able to track down his father.

Earlier in the year, Masuyama decided he wanted to locate his relatives in Japan, so he turned his adoption papers over to a police department clerk who spoke fluent Japanese. She wrote Tokyo police authorities and asked them for help.

A few months later, Japanese police officials located Masuyama's stepfather. They told the LAPD clerk that in Japan, after children are adopted, their names are deleted from the family register in the city census records. But Masuyama's stepfather had asked city officials in 1955 to keep his stepson's name on file. He always hoped that one day his stepson would return.

Masuyama and his mother made the trip together. Before they left, he had a long talk with her, explaining that while he was searching for information about his birth mother and father, that did not change his feelings for her and his adoptive father. They raised him; they were his parents.

When they arrived at the Sapporo airport, they were greeted by his cousins, to whom he had sent family pictures in the spring, and his stepfather. Masuyama, who had not seen him since he was 5 years old, hugged him. The old man, unaccustomed to public displays of affection, stood stiffly.

Later that night, his stepfather pulled out a picture of Masuyama that he had kept in his wallet almost 40 years and told him, in a quavering voice, that he never forgot him. It had been very difficult to give him up for adoption, he explained, but for a half-American child it would have been a hard life in Japan. He knew his stepson would have more opportunity in America.

He told Masuyama a strange story of how his mother met his American father. His mother found out she had a fatal heart disease and went to Nakajima Park in Sapporo and planned to commit suicide. Masuyama's father noticed she was distraught, approached her and they spent the afternoon together. They began seeing each other and, eventually, they married—against her family's wishes. They had been married two years when his father's unit shipped out. She never heard from him again.

Masuyama's stepfather had fought in the Philippines during World War II, and out of a battalion of 400 men, he was one of only 8 survivors. He met Masuyama's mother, Sumiko, when Masuyama was four. When they married, he adopted Masuyama. Sumiko's dying wish was that her son be given to his father's family and raised in America. His stepfather tried to locate the father, but was unsuccessful.

He began crying and told Masuyama that all these years, he had considered him his son, and questioned whether he should have given him up for adoption. But when he received Masuyama's letter in the spring, and discovered he was a homicide detective with the Los Angeles Police Department, he knew he had made the right decision. He told Masuyama that he was proud of him. The entire time they were together in Japan, he bragged to taxi drivers, people in the subways, policemen on the street, that his son was a homicide detective in Los Angeles.

Masuyama then shows Razanskas and Winn a worn, sepia-toned photograph of his parents. His mother, a slender, demure-looking woman, is wearing a kimono, her face is whitened with chalky makeup, and she is carrying a fan. His father, also wearing a wedding kimono, has the same prominent ears and broad forehead as his son.

Masuyama's relatives told him that his father's first name was William, and his last name was pronounced something like "Car." He tracked down the Buddhist temple where his parents were married and tried to find out his father's last name. But the temple did not keep marriage records that far back. He checked city marriage records, but the marriage was never registered with the city.

Although he never did discover his father's last name or how to contact him, he did not regret making the trip. Masuyama tells Razanskas and Winn that at least now he has a few leads. He plans to continue his search. But that will have to wait. Because on his first day back at work, he has a stack of unsolved homicide files on his desk, and he and Reyes are number one on the on-call list.

At 10:30 that night they get the call. But this is not the usual homicide call. This is a "shots fired at an officer" call.

Last year 40 patrol officers in South Bureau were shot at—a record number. The bureau commander wanted to make sure these cases were given top priority, so he assigned homicide detectives to the investigations. These investigations—investigations that are not even officially included in the detectives' caseloads—create even more work for already overworked detectives.

If an officer is shot in South-Central, Robbery-Homicide Division handles the case. If the shooter misses, South Bureau Homicide takes over. There are a number of reason why cops are being fired at so often in South-Central. Assaults against officers across the country are at a record high, so cops are in greater danger now in South-Central, just as they are in greater danger throughout the country. But in South-Central there are other forces at work. Part of it is historical, the decades of friction between the LAPD and the residents. And part of it, some cops say, is California's new "Three Strikes" initiative. Some suspects with two prior convictions would rather risk a shootout with police than face a mandatory 25-to-life sentence.

Razanskas, whose back is much improved, arrives at East 85th Street shortly before midnight. The narrow street is lined with modest Spanish-style houses with red tile roofs, shaded by towering magnolia trees. He spots Masuyama in the distance and, impersonating Inspector Clouseau in the *Pink Panther* movies, calls out, "Kato, you little yellow devil."

Masuyama ignores him. Reyes walks over and a sergeant describes the shooting to the three of them. Residents have been complaining about drug dealing on their street, so two officers from the Special Problems Unit—uniformed officers who drive unmarked cars—were dispatched to the neighborhood. A man sitting on the hood of a car spotted the officers and ran through a backyard. The officers chased him. A few seconds later shots whizzed by the officers. They took cover and called for backup.

Dozens of officers responded, including the SWAT team. One SWAT team member wandered into a nearby backyard and spotted a T-shirt covering a window in an abandoned shack. He studied the shirt and noticed it had a Levi Strauss insignia. He recalled that one of the officers who had been shot at said the suspect had a blue jean insignia on the back of his shirt. The SWAT team crashed through the shack and found the shirtless suspect cowering in the corner.

Masuyama, Reyes and Razanskas flip on their flashlights and search the shack. It is a dirty, ramshackle structure with ripped carpeting and a few splintered drawers from the built-in shelves scattered about the floor. The detectives do not find any evidence in the shack, so for the next hour they scour every backyard in the area for shells, footprints or any other evidence. It is a dark night without a hint of a moon. Every few minutes the skies are illuminated by a flash of light, from the jets cruising low overhead, preparing for landing. The detectives do not find much at the crime scene, so they return to the 77th Street station.

Masuyama and Reyes interview one of the officers who was shot at. He is in his mid-20s, has a crew cut and is extremely nervous. He is tapping a foot and chewing on a cuticle. First he was almost killed. Now he has to recount the story to detectives. He tells them he and his partner were driving eastbound on West 85th Street. "A guy jumped off a car and took off running. We went after him. As he was running I noticed he was reaching into his waistband. I yelled to my partner, 'Watch his hand! It's in his waistband!' We followed him to the rear of the house. I heard him hit one fence. That's when I heard the shots."

Razanskas walks into the room, scrutinizes the officer and snarls, "You're a lying son of a bitch."

The young cop is stunned. He looks to Masuyama and Reyes for help. He turns to Razanskas and sees that he is laughing. He laughs too now, much relieved. Razanskas banters with him for a few minutes. He seems to relax. He recounts the story again to Razanskas, this time with more detail.

"I heard five to six shots. They were coming from a yard south of our location. Maybe two blocks away. I heard the shots whizzing right by me. Man, I could hear those bullets cutting the air." He flick a finger by his ear. "They were passing right by me."

When the officer finishes his statement, a sergeant puts his arm around him, walks him across the squad room and says, "Don't worry. We're going to hammer them tomorrow."

Razanskas walks over to a wall calendar, points to the last week in September and says to Masuyama and Reyes, "That's it." He clenches his fist and pumps it. "Oh yeah. Deer hunting in Wyoming."

The three detectives talk for a few minutes about how they will approach their interview with the suspect, who is waiting in an interview cubicle. Razanskas tells Masuyama and Reyes that the room's tape recording equipment—with the microphone hidden in the wall—is broken. They all shake their heads in disgust.

Razanskas waves the suspect's rap sheet. "He's a car thief and a dope fiend and a burglar," he says, reading the list of offenses. "And that's just the first page." The rap sheet is four pages long. He knows the system, Razanskas tells Masuyama. He is not going to be easy to turn.

The suspect, whose name is Adrian, is a small, slender 20-year-old wearing a gold hoop earring. Masuyama, who is the primary on the case, takes the lead in the interview.

Adrian agrees to talk without an attorney. "Sure I'll talk," he says. "But I don't have much to say."

"Why'd you run?" Masuyama asks.

"My partners—Li'l Monk and Lump—were killed last night by Kitchen Crips," says Adrian, who is a Swan, a Blood set. "So I was paranoid."

"Didn't you know they were police?"

"No. I just saw the lights from the car. I didn't know who it was."

"When did you realize it was the police?"

"After I hopped the first gate."

"Why didn't you stop then?"

"I'm trying to stay as far away from the police as possible."

"What you trying to hide?"

"Nothing."

"Then why'd you run when you knew it was the police?"

Adrian shrugs. "I figured the police were doing the shooting to scare me. . . . That's when I saw that little house in the backyard. The door was open. I went in and sat down."

"The police didn't do any shooting," Masuyama says. "We already eliminated that. All that leaves is you."

Adrian stares at Masuyama coolly. "Well, it wasn't me."

"Maybe you didn't know they were police," Masuyama says. "Maybe you thought they were Kitchen Crips."

Adrian shakes his head. "I would have waited until they got closer before I shot them."

"You say you didn't shoot a gun on Tuesday?" Masuyama asks.

He nods.

"Well, what if our gunshot residue test on you comes back positive?"

Adrian licks his lips and looks down. "I did some shooting earlier in the day."

"What were you shooting?"

"A .357."

"What time?"

"Two o'clock."

Masuyama shakes his head in disbelief. "So when that GSR test comes back positive, what's going to be your story?"

"My partners and me were testing the gun."

"What did you do between the time you shot the gun and the time police chased you?"

"Went to my auntie's house. Messed with a car. Hung out."

Razanskas stands up, stretches and winces. His back is beginning to act up. Sitting on those hard metal chairs is causing him problems.

He exchanges an incredulous glance with Masuyama. Masuyama turns to Adrian and barks, "We don't believe your story. You willing to take a lie detector test?"

Adrian fidgets in his chair. He chews his lower lip and says, speaking quickly, "Yes. But you should know that I been real upset. Since Li'l Monk and Lump were killed. I couldn't eat. So I haven't washed my hands since I shot the gun. At two o'clock."

He sees they are not convinced, so he says, "Look, I ain't going to shoot at no PO-lice. I ain't got no reason to lie. I'm telling the truth, man." He is pleading now. "I thought the Crips were comin'. I just trying to save myself."

"How many times you fire this gun?" Masuyama asks skeptically.

"Four times. In the air."

"Where?"

"In the alley off 83rd and Avalon."

"Why?"

"To see if it worked. My homie just bought it."

"Then why'd *you* shoot it?"

Adrian pauses and thinks for a moment. "Just curious about the gun."

"Who bought the gun?"

"I don't want to put a name on it."

"Who'd he buy it from?"

"A junkie."

Masuyama taps his pen on the metal table. "People said shots were coming from that vacant house where you were at."

"Damn!" Adrian shouts. "I didn't shoot no gun. I didn't shoot at no PO-lice."

"Adrian, listen to me," Masuyama says. "Let's say you didn't know they were police. That's understandable. You took off too soon to see them." Masuyama's tone now is conciliatory, sympathetic. "Let's say you fired at them from several blocks away. And you fired at them because you thought they were Crips. And you were just trying to save your life. I can understand that." He extends a palm toward Adrian. "That's your way out."

Adrian has spent too much time in police interview rooms to bite. He shakes his head. "I didn't fire no gun."

Masuyama nods. "Okay. If that's the way you want to play it. But if that GSR test comes back positive, you've got some serious explaining to do."

The detectives walk out into the squad room. They all agree he is lying. "We had him on the ropes," Razanskas says. "But he wouldn't go down." They decide the case is shaky. They do not have Adrian's gun. Neither officer actually saw Adrian shoot at them. One officer knew which direction the bullets were coming from; one did not.

Masuyama decides to give Adrian a polygraph examination. The results are not admissible in court, but they can be useful anyway and can give detectives invaluable insight into a suspect. Although not 100 percent accurate, at least detectives can get a sense of what part of a suspect's statement is true, what part is a lie. And a skillful polygraph examiner can use the test to manipulate a suspect, to convince him to confess.

Even though it is 3 A.M., Masuyama wants to give Adrian the polygraph now when he is more vulnerable, instead of waiting until morning, after Adrian has been booked and has had time to think about the case.

Fortunately, the department's polygraph investigator, Ervin Youngblood, is a hunting buddy of Razanskas'. And fortunately, he owes Razanskas a favor. Last year, during a pig-hunting trip in the mountains up the coast, Razanskas spotted a good-sized boar with long tusks. He let Youngblood take the shot. Youngblood took it down, mounted the head, and it is now on his wall.

Razanskas calls Youngblood at home. "Get your ass out of bed," Razanskas tells him. "Or I'm going to come over and kidnap your pig."

Youngblood tells Razanskas to meet him downtown. So the three detectives drive Adrian to Parker Center, which is dark and deserted at this time of night. The detectives, with Adrian in tow, take the elevator to the fourth floor, walk down the quiet, dim hallway, their footsteps echoing on the linoleum. Youngblood tells Razanskas that now his pig-hunting debt has been paid. While the detectives brief him on the case, Adrian is on a bench in the hallway, sound asleep.

The detectives wake Adrian and Youngblood takes him into the polygraph room and hooks him up to the equipment. He tells Adrian, "I didn't always sit behind a desk. I grew up on the streets, too. I know what you're going through. One thing you'll find out about me. I'm very honest. I don't play games. So whatever you do, don't play games with me. If you lie to me, that's exactly what'll be in my report."

"I hope this is accurate," Adrian says.

"There's probably no kind of training I haven't had, including the FBI academy," Youngblood says. "Okay? At this point I don't know if you were out there trying to kill a police officer. I know your natural feeling is to say, 'I don't know nothin' about nothin.' But don't blow it. Don't lie. If you lie—I'll know."

After he asks Adrian some elementary questions—his age, address, place of birth—he asks, "Did you knowingly shoot at police officers?"

"No, sir."

"Did you know police officers were chasing you?"

"Not right away."

"Did you have a gun?"

"After I realized it was the police, I threw it as far as I could throw it."

This is an important admission. For the first time, Adrian acknowledges that he had a gun when he took off running.

"So you had a gun, but you didn't shoot it?"

"Yes."

"When did you throw it?"

"When I hit the second gate."

"Did you shoot to stall for time, so you could get away?"

"No, sir."

For the next half hour Youngblood peppers Adrian with questions. At times, it seems Adrian is on the verge of making a confession, but he ends up holding back.

After Youngblood computes the results, he says to Adrian, "There are three possible results: inconclusive, telling the truth, and deceptive. Your tests comes back deceptive. Conclusively deceptive. Yes, you did fire shots at the officers. I'm not going to lie to you and say you're not in trouble. Attempted murder of a police officer is very serious."

Adrian moans. "This fucking machine. It shouldn't determine someone's fate. I'm going to call my sister. I want to talk to someone else. I'm not talking to you anymore."

At dawn, the detectives decide to take Adrian back to the station for booking. They pull out of Parker Center and drive down Main Street, through Skid Row, as hundreds of homeless people on the sidewalk are arising, crawling out of their cardboard boxes, emerging from beneath piles of blankets and newspapers. The detectives are disappointed Adrian did not admit that he fired the gun. But at least he admitted to Youngblood that he had a gun when he took off running. That might be enough to persuade the D.A. to file attempted murder charges against him.

After they book Adrian, the three detectives return to the scene of the shooting. It is a hot morning, the asphalt is sizzling and the detectives pause to pat their foreheads with handkerchiefs as they search through backyards and alleys, hoping to find the gun that Adrian said he tossed. They have no luck, so they head off to Pepy's for breakfast.

Razanskas' back is aching now, and he can no longer stand straight. He slowly crawls out of the Caprice and, stooping, limps off to the restaurant. Usually he is upbeat after an investigation, even an all-night investigation. The thrill of the chase energizes him. But now he is in pain. He knows that after breakfast, after being up since last night, he has to return to the office and work on some overdue paperwork. Then he plans to drive straight to the chiropractor. He is feeling irritated and unappreciated.

He takes his first sip of coffee, turns to Reyes and says, "This department will use you up like a number-two pencil."

Razanskas is back in the office the next morning at 6 A.M. A few hours later, Masuyama stops by Razanskas' desk and tells him he had to kick Adrian loose. The deputy D.A. decided the case was not strong enough because neither police officer saw the suspect fire the gun. Adrian's failed polygraph exam is irrelevant because the results are not admissible in court.

Masuyama is disappointed and angry. He was awakened before midnight, worked all night on the case, and the next day. And it was all for nothing. He tells Razanskas that police in the

Valley recently have been pursuing thieves who steal bottles from curbside recycling bins.

"They'll prosecute you for stealing garbage," Masuyama says with disgust. "But if you shoot at a cop, you get off."

Razanskas spends the next two days trying to track down the stabber and some of the others involved in the Ruben Gomez murder. A relative of Ramon Sanchez, the college student who was arrested for the murder, gave Razanskas a lead. He had heard that a gangbanger named Elias—he did not know his last name—was the stabber. He also heard that Elias had been arrested for beating his wife in late August.

Razanskas drives over to the 77th Street station and gathers a stack of arrest reports—every spousal abuse arrest in the past three weeks. After he sifts through dozens of reports, he pulls one from the stack and shouts, "I love L.A." He is sure this is the right Elias. He lives in the right neighborhood, was arrested on the right date and is the right age.

Elias' girlfriend stated in the report, "He was punching me in the face and stomach. He dragged me down the sidewalk about 20 feet by the hair. He was beating me like he was hitting a man. I'm three months pregnant. My entire body is sore."

Razanskas throws the report down with disgust and mutters, "What an asshole." He finds Elias' booking photo. His face is bruised and cut. Razanskas figures the bruises are not from the fight with his girlfriend. That was too one-sided. The bruises are from the fight with Ruben Gomez and his brother. This is the suspect Razanskas wants. This suspect, Razanskas believes, was the killer.

He puts the picture in a six-pack and the victim's brother identifies Elias. But the victim's son—who was not a good witness because he quickly fled the murder scene—cannot.

Razanskas presents the case against Elias to a deputy district attorney. But she refuses to file murder charges against Elias, arguing that the D.A.'s office is reluctant to file murder charges on "one-on-one" cases. This is a case where it is the witness's word against the suspect's, and there are no other witnesses or evidence to corroborate either side.

Even if the suspect currently in custody fingers Elias, the D.A. still will not file. She says a jury will assume Sanchez fingered Elias to save himself. Razanskas disagrees with the D.A.'s assessment and figures many other district attorneys in California would have filed on Elias.

South Bureau detectives have been grousing all summer about the D.A.'s filing policies. The detectives think the deputy D.A.s are too cautious, too afraid to risk defeat. Detectives think that the D.A.'s office is more interested in pumping up its conviction statistics than in seeing justice done. But the assistant D.A.s say detectives have such heavy caseloads that the quality of their investigations has deteriorated. The D.A.s argue they do not want to take cases to court that they have no chance of winning.

It is the rare suspect that gets any sympathy from Razanskas. But he feels sorry for Ramon Sanchez. Sanchez, he feels, deserves some prison time. But Sanchez does not deserve to get slam-dunked. He does not deserve to take the fall because someone else used a knife.

Randall Rich, Ramon Sanchez's public defender, is preparing his case in a way he has never prepared before. He is studying his client's college transcripts. Last semester, at Cal State Los Angeles, Sanchez received an A in symbolic logic, Bs in geography and history of Western civilization, and a C in geology. The fall semester is beginning soon and Sanchez's financial aid check is waiting for him at school.

Rich has had a number of sleepless nights because of this case. His client has spent his life being a dutiful son and a good student. He stayed away from gangs. He worked part-time and helped his family pay the bills. He studied hard and went to college. Then he gets into an altercation that ruins his life. Sanchez did not start the fight. He spent an hour trying to flee. Someone else stabbed the victim. But now he is locked up in jail, facing decades in prison. And his only hope is Rich.

Rich feel tremendous pressure. He knows that if he blows this case he will forever be haunted. He believes Sanchez is being overcharged by the district attorney. Sanchez probably should face some jail time, Rich believes, but not a murder rap. Rich recently woke up in the middle of the night, in a cold sweat, and muttered to himself, "Jesus. I have to do right by this guy. I hate to see what'll happen to him in the joint."

On Monday morning, a week after Labor Day, Winn is preparing to testify in the preliminary hearing for her first homicide—the Felipe Angeles Gonzales case. Gonzales was murdered in late March, but after everything Winn has been through this summer, the murder seems years ago.

Winn is worried. Even though she cleared the case, if her investigation does not stand up in court, and the judge refuses to hold the suspects over for trial, all her work will have been for nothing.

At the preliminary hearing, Winn is wearing a peach-colored linen suit and sits with the deputy district attorney. The two suspects, Obie Anthony and Reggie Cole, who are wearing orange jump suits, sit across from her, with their public defenders.

Three witnesses testify against the suspects. A friend of the victim, who also was wounded in the shooting, identifies the two suspects. John Jones, the apartment manager, identifies both suspects and testifies that one of the suspects was shot as he fled the murder scene. A hospital guard testifies that he saw one suspect, whose leg was heavily wrapped, limp into the hospital, with the other suspect supporting him. They both left the hospital when a receiving nurse began questioning them about the wound.

But the suspects' attorneys stress the inconsistencies of the witnesses' statements. The hospital guard had picked out only Anthony from a six-pack photo display, but had picked out both Anthony and Cole from a live lineup last month. He had previously said Anthony was the one who limped into the hospital. Now he says Cole was actually the one who limped and Anthony accompanied him. Cole's public defender acknowledges that his client had been shot in the leg—but the shooting was six years ago in Louisiana, he says, not after the murder.

The apartment manager picked out Anthony and Cole in both the six-pack and the live lineup. But Anthony's public defender points out that the apartment manager is facing criminal charges in an unrelated case and may be cutting a deal in exchange for testifying in this case. The D.A. denies a deal was offered.

Finally, the wounded witness picked Anthony's photograph out of the photo display, but he was unable to identify either suspect in the live lineup last month. And, at the lineup, he picked out one man who was *not* involved in the murder. Now at the preliminary hearing he picks out Cole and Anthony without hesitation.

"As you sit here today in court," Anthony's attorney asks, "do you have some doubt that the man next to me was at the scene?"

"No . . . ," the witness says softly. "I am . . . traumatized by all that happened to us. . . . And even in my dreams those things come to my mind all the time. They appear. I see the people. I see everything all over that happened. And I recognized him."

The judge determines there is enough evidence against the suspects to hold them over for trial.

Winn feels a sense of accomplishment, and relief, as she saunters out of the courthouse and into the morning glare. Now she can rest easy about the case, at least for a few months. She still has to face the final hurdle—the trial.

Unlike the preliminary hearing in the O. J. Simpson case earlier in the summer, with its overflowing courtroom and legion of reporters, only one spectator attends this hearing—Anthony's ex-girlfriend. She pulls $5 out of her purse and gives it to Anthony's attorney, so Anthony will have a few dollars to spend in jail. Anthony, whose hands are shackled, turns to her, before the bailiff leads him away, and mouths, "I love you." She musters a weak smile and mouths, "I love you too."

Chapter 18
An Unfortunate Death Situation

Friday, September 9

Fridays at South Bureau Homicide are devoted to paperwork and report writing. Detectives are allowed to dress casually, allowed to wear, in LAPD jargon, "soft clothes."

Razanskas reluctantly plans to spend the day in the squad room, in the hopes of making some progress on his mountain of paperwork. He is happiest when he is out on the street, and always seems dispirited and bored at his desk. He never can manage to write an entire report in silence. When a detective wanders by, he quickly looks up, grateful for the opportunity to needle someone and get a moment of respite from the tedium of paperwork.

The solitary nature of report writing, however, suits Winn. She is comfortable spending hours hunched over her laptop, lost in thought, crafting her reports. But Winn is getting interrupted more frequently these days. The other detectives have discovered she is an expert at analyzing checking records and banking transactions, at detecting forgery and fraud. She mastered these skills at bunco forgery, and now detectives frequently stop by her desk for advice.

On this Friday, Lieutenant Robleto wanders by and notices Winn and Razanskas are both wearing jeans and cowboy boots. He stops and puts his hands on his hips. "If I catch her chewing," he says to Razanskas, "you're out of here." Winn tells Robleto that her cowboy boots bear little resemblance to Razanskas'. She did not buy them at some cheap western store, she tells the lieutenant. She paid $625 for her black lizard boots at a tony Brentwood bootery.

When the lieutenant returns to his office, Razanskas tells Winn he has an idea. For the next few minutes, they huddle in a corner, whisper, nod their heads and laugh.

After lunch, Winn walks into the lieutenant's office, as all the detectives in the bureau watch. A Skoal can is outlined against her jean pocket and she is carrying the plastic cup Razanskas uses for spitting. She asks the lieutenant a question about one of her cases and, in an exaggerated motion, spits into the cup. The lieutenant jumps out of his chair and waves his hands in mock outrage. He throws her out of his office. The detectives in the squad room burst out laughing.

Winn struts back to her desk. She and Razanskas grin at each other. They exchange a high five.

Razanskas' high spirits do not last long. Robleto stops by his desk, on his way out, and reminds Razanskas that he has several 60-dayers that are long overdue.

"I want those sixty-dayers and I want them soon," Robleto says, tapping a forefinger on Razanskas' desk.

Robleto takes the 60-dayers very seriously. He was a homicide detective himself once, and now he is a demanding lieutenant with exacting standards. After he reviews a 60-dayer, he sends it downtown to LAPD headquarters. If a detective is late on a 60-dayer, that means the lieutenant also is late. It makes him and his unit look bad. Robleto needs the 60-dayers to stay apprised of unsolved cases. It enables him to ensure that detectives are not letting their investigations slide. And, ultimately, it enables him to ensure that his unit is upholding their responsibility to the victims' families.

Razanskas digs out a few old murder books and a legal pad.

He writes for a few minutes, looking forlorn and out of his element. He stops, stands up, stretches and turns to Winn.

"Paperwork," he says with distaste. "I hate this bullshit."

In mid-September, not long after American troops land in Haiti in order to restore democracy, a group of community activists call for an invasion of South-Central. South-Central, they argue, needs U.S. troops as much as any foreign country. People are afraid to leave their houses at night. Police cannot control the gangbangers and criminals.

A local physician who heads the group suggests that former President Jimmy Carter—who negotiated an agreement with Haiti's military leaders—and retired General Colin L. Powell come to South-Central and warn the criminals that the Army is on the way. Carter also could use his diplomatic skills to ease tensions between Latinos and blacks.

Clinton should initiate in South-Central something similar to the Marshall Plan, the doctor argues. If the United States could finance the rebuilding of Germany after World War II, it also has a responsibility to finance the long-term rehabilitation of South-Central.

Although this call for an army occupation is largely symbolic, it underscores the way many in South-Central feel. They know the nation is spending billions in foreign aid. They also know that politicians do not have the will to improve conditions in South-Central. Nor are they willing to spend much money here. What people are saying is: *We have a crisis here. But nobody cares. So do something. Even if it means making the neighborhood an armed camp.*

The hysteria over the O.J. case is growing, and, for once, South Bureau detectives are grateful their work is largely ignored. An article by Robert Shapiro, Simpson's defense attorney, has been Xeroxed and passed around the squad room.

"To describe an unfortunate death situation, I use the term, 'a horrible human event,' " Shapiro wrote in an article for a criminal defense lawyer magazine. "Come up with phrases that you believe in and are comfortable saying. Repeat them continuously, and they will be repeated by the media. After awhile, the repetition almost becomes a fact. That is your ultimate goal."

Now, when a South Bureau detective picks up a gruesome murder, he sarcastically refers to it as "a horrible human event" or "an unfortunate death situation."

The unrelenting barrage of Simpson news has unnerved Erlinda Acuna. There is so much talk about murder, she constantly is reminded of her son's murder. When she hears people criticize the detectives involved in the Simpson case, she wonders if the homicide detectives who investigated her son's murder made a mistake.

At Loved Ones of Homicide Victims, Acuna's friends urge her to stop trying to solve the murder. It already has *been* solved, they tell her.

But Gizmo, the man convicted of her son's murder, has been writing to her all summer from prison and continues to insist he is innocent. Acuna's friends at Loved Ones say this is just a scam. They tell her to ignore the letters. But Acuna cannot ignore them until she is sure.

She is still disturbed by Gizmo's claim that Ernie's cousin Donna knows he is innocent. Acuna has put it off for months, but at the end of the summer, she finally calls Donna. And now, on a bright, breezy afternoon, she nervously awaits Donna's arrival. While she waits, she talks about Ernie's death.

The family had been living in South Gate, a working-class neighborhood on the outskirts of Los Angeles. But when Acuna and her husband—Ernie's stepfather—divorced, she and her children moved in with her mother. Her mother, who owns a small house a few miles south of downtown, warned her not to return to the neighborhood. She told her it had changed since she was in high school. In those days the two rival neighborhood gangs, Primera Flats and Clanton, used to fight. Now the neighborhood gangs spray the streets with bullets. The gangs will cause problems for your children, her mother warned her.

The small house is in the back of a lot behind another house. Acuna, her five children and her mother share the tight quarters, and the house is filled with the clutter of young children. The living room and hallways are strewn with toys, basketballs, schoolbooks, jump ropes, homework papers, pencils, erasers, lunchboxes.

Now, Acuna says, tears streaming down her face, her mother blames her for Ernie's death. But at the time she felt she had no choice but to move back home. She had no money and nowhere else to go.

In South Gate, Ernie was a good student and played on the freshman football team. During the summer he spent his days at the park playing baseball. But in his new neighborhood, no one seemed to care about sports. Many of the boys were members of the Ghetto Boyz, and their interests were limited to selling crack and gangbanging.

As soon as Ernie moved to the neighborhood, the Ghetto Boyz tried to recruit him. But Ernie was afraid of the gangbangers. He stayed inside after school and played video games. He always had been close with his mother and he helped her raise the younger children. Ernie was so obedient some of Acuna's friends thought he was a mama's boy.

Acuna was a teenager when she became pregnant with Ernie. Her boyfriend wanted her to get an abortion. She refused and he left her. Ernie met his father only once. Ernie and his mother were eating hamburgers at a Carl's Jr. when his father wandered by. Acuna introduced him to his son, who was 12 at the time. They shook hands, but Ernie was too shy to say anything.

After Ernie met his father, he would stop his uncle—his father's brother—when he spotted him on the street. "I want to see my dad," he would tell him. "You know where he's at. Tell him to come around." His uncle promised to pass along the message. Ernie was angry and hurt that his father, who was now married and had three children, never made the effort to see him. Acuna recognized that her son was in great need of a father figure, so she called Big Brothers. But she was told Ernie was too old for the program.

Every time Ernie left the house in his new neighborhood, a group of Ghetto Boyz who hung out at the park across the street would yell at him, call him a punk or a buster. They would shout, "You better get *in* with the Boyz or *out* of the neighborhood." Sometimes they would try to rough him up as he passed by.

Five months after Ernie moved to the neighborhood, he finally relented. But he did not join the gang because of the daily hazing. Acuna believes he relented because of his cousin, Mario. Mario, who lived next door and was five years older than Ernie, was a member of the Ghetto Boyz. Ernie looked up to him. He became the father figure Ernie had been searching for.

In January, Ernie was jumped into the gang. Four months later he was killed.

Although several witnesses testified against Gizmo, there was some confusion after the shooting and at the trial. Gizmo was a member of 29th Street, a gang that was at war with the Ghetto Boyz. Gizmo and his best friend, TC, another member of 29th Street, look so much alike many people confuse the two. At the trial, Gizmo's attorney showed a photograph to a witness and asked if this was the killer. The witness said yes. The attorney asked if the person in the photograph was in the courtroom. The witness pointed to Gizmo. The picture, however, was of TC.

After Acuna received a few letters from Gizmo, she talked to a Ghetto Boyz *veterano*. He had never talked with police, but he told Acuna he saw the murder from a distance and he thought it was TC who did the shooting.

Acuna believes Donna is the only one who can clear up the confusion. She was there. She can identify all the gangbangers in the neighborhood.

Donna arrives in the late afternoon, carrying her 3-year-old boy. On her right hand, just above the knuckle, she has a tattoo: "ERNIE R.I.P." Donna sits on the sofa, lifts her son onto her lap and looks up at Acuna.

"You know that Gizmo's making me crazy," Acuna says.

Donna nods.

"I need to know if you're sure," Acuna asks. "Then I can be sure."

"I'm sure."

Donna tells Acuna it was a Thursday night, about 10 o'clock, when she and three friends were "kicking it" at the park. She saw Ernie standing on the sidewalk, leaning over and talking to some friends in a car. A girl was sitting on the hood.

"I saw a car come by real slow. It was a 280Z. It was red and it had primer on it. At first, I thought it was a friend of Ernie's. Gizmo got out of the car and asked Ernie, 'Where you from?' Ernie just looked at him. Gizmo said, 'Fuck the Ghetto . . . '

"That's when Gizmo shot him. I ran toward Ernie and stopped at the sidewalk. I saw Gizmo with a black gun. Ernie tried to crawl and to get up. Gizmo yelled, 'You going to die, *puto*.' He shot him a few more times while Ernie was on the ground."

Acuna goes limp in her chair, likes a marionette whose strings have been cut. She sits in silence for a few minutes. Finally she asks Donna, "You sure it was Gizmo?"

Donna nods. "I was on the sidewalk, only a few feet away. They were under a streetlight. I could see real good."

The girl who was sitting on the hood of the car was the witness who confused Gizmo and TC in court. Acuna tells Donna that if one witness confused them, maybe she made a mistake, too.

Donna reminds her that at the trial, when the defense attorney showed her a picture of TC, she was not confused, like the other witness. She did not say it was Gizmo, like the other witness. She told the defense attorney the man in the picture was TC.

"That girl's not from around here," Donna tells Acuna. "If you've never seen either of them, you could confuse them. But I know them. And I know all about Gizmo. I was friends with a girl who knew him. I use to hang at her house and Gizmo used to try to pick up on me. I know him. He's with 29th Street. I know they look alike, but I can tell them apart. TC looks a little Chinese and has lighter skin than Gizmo. Gizmo looks part black."

Acuna asks her about the letter Gizmo wrote. He claimed he talked with Donna on the telephone and that she knows he is not guilty.

"He's full of shit," Donna says. "I did talk to him on the phone. He kept saying that it wasn't him. I just told him, 'I know what I saw. And I saw you.' "

Acuna thinks about what Donna has said. She stares out the window, nodding.

Donna lived with Acuna and her children for six months before Ernie's death. She and Ernie became very close. "When I went to court, Gizmo's homies said to me, 'You a fucking rat. We going to get you.' People called me at home and said, 'You going to die, bitch.'

"Even the Ghetto Boyz didn't want me to testify. They said they'd take care of it themselves. But I loved Ernie. He was my cousin." She dabs at her eyes with a tissue. "I could of been like everyone else around here and refuse to talk to the cops. That would be the easiest thing to do.

"After I talked to the detectives, I was scared to walk the streets. Not for myself, but for my family. I was scared that 29th Street would go after them for revenge. But I wouldn't let it slide. I wanted to see some justice. For Ernie."

She runs a hand through her hair and looks up at the ceiling for a moment. "You ask me if I'm sure. Well, I wouldn't go through all this if I wasn't sure. If I put an innocent man in prison, I wouldn't be able to sleep. But I know it was Gizmo."

Donna leaves and Acuna slumps in her chair. She is exhausted. Her health has deteriorated since Ernie's death. She is always tired and now takes medication for high blood pressure.

A few days after Ernie was killed, his best friend avenged his death. He killed a 29th Street gangbanger called Chopper. Ernie's friend, who was 15, was arrested and is now serving a murder sentence at a juvenile facility.

Ernie was killed across the street from where Acuna and her children live. Every day Acuna, who still cannot afford to move, feels a twinge, a tightness in her chest when she passes the spot. But she made sure her two teenage sons will not share Ernie's fate. They now live with their father in the suburban San Gabriel Valley.

When Acuna's mother returns from work, they talk about what Donna has said. Acuna tells her mother she feels better now. She is less confused. She is sure Gizmo was the killer. But she tells her mother, after a long pause, she still is not 100 percent sure. Maybe 90 percent sure.

She decides that her next step will be to fill out the prison visiting form that Gizmo sent her. She will visit Gizmo. She will ask him if he killed her son.

Chapter 19
Slick

Monday, September 19

The last week of summer is finally here and Razanskas and Winn are number one on the on-call list.

Everything is ready for his hunting trip, he tells Winn, except one thing—his back. So he plans to squeeze in a few more visits to the chiropractor.

Last week Razanskas cleaned out his freezer and brought Winn a half-dozen packages of frozen venison and antelope sausage—the final remains from last year's hunt.

On Monday morning, Winn tells Razanskas, "That sausage has it going *on*. I've been eating it all weekend. I never tasted sausage that tasty."

He beams. "When I kill Bambi next week, I'll bring you another batch."

Late Monday afternoon, after work, the chiropractor is manipulating Razanskas' back when he suddenly stops. "Is that your beeper?" the chiropractor asks. Razanskas checks. The message is the phone number at South Bureau Homicide and the number 187. He slips on his shirt, slides off the table and heads back on the freeway.

He meets Winn at the Southeast station at 6 o'clock, and they drive over to a house on East 94th Street. Lieutenant Fletcher and the night watch detectives are standing on the sidewalk, about to give them the rundown. But before Fletcher begins, Razanskas crouches right where they are standing and picks up a small plug of something that looks like brown paper. The uniformed officers, the night watch detectives, the lieutenant and Winn had all missed it.

It is shotgun wadding from the murder weapon.

A man was sitting on the porch at a friend's house. A Cadillac slowed in front of the house, the driver pulled out a shotgun and blasted the victim in the chest. He died at the hospital.

Razanskas and Winn search the street for evidence. It is almost dusk now, cool and misty, with a hint of fall in the air. Summer is coming to an end and the days are getting shorter. The sun sinks toward the ocean, the dying light soft and diffuse, the light of fall, not the sharp, harsh light of midsummer. Jets crisscross the darkening sky, leaving gauzy white contrails behind them.

Many of the houses on the street have a down-at-the-heels, countrified feel to them, with patches of dirt instead of lawns, and large dogs that kick up swirls of dust and snarl and slobber at the front gates. A man who lives across the street from the murder scene works under the hood of his car and pays little attention to the detectives. Children roller skate along the edges of the yellow crime-scene tape. A uniformed officer plays with a puppy that has crawled beneath his squad car.

Razanskas spots a few shotgun shells scattered in the street and circles them with chalk. He and Winn walk up to the front porch of a narrow, mustard-colored house with chipped and peeling paint and a few withered rose bushes in front. Razanskas finds more shotgun wadding on the porch. Next to the heavy metal security door is a sign: *No Jehovah's Witnesses.* A wall is stippled with tiny blood drops gleaming under the porch light. The detectives walk inside and see that the living room carpet is smeared with blood, where someone dragged the body from the porch. Razanskas searches a bedroom facing the street and spots an enormous green Gumby riddled with shotgun pellets. He hoists Gumby over his shoulder and carries it out to his squad car. He wants the shotgun pellets for evidence.

Fletcher tells Razanskas and Winn that the night watch detectives took a few witnesses back to the station. He asks who wants to interview them. Razanskas points to Winn. "Ask her. She's running the show tonight. She's the boss."

Winn, who is the primary, decides she will do the interviews and drives back to the station. Razanskas will finish up at the scene.

A witness named Darryl tells Winn that he was at his girlfriend's house when the victim—Erick Johnson—and his friend Cornel stopped by. The three of them were on the porch, drinking beer and talking about the upcoming Monday night football game. He cannot give Winn a good description of the man who shot Erick. "Erick was no gangbanger," Darryl tells Winn. "A bunch of gangbangers usually hang out on the curb near the house, but they weren't there today. This guy in the Caddy was probably lookin' for 'em."

Winn signs on to a computer and checks out Johnson's record. He is not listed in the computerized gang file. He was 27 years old and he had never been arrested. Now she believes Darryl.

She brings Cornel into an interview room. He is wearing blue shorts, a white T-shirt and has two diamond stud earrings. His front teeth are rimmed with gold dental work. He is from New Orleans, he tells Winn, and he moved to Los Angeles five years ago. "I met Erick in the neighborhood," he tells Winn. "I was new, but Erick grew up here. He helped me out. He told me to watch out for this and that, to stay away from this place and that."

"You into gangs?" Winn asks him.

"Naw. I'm thirty-two. I got three kids."

"Tell me what you saw," Winn says.

"I was walking down the driveway to the front gate when I saw a Cadillac slow down. It pulled even with the gate. The driver's window went down. I looked right into the driver's face. Then I saw the barrel of the shotgun. The driver was holding it. The car never actually stopped. It just cruised real slow. I heard four shots. Boom. Boom. Boom. Boom. I couldn't hear anything for a few minutes afterwards. The shooter looked right at me. I was that close."

Cornel is still shaken by the murder. He closes his eyes and drops his head to his knees for a moment. He tells Winn the driver had a round, fat face. His hair was short, almost bald, and he had a pencil-thin mustache. He was in his mid-20s. His chest and arms were thickset, muscular. Cornel got such a good look at the shooter's face Winn decides to set him up with a police artist so they can create a composite drawing.

Cornel also gives Winn a detailed description of the shooter's Cadillac. It was a white four-door sedan DeVille, an older model. The car had original Cadillac hubcaps, but the tires were distinctive, Cornel tells Winn. They are made by a company called Vogue Tyres. They are white walls with a narrow gold strip bordering the white.

Winn knows she has found a rare and valuable commodity—a cooperative eye witness with a good memory. Cornel tells Winn that Erick Johnson was a close friend of his. He wants to help her, he says, anyway he can.

Winn and Fletcher drive over to see the victim's mother, who lives a few blocks from the shooting. It is dark now, the moon is almost full, and a cool breeze is blowing in from the ocean. The mother already has heard the news, and she is surrounded by her other children. The walls of her small house are covered with portraits of Jesus, a photograph of Erick holding his newborn son, and pictures of her children and grandchildren and their athletic trophies.

"They taking a life today like it's nothin'," the mother tells Winn. "It's too much around here. Too, too much." She collapses onto the sofa and buries her head into a pillow as her children try to comfort her. Winn crouches by the sofa. "I'm very sorry for your loss," Winn tells her. "We're doing everything we can. In fact, we're going out right now to follow up on some leads."

Razanskas is still busy at the homicide scene, so Winn and Fletcher decide to look for the Cadillac. They cruise around the neighborhood, driving slowly so they can see the cars parked in driveways and open garages and backyards. Winn and Fletcher take note of the graffiti on the sides of garages and, after studying which gang names have been crossed out and which names were spray-painted above, determine that three gangs in the area are at war—Main Street Crips, Q-102 Crips and 97 Street Crips. This is not unusual because some Crip sets fight each other in addition to fighting Blood sets. But most Bloods save their hostility for Crips.

"This is a solver," Winn says to Fletcher. "Our wit got a good-ass look at that Cadillac, right down to the tires. I want to arrest that motherfucker by this weekend."

They drive around the neighborhood for a few minutes, when a call comes crackling over the lieutenant's radio: "Ten shots fired. Two down. 118th and Main." The Erick Johnson murder will have to wait. Fletcher and Winn turn onto Main and speed south, past tire shops that sell retreads and stay open until midnight; past soul-food restaurants, taco stands and Salvadoran markets; past liquor stores, where men congregate out front, smoking and drinking malt liquor out of paper bags; past boarded-up, graffiti-strewn storefront churches and vacant lots. They speed beneath the Century Freeway overpass; past a stand of luxuriant, pungent eucalyptus trees, an anomalous sylvan touch amid the industry and asphalt, and pull up in front of an apartment building, its sides covered with graffiti, surrounded by a rusted, sagging chain-link fence.

A wounded man is on the street, covered with blood. A friend stands over him shouting, "Where's the ambulance? Where's the damn ambulance?" Another friend paces back and forth and yells, "I'm getting the fuck out of L.A.!"

A sergeant at the scene tells Fletcher and Winn that two men had just returned from the store and parked in front of their apartment. A car pulled up next to them and the passenger jumped out. He aimed his .45 into the driver's window and began firing. The victim in the street was shot in the buttocks. A roommate carried the other victim, who was hit in the back and the side, to their apartment.

Winn and Fletcher enter the apartment. The victim is on the kitchen floor, his T-shirt covered with blood. His breaths are short and hoarse. His roommate is crouching next to him, whispering in his ear, "Keep breathing! Keep it going, baby."

The television is still on and the Monday night football game is blaring. The Dallas Cowboys and the Detroit Lions are tied, there are seconds left in the game and Detroit is lining up for the winning field goal.

"You got to fight, baby!" the roommate whispers to the victim, whose breathing is becoming more labored. "Come on, dog. Don't fade on me. Breathe, baby."

The paramedics rush into the room, strip off the victim's shirt, pump his chest and place an oxygen mask over his mouth. Fletcher puts an arm around the roommate, leads him out of the kitchen and says softly, "They're doing the best they can."

At the moment a Dallas player blocks a 57-yard field goal attempt, and the crowd roars, the victim's eyes flutter. His chest stops heaving. He is dead.

The paramedics wheel the victim out of the living room as Detroit and Dallas line up for the overtime kickoff.

A neighbor tells Fletcher and Winn that the victim was 20 years old and he used to be a Rollin 20. But he found religion last year and moved into this apartment. The victim's four roommates are all deeply religious and they held Bible study sessions several nights a week. The victim's Bible is still in the back seat of the car.

Razanskas arrives at the scene and tells Winn they caught a break on the Erick Johnson murder. A man driving a van, a few blocks from the murder, clipped a motorcycle, Razanskas tells her. Neighbors began beating the driver and police arrived. A few minutes later, an anonymous female called the Southeast Division station. She told the desk officer that the shooter from the East 94th Street murder was riding the motorcycle that had been clipped. She told him where he lived.

Officers pick up the suspect and his brother, because Cornel said there had been a passenger in the Cadillac. At midnight, Razanskas and Winn take Polaroid photographs of the two suspects at the Southeast station and put together a six-pack. They drive to the box factory in East Los Angeles where Cornel works the graveyard shift. But the foreman tells them they just missed

Cornel. He had tried to work, but he was too upset and asked for the rest of the night off. The detectives return to the station, call Cornel at home and ask him to stop by and look at some six-packs.

While Razanskas is waiting for Cornel, he walks out to the car and carries the four-foot stuffed Gumby to the squad room. A motorcycle officer spots Razanskas, screeches to a halt and shouts, "You've finally found your calling—Sesame Street."

Razanskas lays Gumby on his desk and says to Winn, "I'm doing the autopsy now." She ignores him.

"I'm serious," he says. "Those shotgun pellets are evidence."

He probes Gumby with his fingers and circles several spots with a black marking pen. "Multiple gunshots wounds to Gumby's legs," he calls out, like a medical examiner listing his findings. "One through and through. One no-exit wound." With a penknife he makes a few cuts. "One incision in Gumby's left leg; one incision in Gumby's right leg," he calls out.

Two women from the cleaning crew, who speak no English, are mystified. They stop emptying trash cans and watch Razanskas work. He sticks a hand in an incision and digs through the stuffing for a few minutes. Finally, he finds a few shotgun pellets. When he is through, he lays Gumby out on the floor and places his Beretta next to Gumby's hand. He takes a Polaroid of Gumby with the gun. He plans to make up a gag wanted poster with the headline: "Who Shot Gumby?"

Cornel arrives at 3:15 A.M., along with Erick Johnson's girlfriend, who is the mother of his two young children. She is wearing purple house slippers.

"It's like a dream," she tells Winn as she puts a trembling hand over her mouth. "It doesn't seem real. Me and Erick got a little girl and a little boy. There's no way I can break it down to them."

Winn takes Polaroid photographs of the suspects in custody, compiles a few six-packs and takes Cornel to an interview room to sift through them. But she is not optimistic because neither suspect fits Cornel's description of the shooter. She is right. Cornel does not pick out either of them. The tipster either heard a bogus rumor or was trying to set up the suspect.

As long as they are in custody, Winn figures she might as well question them. They live just a few blocks from the shooting. They're dressed like gangbangers and might know something.

Winn and Razanskas drag chairs into the interview cubicle.

"You ever been arrested?" she asks the younger brother.

"No."

She shakes her head. "I *know* you've been arrested. I ran your rap sheet."

He smiles sheepishly. "Okay. I've been arrested. But I've never been arrested at *this* station."

She glares at the brothers. "Let's get something straight. I don't want any more lies. If you lie to me, I'll come down on you two like a vengeance."

The detectives take the older brother into a separate interview room. Winn says to him, "Read my lips. You got eight thousand dollars in warrants out for your arrest. You must have a lot of traffic tickets. Now I'm very interested in solving this murder. You understand what I'm sayin'?"

He nods.

"You hear about that murder on 94th Street?"

"I don't affiliate with people involved in that."

"I don't care who you *affiliate* with," Winn says. She describes the shooter and she describes his Cadillac.

"You know anyone like that?" she asks.

"Yeah, I think I seen the guy around. But I don't know his name. I don't know where he stay at. But you cut me loose, I'll try to find out for you."

Winn stands up. "I'm going to leave you alone in here for a while. Maybe that'll refresh your memory."

She and Razanskas return in ten minutes. "Your memory any better now?" she asks him. "You decided whether you want to spend the night in jail or at home?"

He nods. "I think I know the guy you want. They call him Slick." He does not know Slick's name or where he lives. But Winn is satisfied. This might be enough.

Winn studies him for a moment and says, "If you screw us on this, I'll come looking for you. You don't want that. You *definitely* don't want that."

"No, man. I'm telling you what I know."

Winn and Razanskas take the man and his brother back to their neighborhood, but drop them two blocks from home so no neighbors will see them with detectives. Back at the bureau, Winn checks the computerized gang moniker file. She finds a number of gangsters named Slick, but they live in the wrong neighborhood, drive the wrong car or do not fit the physical description. One of the last listings, however, looks promising. He is a Main Street Crip and his street names are Devil, Slickdog and Slick. Winn checks his arrest record.

"Yesss," she shouts.

She walks over to Razanskas' desk. "This one looks *real* good," she tells him, waving Slick's four-page rap sheet. "He's been arrested several times for armed robbery. He was arrested for carrying a gun. Right down the street from the shooting. And he was picked up not long ago driving a car. Guess what kind?"

"A Cadillac," Razanskas says.

"Yes. A Cadillac," Winn says. "White. Four-door. Sedan DeVille."

Winn tells Razanskas that she plans to get a booking photo of Slick and see if Cornel can identify him.

It is now 8 A.M. They have worked straight through the night. Razanskas tells Winn he is starving and invites her to join him at Pepy's. Although she does not like to start the day with a heavy breakfast, and is not fond of Pepy's, she is hungry, and in such a good mood now after tracking down Slick that she agrees to join Razanskas. They drive off to Pepy's on a chilly overcast morning without a hint of sun. It feels more like January than September. Razanskas' eyes are bloodshot and the lids heavy. He has an unhealthy gray pallor. His back aches and he fidgets in his seat as he drives, trying to get comfortable.

"We've got about five new trainees coming in during the next few weeks," he tells her. "I'm going to ask the lieutenant to give me one of them."

Winn had been yawning, but this jolts her awake. She casts a nervous glance at him.

"I'm going to be up front with the lieutenant," he says. "I'm going to tell him that you're ready to go out on your own. You're at that level now."

At a stoplight he grabs a pinch of Skoal, the wintergreen smell filling the squad car. "I have to tell you, you've made the fastest progress of any trainee I've ever had. You don't need a supervisor any more. You're ready for your own partner."

Winn is embarrassed and does not respond. They drive in silence for a few minutes.

During breakfast neither talks about their partnership, which will soon be coming to a close. It is a subject that could elicit emotion. And since neither is comfortable with emotion, they avoid the topic.

They return to the bureau at 9:30. She asks him, "Should we call it a day?"

"Don't ask me," he says. "This is your case. You're on your own now."

She nods. "Let's go home."

Chapter 20
Wyoming

Wednesday, September 21

Winn and Razanskas are back in the bureau the next morning at 6 A.M. She obtains a booking photo of Slick, compiles a six-pack and shows it to Cornel in the afternoon. He immediately points to the photograph in the top left corner—Slick's photograph. Winn is so caught up in the chase that she takes the murder book home with her Wednesday night. She plans to spend the evening writing the warrant for Slick's arrest.

Razanskas has three 60-dayers that are long overdue, and the lieutenants want them completed before Razanskas leaves for his hunting trip. The 60-dayer from the body dump case he picked up in the beginning of the summer is two weeks overdue. A car-jacking case from the spring is two months overdue. And a street shooting case from early spring is four months overdue.

Razanskas missed a night's sleep on Monday and he is still exhausted. He is having a hard time keeping his eyes open Wednesday morning when he hunches over his desk and begins scrawling a 60-dayer on a yellow legal pad. He writes a few paragraphs, but gets sidetracked by a four-year-old murder case that he cleared earlier in the summer when he picked up the suspect in Oregon. The preliminary hearing is scheduled for next week. He will be hunting, but he has to make a few phone calls and ensure that the witnesses will be available to testify.

Razanskas does not expect to get much sleep this week. Masuyama and Reyes are on the weekday rotation, which means Razanskas is on call again.

Most murder calls come in the middle of the night. But Razanskas catches a break. Masuyama and Reyes pick up a case midmorning on Wednesday, right after Razanskas returns from breakfast at Pepy's.

The three detectives meet in the driveway, in the shade of an enormous avocado tree, next to the victim's apartment. The detectives have to watch where they walk to avoid the overripe avocados that have splattered on the cement.

The victim is a 17-year-old Belizean who was stabbed several times on the sidewalk in front of his apartment. Hc staggered down the street and banged on an apartment door for help. The woman who lived there refused to let him in, but she did call paramedics. The victim staggered back to his apartment and neighbors directed the paramedics to his house. He died at the hospital.

The detectives linger by the victim's front door, which is facing the alley. Razanskas says to Masuyama, "If he lived here alone the place is yours. If he has a roommate and the roommate is a suspect, you need a search warrant."

Masuyama, who is the primary, talks to some neighbors and determines that the victim lived alone and his street name is Sugar. The front door to Sugar's apartment is open and the detectives look inside. The small apartment is strewn with dirty clothes, videotapes are scattered in the bedroom, and dirty dishes fill the sink. The television is still on. In the kitchen, there is a single drop of blood on the linoleum floor.

Masuyama leafs through Sugar's telephone book. He finds the listings for both the suspect, Alton, and the victim, Bernard, in the Belizean body dump case that he picked up in July. He now suspects that the murder is drug-related.

Masuyama approaches a man who lives in the apartment next door and asks, "Did you see him after he was stabbed?"

"Yeah. He came staggering back to his apartment. I kept asking him, 'Who juked you? Who juked you?' He told me, 'I know his face, but I don't know his name.' "

Razanskas is not surprised. He knows that the knife is an intimate weapon, and many stabbing victims know their killers.

The neighbor looks shaken. He wipes the sweat off his forehead with a palm. "He asked me for some water. But I wouldn't give him any. I didn't think it would be good for him."

Razanskas, Masuyama and Reyes walk outside, into the morning glare, and slip on their sunglasses. This is the cusp of the morning, when soft ocean breezes and wispy clouds give way to a dry, baking heat. They study the spot on the sidewalk where Sugar was stabbed and crouch beside a pool of blood oozing onto the lawn.

The detectives follow the blood drops down the sidewalk, past low-slung apartment buildings and brown lawns. In the distance, smog shrouds the hazy contour of the Coliseum. Following the blood drops is slow, careful work because there are so many berry, paint and chocolate stains on the sidewalk that have to be dismissed. They follow the trail to an apartment, where Sugar banged on the door and asked for help. There is a large red smear on a wall by the door. This is where Sugar leaned for support. The detectives follow a few drops of blood to a dirt alley, behind the apartment. The alley is filled with cigarette lighters, plastic bags and small glass pipes.

"I don't want anyone to think drugs were consumed here," Razanskas says sarcastically. "That would be an unfair conclusion."

They come to a section of the alley directly behind Sugar's apartment. There is an eight-foot high fence separating the alley from the apartment. The trail of blood has ended. The detectives cannot figure out how Sugar got back to his apartment so quickly. "I'll be goddamned," Razanskas mutters. He spots a few bloodstains on the fence. He motions to Masuyama. "This guy actually jumped the fence after he was stabbed."

They return to the apartment and Masuyama calls in the victim's name to the bureau. He discovers Sugar was a drug dealer with a no-bail warrant out for his arrest. The detectives talk to a few of Sugar's neighbors and friends. Now they understand how he picked up his nickname: Sugar has three girlfriends. One had his baby two weeks ago. Another is eight months pregnant. A third lives a few blocks away. The detectives return to Sugar's apartment, and while they discuss his active love life in wonderment, a fourth woman calls. She tells Masuyama she met Sugar yesterday and wants to talk to him.

Lieutenant Fletcher walks in and tells Razanskas to return to the bureau and get to work on his 60-dayers. Masuyama and Reyes, Fletcher tells him, can finish up.

On Friday morning, September 23, the first day of fall, the autumnal equinox, Razanskas bounds into the office. He is so excited about his hunting trip, so relieved summer is finally over, that he cannot concentrate for more than a few minutes at a time. He tells anyone in the squad room who will listen about the hunting trip, the route he will take to Wyoming, the weather he expects, the beauty of high country, his new spotting scope that he will try out.

In the early afternoon, he finishes the second of the three 60-dayers that are long overdue. The last one will have to wait until he returns from Wyoming. He slips away from the bureau and visits an officer at the Southwest Division, one of his hunting buddies. When they meet in the parking lot, both are grinning.

At the end of his shift, Winn takes him to the Southeast Division station, where his truck is parked. Winn drives east on Vernon, past check-cashing shops, used-car lots, vendors selling oranges at street corners, empty lots where buildings were torched during the riots and never rebuilt.

Razanskas takes a pinch of Skoal, surveys the surroundings and says, "I can already smell that sage. I'm already starting to forget about 60-dayers, subpoenas and murder books."

She pulls up in the Southeast Division parking lot. They shake hands.

"Have a great time," she says.

He climbs out of the car and gives her the thumbs-up sign.

On Monday morning, Razanskas pulls his red Toyota pickup truck with the oversized tires into his driveway. His hunting gear is neatly packed in boxes, stored in the garage. His Finnish deer hunting rifle—a .270-caliber Sako—his backup rifle and his ammunition are stored in huge metal gun safes.

He lives in a tract of 1970s split-level ranch-style homes, about 45 minutes south of Los Angeles. He walks back and forth from the garage to the truck, loading his hunting clothes, field knives, sleeping bag, binoculars, down jacket, boots, thermal underwear, water jugs, propane lantern, canteen, backpack. He chatters as he packs. He talks about the pocket of aspen trees where he and his buddies set up camp every year. He talks about how much he enjoys waking before dawn, perching on a hillside, waiting for deer and watching the sunrise.

Later, his wife Ada talks about how he wears down over the course of a year, how much good the hunting trip does him. By the end of summer, she sees how pale and drawn he looks, how much weight he has lost, how little energy he has. She is grateful he has something that can rejuvenate him. His sense of humor, she feels, relieves the daily stress of the job. The hunting trip relieves the cumulative stress.

She is a nurse and understands the nature of his work. Still, when they first married, she had a hard time adjusting. He would be gone 24 hours, sometimes 48 hours. He never had time to call home. On extraditions, he would be out of town for days. When he had to serve warrants, he would be up at 2 or 3 A.M.

She learned to compromise. And Razanskas, after two failed marriages, also learned to compromise. Now, when he is busy, she stays busy by spending more time at work and attending conferences. He tries to work less overtime and fewer weekends.

Still, she worries about his health, and she worries about the danger on the street. She wants him to retire. Sometimes, when he is tired and frustrated by the job, he talks about leaving the LAPD and moving to Colorado. But when he returns home strutting, after he has cleared a case, she knows he will not be ready to retire for years.

When Razanskas finishes loading his truck, he drives to a cop friend's house in Downey, where his hunting buddies are meeting. His friend tells him there were seven murders in South Bureau over the weekend. Razanskas claps him on the back and says, "That's the last talk about murder I want to hear for the next few weeks. All I want to talk about now is hunting."

It is midafternoon now, warm and muggy with billowing clouds overhead. Hurricane Olivia is hovering off Baja, blowing hot, humid air up the coast. Razanskas figures if they drive straight through, with only breaks for meals, they will arrive at their camp by nightfall tomorrow.

Razanskas drives off, his hunting buddies in a pickup truck right behind him. They pull onto a freeway ramp, past a man holding a sign: *Homeless and Hungry—Will Work For Food.* The clouds and heavy smog coalesce, blotting out the sun and creating an eerie midafternoon twilight.

Razanskas drives north for fifteen minutes, and when he pulls onto the Pomona Freeway and heads east, he pumps a fist in the air. He is on his way now. He will be out of the smog and into the bracing, pristine air of the high desert in a few hours, and then he will traverse Nevada and Utah and Colorado, head into the Rocky Mountains and on to Wyoming.

Chapter 21
Face to Face

Monday, September 26

Razanskas is gone, but his partnership with Winn is not over yet. She knows they will work at least one more homicide together when he returns. Then she will have to find a new partner.

On the Monday Razanskas leaves for Wyoming, Winn is trying to track down Slick. She discovers through utility records that his last address was his sister's house on 113th Street. He is not living there anymore, but she has driven by a number of times anyway, hoping to spot Slick's Cadillac. She also tells patrol and the gang unit to watch for the car.

In the afternoon, Winn discovers that a witness—and intended target—from the crack house double-murder she picked up in mid-June was killed over the weekend. Li'l Sambo, the enterprising 15-year-old Front Street Crip who had set up his drug operation, did not make it to 16.

Winn is not surprised when she hears that Sambo is dead. Sambo was too young to even drive a car, but rivals had tried to kill him three times during a four-month period. Sambo had been shot in the leg in May during a drive-by. A month later, he narrowly escaped death at the rock house, where his uncle and another man were killed. Last week he was shot again during a drive-by. This time, the killer wanted to make sure he was dead. His body was riddled with bullets, and detectives recovered 24 shell casings at the scene. Sambo died at the hospital early Sunday morning.

Winn's key witness from her March homicide calls. John Jones, the apartment manager, tells Winn he has been threatened for the second time. He was standing by his front stoop when a Five-Deuce Hoover Crip walked by, held his fingers like a gun, aimed at him and pulled the trigger. "Five-Deuce is going to get you. Don't take your ass to court," the gangbanger whispered and walked off.

Winn offers to relocate the witness and his family, but he tells her that he is trying to purchase the apartment house he manages, so he cannot move. He asks Winn if he can carry a gun to protect himself. "You're an ex-con, so I can't advise you to carry a gun," she says. "But, at the same time, you have a right to protect your family." She tells him to call her if he has any more problems and to seriously consider her offer of relocating him.

Winn spends the rest of the week searching for Slick. She is going to request that the district attorney file murder charges even though she has not yet tracked him down. But convincing the D.A. to file against Slick is, in some ways, a more onerous task than finding Slick. Winn knows deputy district attorneys usually will not file murder charges in cases when there is only one witness. And her only witness is Cornel. But she figures she has a chance because Cornel was such a good witness. She plans her presentation to the D.A., but every time she thinks about what she is going to say, she anticipates the D.A.'s rejection and becomes increasingly angry.

Winn talks about her case with another detective, who also grew up in South-Central. He recently had what he considered a good case rejected by an deputy D.A. who is notorious for his frequent rejections.

"After he refused to file on my case, he starts talking about the trip to Portugal he's got planned," the detective tells Winn. "Then he sees that I'm real unhappy, so he says to me, 'Don't worry about it. We both got good jobs. We can go home to our nice neighborhoods and forget about the case.'

"I was so stunned that all I could say was, 'Well, not everyone's so fortunate.' It was no big deal to him. Like people are killing each other all the time here, so who cares. I've seen a lack of concern, but that took the cake. How can I go back to the victim's family and tell them, 'I know who killed your son and your brother, but I have to drop it.' I feel like throwing the bloody pictures of my victims on this D.A.'s desk and saying, 'Did you enjoy your trip to Portugal?' "

Winn nods. "Every day when I'm coming in to work I see all these people around here, driving to their jobs, walking to school, trying to live their lives. And they have to deal with these predators every day," she says indignantly. "But people like your prosecutor could care less. If this was the Westside, things would be a lot different. I can tell you that.

"I got a good case I'm working up for the D.A. right now. I know they're going to give me a hard time on it. But they better not reject me. I'm ready for battle."

On Wednesday morning, Winn drives down the Harbor Freeway to the D.A.'s Compton office. She presents her case to a tall, blond deputy D.A. Winn is impassioned and dramatic, jabbing her forefinger, pounding on the desk, standing up and pacing, like a defense attorney playing to the jury in a death penalty case. When she finishes, the D.A. asks about Slick's record.

"He's an asshole," she says. "Burglary, armed robbery, selling drugs, carrying a concealed weapon."

"Does Cornel have a criminal record?"

"No. He's had a steady job for five years."

"Is he intelligent? Does he make a good impression?"

She nods.

"Will he get scared and flake out?"

"He and the victim are longtime friends."

"Does the suspect exactly match Cornel's description?"

"Exactly."

The D.A. pauses for a moment, lost in thought. "You've got other witnesses who were there, but who can't ID the suspect. That's a point for the defense. When we go to trial we only have one guy who saw the suspect's face. The others will be saying, 'I got a look, but I'm not sure.' I've got a lot of cases where I've been burned before because of a single ID."

He tells Winn it is imperative that she find Slick and his Cadillac. And he wants Cornel to identify him in a live lineup.

"How unusual are these tires?" he asks.

"Very," she says. "They're real throwbacks."

"You're going to have to find that Caddy. And you're going to have to improve this case. If you don't, some D.A. will be out there in trial on a wing and a prayer."

"I don't understand what you're doing," Winn says angrily. "I got a witness who sees this killer pull a shotgun out and shoot my victim."

"You say you don't know what I'm doing," he says. He is angry now, too. "I'm trying to get a good enough case to convict this guy."

The D.A. tells her that he is concerned that Slick's Cadillac was a 1979, but Cornel said he thought the Cadillac was an '85 or '86. He suggests she show Cornel pictures of Cadillacs from 1979 to 1985 and ask him to pick out the year.

"Okay," she says. "I'll show Cornel the pictures of the Cadillacs. Then what?"

"Get the Cadillac within forty-eight hours of the suspect's arrest. And get a live lineup."

"I'll do that."

"But after you arrest him, if there's no live lineup and no Caddy, I'm going to seek dismissal." He stands up and walks to the door. "I got to get to Seal Beach by twelve-fifteen."

Winn sits in the office for a few minutes after he leaves. She had been so prepared for rejection, so prepared to be outraged, that now she is stunned when she realizes the assistant D.A. has agreed to file murder charges against Slick. She does not know how to react. So she sits in silence as the D.A. walks out the door.

She gets up to leave and notices a note taped to the wall. A murder suspect awaiting trial wrote the note to a friend, but it was seized by a bailiff. The suspect waxed poetic about a woman he just met from Sybil Brand Institute—the women's jail.

"I met this bitch from Cybil Bran," he wrote. "Light skin, healthy and thicker than a motherfucca. In for murder. I'm like yeah. I knew we had something in common. We switched 411. She soppose to write this week."

Winn laughs as she reads the note and makes a few Xerox copies. She knows her girlfriends will be amused by this love story. A young couple fall in love when they discover they share a common interest. Murder.

When Winn returns to the office, she calls Erick Johnson's mother to let her know that the D.A. has filed charges against the suspect. Johnson's mother thanks her and tells her she is much relieved.

The family is still mystified why Erick was murdered. They heard the intended target might have been Darryl, who Erick was visiting that afternoon. In fact, Darryl has disappeared and Winn cannot find him. The shooting was at Darryl's girlfriend's house, and the family heard that one of the girlfriend's teenage sons might have been the intended target. They also heard the shooting might have been a random drive-by, a payback for a gang murder in another neighborhood.

Erick's friends were stunned when they heard he was killed in a drive-by. He was not the type who would hang out on the street corners with the gangbangers. He lived with his girlfriend and two young children in Ontario, a suburb 40 miles east of Los Angeles. They did not want to raise their children in the city. He had been laid off from his job as a security guard and was spending a few days a week during the summer at his mother's South-Central house. She has diabetes and failing eyesight and Erick had been caring for her.

When he returned to his old neighborhood, he liked to play dominoes with his friends and water the roses in his mother's yard. He landscaped the yard years ago and won a gardening award from the city. His mother still has the trophy on her mantel. He took pride in the lush lawn he put in, the red, yellow, pink and violet rosebushes he tended, the thick stands of philodendron he planted to shade the yard.

He was so well liked, more than 300 people came to his funeral, including a few teachers from elementary and high school. At his wake, his 3-year-old son, Erick, Jr., who now wears his father's gold earring, tried to climb into the coffin. He could not comprehend that his father was gone. Later that night, he picked up the telephone and tried to call his father so he could tell him to come home.

Erick's 5-year-old daughter, Danielle, who is missing her front teeth and has pigtails, lingered by her father's open casket. She kissed him and held his hand. Finally, she told her mother, "I want to die, so I can be with my daddy in heaven."

Now, Danielle's mother often finds her crying in her bed, the blankets pulled over her head. When her mother pulls the covers back, Danielle tells her that she tries to muffle her cries. She does not want to upset her.

Every day, Erick, Jr., talks about his father. And every day he tells his mother, "I want to find the man who shot my daddy. I want to kill him."

The summer is over and it is time for Erlinda Acuna to meet Gizmo, the man convicted of killing her son. Now, to be certain that Gizmo is guilty, she has to talk to him herself.

On the drive to the prison, she recalls that Ernie had a premonition he was going to die. His uncle had died earlier that year. A few months later Ernie told a friend at the park, "I'm going to be next. I know they're going to kill me."

Early in the morning on the day he was killed he had a nightmare and his shouts woke up Acuna. "No! No!" he shouted. "Motherfucker! Don't!" She stood over his bed and prayed. She woke him, but he would not tell her what was troubling him.

He had begun carrying a .357-magnum for protection. On the night he was killed, he was standing out on the street, talking to some friends when he became spooked by the patrol cars cruising by. He did not want to risk getting patted down. He ran into the house and put his gun away. An hour later, he was killed.

At midmorning, Acuna arrives at the Calipatria State Prison, about 200 miles southeast of Los Angeles. The prison, set in a dusty, desolate patch of desert, is composed of dozens of gray cell blocks, which rise abruptly from the sand and scrub. The cell blocks, surrounded by double chain-link fences topped by razor wire, face the towering peaks of the Chocolate Mountains, their faded brown escarpment silhouetted against a brilliant turquoise sky.

Acuna climbs out of the car and is assaulted by a furnace blast of desert heat. She catches her breath and walks across the parking lot to the visitors' desk. A guard tells her that Gizmo violated a prison rule and is not allowed face-to-face visits. Acuna will have to talk to him behind glass. She is relieved. She still will be only inches from him, but the glass will give her the slight measure of detachment that she feel she needs.

While she waits for Gizmo, she is too nervous to sit. She considers calling the whole thing off and walking out. She paces back and forth, prays and asks God whether she should leave. While she is praying, she senses the warmth of Ernie's spirit enveloping her. She feels Ernie wants her to continue.

A guard brings Gizmo to the visiting room. He sits behind the glass barrier and waits. When Acuna spots him, she shudders. "Holy Jesus," she whispers. "Please help me through this." She takes a deep breath, slowly exhales and walks to the glass. She picks up the telephone and Gizmo picks up his phone.

"You know why I'm here," she says in a slow monotone.

He nods. "To talk about Ernie's death. I want to tell you right off that I didn't kill Ernie."

The name Gizmo fits him perfectly. He is short with a wide-eyed, innocent boyish look. His prison blues are baggy and ill-fitting, and although he is 22, he looks like a child wearing his father's clothing. Only his tattoos give him away. He has 29th Street tattooed on his hand, his elbow and spelled out on his fingers.

Acuna begins by asking him, "Why did you wait so long to contact me?"

"Part of it is my appeal," he says. "I been working on it. It ain't right that I'm in here for something I didn't do. But that's not all of it. I wanted you to know that it wasn't me. It's important to me that you know that."

She glares at Gizmo. "I want you to know what this has done to me," she tells him. "I was home the night Ernie was killed. I heard the shots. I heard Donna scream, 'Ernie. Ernie. They shot Ernie in the head.' When I saw Ernie, I knew he wouldn't want to live as a vegetable. So I prayed. I said, 'God, you gave my son to me. If he is not going to wake up, you can take him. I want you to let him go with you in peace.' "

She wipes her eyes with a palm. "Since Ernie's death, I'm not the same person. Look at me. I've gained forty pounds. I'm taking high blood pressure medication. This has made my life a living hell."

Gizmo looks shaken. His lower lip trembles and his eyes are watery. He is trying not to cry.

She puts the telephone down and surveys the visiting room, where families are sitting at tables, sipping Cokes and talking. Now is the time, she decides, to put the question to him.

"If you didn't do it, who did?"

He licks his lips. "There's another Gizmo. He's from 39th Street. Before Ernie's death, his brother was killed. I heard he came by that night and shot Ernie."

Acuna frowns and shakes her head. She tells him she already talked to a homicide detective about Gizmo from 39th Street. He looks like an Indian, the detective told her, with long straight hair. He bears no resemblance to the witnesses' descriptions of the killer. The detective checked him out and dismissed him as a suspect.

"Look," he says, "I'm not saying he did it. I'm just saying I *heard* it was him. I'm just passing the information on to you."

"I'm asking *you* who did it," she says. "If you didn't do it, you gotta know who did."

It was the day after his birthday, Gizmo tells her, so he remembers the day well. That night he was "kicking it" out on the street with his friend Trino. A dark Buick Regal pulled up next door and picked up a gangbanger who lived nearby. He tells Acuna the gangbanger's name.

A few minutes later he heard several gunshots. Then his friend Crazy came by and told them that the passenger in the Buick Regal just killed Ernie.

"Why didn't you tell anyone about this earlier?" she asks.

"I was afraid. You can't be known as a snitch in the joint."

He had claimed in his letters that Donna—the key witness in the case—knows he is not the killer. Acuna tells him that she has talked to Donna. She tells him that Donna says he is lying, that she saw him kill Ernie.

He waves his hands and shakes his head. He tells Acuna that Donna has not been honest with her.

They talk about his life and how he grew up. His mother had six children with three different fathers. Gizmo's father is black, and he rarely saw his son. His mother is Latino. She abandoned her children when they were young, and they were raised by their aunt and grandmother. Occasionally their mother would return and take her children back. These were the worst times for Gizmo and his brothers and sisters, the times they dreaded. If they cried because they wanted attention or were hungry, their mother would beat them. She would haul off and punch them in the face. She would pummel them with her fists them until they were too terrified to cry. Gizmo once was beaten with an extension cord so badly he had a dozen deep, bloody gashes on his back. His aunt, Elda Noriega, eventually rescued Gizmo, brought him to her house and called county social workers. She was afraid his mother was going to kill him.

Noriega felt sorry for all the children, but it broke her heart when she picked up Gizmo. He was a quiet, sweet child who was so desperate for affection that he would rub up against her leg until she gave him a hug. Noriega is convinced Gizmo's mother had children for one reason—to make money. She collected welfare for each of her six kids and let Noriega and her mother take care of them. The only time she paid attention to her children was when they could make money for her. When Gizmo was in elementary school, his mother took him to the Glendale Mall and taught him to shoplift. If he was caught, she would beat him. At 12, she sent him out on a street corner to sell crack for her. During the next few years he was in juvenile hall a half dozen times. When he was 15, he joined 29th Street. The *veteranos* of the gang, Gizmo's relatives felt, were better role models than his mother. His homies began calling him Gizmo because he reminded them of a character in the movie *Gremlins*.

At the time Ernie was killed, Gizmo was too poor to rent an apartment. He lived in a beat-up Ford Van—parked in his great-grandfather's backyard—with his girlfriend, their two babies and his two younger sisters. His mother was arrested for selling drugs and is now in a Las Vegas jail.

Acuna has known about Gizmo's family for years. People in the neighborhood told her about his brutal childhood. Acuna is a guileless, ingenuous woman, and now she feels sorry for Gizmo. She is a devout Catholic and hatred is an emotion she will not allow herself to indulge in.

She tells Gizmo to continue reading the Bible, to put his faith in Jesus. Her tone is maternal now. For a moment, she forgets why she is here. "If you need help, ask Him for help," she tells him. "He will hear you. Sometimes we don't get our answers from God right away. Sometimes it takes time. So stay with it. Keep your faith in God. He will provide you with answers."

Acuna sighs and presses her face against the glass. "God knows everything we do," she tells him. "And He knows everything that's going to happen before it happens. God knows if you're telling the truth. So I'm asking you. In the name of God. Did you kill my son?"

He looks at her, wide-eyed and earnest. "No. I did not kill your son."

She drops the telephone and leans her head against the wall. She stares across the visiting room for a few minutes. Finally, she picks up the phone and asks him a few more questions about the night her son was killed. They talk for about ten minutes, and she tells him she is going to think about what he has said.

Gizmo hangs the phone up and waves. A guard leads him away.

Acuna is so drained as she drives off from the prison that she cannot think clearly. She does not know whether to believe Gizmo. But after driving for a few hours, she begins to analyze what he told her. She recalls how, at first, he tried to convince her that Gizmo of 39th Street killed Ernie. Now she remembers that Gizmo of 39th street was killed last year. He cannot defend himself. He is a convenient scapegoat.

She recalls that Gizmo said the killer was in a dark Buick Regal. But witnesses said the car was a red 280Z. Gizmo was not even close. She thinks about his other inconsistencies, the other things he said that, now, do not make sense to her.

Acuna realizes that in the visiting room she was taken in by Gizmo. He seemed so small, so vulnerable, so sincere. His life had been so hard. She pitied him. Part of her wanted to believe him.

But now, hours after the visit, as she drives into the sunset and nears Los Angeles, she comes to a conclusion. For the first time since she received his letter in June, she has found some peace of mind. She knows that Gizmo killed her son. She is sure.

Chapter 22
The Edge of the Carving Knife

Monday, October 10

Razanskas returns from his hunting trip and is back at work during the last gasp of the southern California summer. All weekend it had been blazing hot. The Santa Ana winds kicked up and began ripping down the mountain passes, through the city and on to the sea. On Saturday, it was 100 degrees downtown. Sunday it was 99.

On Monday it is still in the high 90s. Brush fires are raging in the Antelope Valley. The beaches are jammed. The air is crackly and bone dry.

Razanskas' desk is piled high with crime reports, phone messages, subpoenas, and other paperwork that has accumulated during his absence. But he is in such a good mood he does not mind. He is tanned and relaxed and looks rested. His back is straight. He walks without pain.

"Well, how'd it go?" she asks.

He grins. "It was tremendous. A million stars out at night. The leaves were changing. Saw a few eagles."

"Did you get your deer?"

"Opening day was Saturday, the first. I got it the next day. It rained in the morning. We had breakfast. Then my buddy beat the bush and chased two deer out of the aspens. I was about seventy feet away. I shot one in the side. Took his lungs out."

"It was busy as hell around here that weekend," she says. "We had about ten homicides."

"Sounds like it was opening day here, too."

She briefs him on the Slick case and tells him about her meeting with the D.A. Razanskas asks her when she thinks she can pick up Slick. She smiles. She tells him Slick is already in custody. He ran a red light last week at Century and Figueroa, patrol officers discovered there was a warrant out for his arrest and they brought him in. Cornel identified the Cadillac Slick was driving. Winn is setting up a live lineup for later in the week.

"After Cornel IDed the Caddy, I called Erick Johnson's mother," she says. "I told her we got the guy in custody. She shouted, 'Praise God!' She got real emotional and started crying. I felt for her. I was glad I could do something to help her."

Winn and Razanskas are interrupted by a lieutenant who assigns them a new case. Razanskas has been back at work half an hour and he already is working a homicide. He was looking forward to a leisurely breakfast at Pepy's with his buddies, where he planned to regale them with tales of his hunting trip. Instead, he and Winn grab an empty murder book and hop into the car.

The victim, a 58-year-old woman who had diabetes and heart disease, died at the hospital on Sunday. Detectives initially suspected that her caretaker killed her for her social security checks. Their suspicion was aroused by a note the victim sent to a relative: "I want to leave," the victim wrote. "Louise is mean to me. She got my money and I want to leave. I don't have money. Betty come get me. . . . I want to see my uncle and Mary. . . ."

Winn, who learned how to analyze handwriting at bunco forgery, studies the writing on the woman's checks and determines that she endorsed them herself. The victim's doctor tells them that the caretaker seemed conscientious and that the victim was always clean and looked well cared for. Her relatives do not have any evidence that the woman was murdered.

At about 7 o'clock Monday night, the detectives conclude the case is not a homicide. The woman died of natural causes. Razanskas no longer looks relaxed and rested. He has been up since 4:20 A.M., has spent 12 hours racing from interview to interview on a day in the high 90s. He has not had time to stop for lunch or breakfast or dinner.

"Typical first day back," he tells Winn, as they walk through the garage to their cars. "As soon as you return from vacation, you're nothing but fresh meat."

On Tuesday, Razanskas and Winn are first on the on-call list. This could be the last murder they work together. Razanskas will soon pick up a new trainee and Winn will get a new partner. Winn passed her written detective exam earlier in the year, and last month she found out she passed her orals. In a few months, when her name comes up on the detective waiting list, she will get her badge. Winn has decided that homicide is the ultimate criminal investigation and that the homicide detective is the ultimate criminal investigator. This is it, she decides. This is where the greatest challenge lies. This is where she belongs.

At South Bureau Homicide, when detective trainees get their badges, they are shipped out to gain experience at other divisions. The lieutenants at South Bureau want to make an exception with Winn. They are trying to figure out a way to keep her. They feel she has the makings of a superior homicide detective. And she is viewed as a comer in the department, a detective who has the brains and the moxie to rise through the ranks and, one day, make it to the upper reaches of the LAPD hierarchy.

Razanskas discovers that his position as the dean of South Bureau Homicide detectives is a tenuous one. The two lieutenants call him into an office for a meeting and criticize him for falling so far behind on his 60-dayers, for writing the ones he did turn in too hastily, for not doing enough follow-up work on a few of his unsolved cases. They acknowledge that he is one of their best detectives at crime scenes, that no one is better at establishing rapport with intractable witnesses, that his knowledge about firearms and trajectories and ammunition types is an invaluable resource.

But, they tell him, he is burnt out.

"You either get your shit together," a lieutenant tells him, "or you're gone."

They tell him no one should work homicide in South Bureau more than five years because the hours are too long, the pressure too great. He has been investigating homicides in South-Central for almost 15 years.

But Razanskas tells them he does not want to leave. He is a South-Central homicide detective. He does not want to do anything else.

The lieutenants tell him they will review his caseload again at the end of the year. If he has been able to "refire his engines," he can stay. If not, he will be on a robbery or auto theft table at another division, or in a homicide unit at a less busy station.

Razanskas staggers back to his desk and falls into his chair. "Jesus," he tells Winn. "They reamed me big time."

Fortunately, working homicide for so many years has given him a thick skin and a sense of perspective. He has seen thousands of bodies on the street. He has told countless parents that their sons have been murdered. A poor job review will not destroy him.

Winn feels bad to see Razanskas so down. She has grown to like him and is already nostalgic about their partnership. It seems to her their partnership lasted much longer than seven months. She no longer thinks of him as a supervisor. She regards him as her partner now. So she comes to her partner's defense.

"I want you to know that I'm behind you," she says. "I don't think you're burnt out. And I'll tell anyone that."

The Santa Anas are still blowing Tuesday night, and Razanskas and Winn are waiting for the call of death. California writers often call upon the Santa Anas to evoke an edgy, unsettling mood, a mood with undertones of malice and murder.

"There was a desert wind blowing that night," Raymond

Chandler wrote in the short story "Red Wind." "It was one of those hot dry Santa Anas that come down through the mountain passes and curl your hair and make your nerves jump and your skin itch. On nights like that, every booze party ends in a fight, meek little wives feel the edge of the carving knife and study their husband's neck."

On this hot Tuesday night, a sister feels the edge of the carving knife and stabs her brother. Razanskas, who is the primary on this one, gets a gift for his last homicide of the extended summer—a domestic dispute. A slam-dunker.

The first murder he and Winn worked together was in late March. There have been 196 murders in South Bureau since then. This is the bureau's 276th murder of the year.

Razanskas pulls up at the station, his truck still covered with mud from the back roads of Wyoming. He meets Winn in the parking lot, and they drive to the murder scene. The night watch detectives and Lieutenant Fletcher are in their shirtsleeves. The Santa Anas carry the smell of dust and freshly mowed grass.

Razanskas is energized now and has put the job review out of his mind. After all these years, he still gets excited by a homicide call, still is intrigued by what kind of case will be awaiting him, by the uncertainty and the promise of what the night will hold. He and Winn approach a rookie patrolman, who tells him a 39-year-old man named Bobby Winston was stabbed to death. The patrolman arrested the victim's sister, and she now is in custody at the 77th Street station. Razanskas looks him up and down and asks if he tested the suspect's hands for gunshot residue. The patrolman looks worried.

"Uhh . . . no . . . ," he stammers. "We didn't have any kits."

Winn tells the patrolman that Razanskas was pulling his leg. Because the victim was stabbed there was no need to test for gunshot residue. The young patrolman laughs nervously.

The detectives walk over to the patrol sergeant, a buddy of Razanskas' from his days with the gang unit. "Hey, Sarge," Razanskas says, "those gang days sure seem like a long time ago. Who would of thought you and me would still be on the street, all these years later."

The sergeant tells them that the Santa Anas are creating havoc on the streets. It is so busy, he says, the patrol officers are ignoring everything but the urgent "hot shot" calls. The sergeant tells them that their homicide suspect lives in a small trailer behind the main house. The suspect claimed that her brother burst through the front door and she stabbed him in self-defense. Razanskas and Winn walk to the backyard and check out the small white trailer, beneath an arbor of ivy. The inside is a jumble of dirty dishes, old newspapers and crumpled clothing. The murder weapon—two kitchen knives taped together to make a double blade—is on the stove. While they check out the trailer, Razanskas tells Winn about a jealous wife who he suspected had killed her husband. He wanted to test the wife's hands for gunshot residue, so he asked her when she last washed her hands. She stared at Razanskas and said flatly, "Right before I shot the son of a bitch."

Earlier in the summer, Winn would have ignored Razanskas' story. She would have been irritated by the distraction. But she has been to so many homicide scenes this summer that murder is now becoming routine to her, too. She is relaxed enough to respond with an anecdote of her own.

"I was working patrol in Hollenbeck and I was patting down this chubby woman," she tells him. " 'You pregnant?' I ask the suspect. She giggles and says demurely that she's just a little overweight. I pat her down some more, jump back and yell, 'Hey, you're not pregnant. And you're definitely NOT a woman!' "

Winn and Razanskas chuckle while they search the trailer. When they finish, they follow a trail of blood drops from the trailer, up the driveway, through the house and into the victim's bedroom, where he collapsed.

The house has a manicured front yard framed by jade plants and African lilies with violet blossoms. The street is lined with well-kept orange, yellow, lime green and pink stucco bungalows, which look like blocks of pastel sherbet set atop the lawns. Inside the house, where the victim lived with his mother, the sofa and chairs are covered in plastic. On the living room wall there is a tribute to the victim's and the suspect's mother. Her children nominated her for a Mother of the Year contest years ago, and their handwritten entry is encased in a large wooden frame. They wrote: "My mother did all that she could to raise her children in every sense of the word. Along with providing us with a strong religious background, she instilled in us morals and values that she felt were acceptable and that would provide us with the solid foundation from which to build as we enter adulthood. She always put our needs before hers. My mother is a person with no hate, only love in her heart."

The mother, who is wearing a pink nightgown, sweatshirt and powder blue house slippers, is pacing on the sidewalk in front of her house. She is waiting for her other daughter to return from the hospital. The mother does not yet know that her son is dead, and Razanskas wants to interview her before he informs her. He walks over and asks her to describe the events leading up to the stabbing. She explains that her daughter, Angelic, is a schizophrenic. A few months ago she stopped taking her medication and stopped seeing her doctor.

"Angelic wouldn't go," the mother says. "Nothing I could do to make her go. She needs her medicine. Nothing I could do to make her take her medicine. I went to the hospital out here and told them she needed help, that she was acting worse and worse and I didn't know what to do with her. But they told me there was nothing they could do. I asked them why. They said it was because she hadn't done nothin'. Well, she's done somethin' now."

She tells the detectives that the electricity went out on their street a few hours ago. Angelic, who was in the trailer, was convinced that her family turned off her lights. She began screaming, so her mother sent her son to calm Angelic down and assure her that the utility company would soon turn the lights back on.

"They started arguing," the mother says. "Next thing I see, my son staggers back into the house and says, 'I'm dying.' He falls in his bedroom. My daughter comes out and tells me she cut her brother in the heart."

She leans against her car and breathes deeply, trying to calm herself. A block away, someone fires a few rounds from a semiautomatic pistol. Several sirens wail simultaneously. A constant stream of calls crackle over a patrol car radio: "Shots fired . . . Suspect with shotgun . . . Attempted 211 . . . Two suspects fleeing eastbound on alley . . . Man down . . . Suspect with handgun . . . 211 armed . . ."

The victim's other sister speeds down the street, pulls her car in front of the house, screeches to a halt and hops out. She runs over to her mother. "He's dead!" she wails. "The doctor said she killed him." Her mother falls onto her car and beats her fists on the hood. She drops to the ground and sobs. The woman has now lost two children. Bobby is dead. Angelic will face life in prison.

Winn tries to comfort her. A neighbor calls the woman's pastor. When he arrives, Razanskas and Winn drive over to the 77th Street station to interview Angelic.

She is waiting in an interview room slightly bigger than a telephone booth. Insulation panels have been chipped off and gang graffiti is scratched into the walls. Angelic is 35 years old and pudgy. She is wearing jeans, a blue T-shirt and a brown pinstriped vest. In another interview room, someone is pounding on the door.

"There are two sides to every story," Razanskas says to her. "I'm sure you have your side. I'd like to hear it. But first I'd like to advise you of your rights."

After he reads Angelic her rights, she says, "Being as I'm innocent, I don't mind talking. So I'll tell you that I had to stab the boy."

"Tell us what happened," Razanskas says softly.

"He came into the trailer hollering and screaming. I told him to get off my property. I stabbed the homeboy because he almost tore my door off, like he was coming to rape me."

Her eyes are wild and her face is twitching. Razanskas wants to determine her mental state, so he asks her if she knows that the man she killed was her brother.

"I don't claim him no more."

"Is that your mother who lives in the front house?" he asks her.

"She's an orphan mother."

"Do you know your brother is dead?" Winn asks.

"Well, I died and God brought me back to life. Anyway, I don't have no sorry blues for the brother. He's a menace to society."

Angelic stares at Winn for a moment and launches into a rambling monologue. "I watched *All My Children* today and took a bus downtown. The bus driver had a scorpion voice. . . . I went back to the trailer and smoked some cigarette butts. . . . After dark, the homeboy came through the trailer. He sabotaged the electricity. The fool was yelling about some shovel. I heard a clicking sound from him, like he had a gun. I yelled at him to clear away from the trailer. When I told the homeboy to back off, he became a death threat. He's a lunatic. He almost tore the door off. That's when I grabbed the knife and stuck him in the chest. I yelled to neighbors to call an ambulance. I told 'em all I'm innocent. I don't want no bad record."

Razanskas and Winn confer outside the interview room. "The issue here is her mental capacity," Razanskas tells Winn.

"She's a schizo," Winn says.

"Yeah," Razanskas says. "But she was slick enough to slip in that she thought her brother had a gun and she thought he was going to rape her. That indicates she knows what she did and is already scrambling for a defense. We'll file the case and let the D.A. make the final call."

They drive east on the Santa Monica Freeway and take Angelic to the county hospital's psychiatric ward for evaluation. She sits quietly in the back of their squad car staring into the darkness, a glazed look in her eyes. After they check her in, they drive over to Martin Luther King, Jr./Drew Medical Center so they can study the body of the victim. Razanskas tells Winn that when he was a young patrolman most of the murders he saw were set off by domestic disputes. But now all he sees are robbery murders, dope murders, gang murders. This is the first domestic homicide he has worked in two years. He is grateful, he tells her, for the case. He could use a slam-dunker now.

They meet a police photographer at the hospital and enter a refrigerated morgue. Razanskas removes the plastic body bag and studies the single knife wound, about a half-inch wide, beneath the victim's nipple. Winn examines the victim's hands and arms.

"No defensive wounds at all," Winn tells the photographer. "That shows he was surprised."

Razanskas nods approvingly. Winn has learned well.

It is still dark when they finish at the hospital and drive back to South Bureau. "The next time I'm out on a murder it should be well into October," Winn says. "It'll be cold at night. I'll have to dig out my long coat."

"Want to get some breakfast at Pepy's?" he asks.

She shakes her head and smiles. "One breakfast a month at Pepy's is enough for me."

He drops her off at the bureau and watches her walk through the dim, deserted parking lot, her low heels echoing on the cement. He is in a bittersweet mood as he watches Winn disappear through the bureau door. He is proud of her progress and glad he could teach her about homicide. He knows if he stays with the LAPD long enough, he may end up working for her. But at the same time he thinks of his own uncertain future. He never thought that after all these years, after all the murders he has cleared, he would have to fight to keep his job. But if that's the way it is, he decides, that's the way it is. He loves the work. He cannot imagine investigating any crime but murder. He will do whatever he has to do to stay at South Bureau Homicide.

Razanskas pulls out of the parking lot and heads west, toward the ocean, to Pepy's. The restaurant is deserted at this hour, so he does not have to worry about the Beretta in his shoulder holster offending any diners. Instead of sitting at his regular table—in the dim lounge in back—he sits at a front table by the window and throws his sports coat over a chair.

A waiter greets him and brings him the usual—steak and eggs. Razanskas stares out the window and watches the sky lighten, ignoring his breakfast. A gauzy bank of fog rolls in and hovers over the golf course across the street. It reminds him of the sunrises in Vietnam, with the mist rising from the rice paddies. The fog soon thickens and covers the horizon in a vaporous veil. Car windshields on the street become damp and speckled with droplets.

The Santa Anas have died down. A cool, salty breeze blows in from the sea.

The summer is over.

Epilogue

As of this writing, about two years after Pete Razanskas and Marcella Winn first became partners, most of the cases they investigated during the summer have wended their way though Los Angeles County's vast criminal justice system:

—Obie Anthony and Reggie Cole, the two suspects in Winn's first homicide case, were both convicted of first-degree murder. They were sentenced to life imprisonment without parole (LWOP), which the detectives call El-Wop.

—Winn's second case, the crack house double murder, remains unsolved.

—Glenn Mason (No Neck), who was tried for the murder of Li'l Boy's father and another man, was convicted of two counts of first-degree murder and sentenced to LWOP.

—The murder of John Robert Elliot—the first body dump of the summer—remains unsolved.

Epilogue

—The trial of J-Bone, the 17-year-old suspect who killed Hector Hernandez in front of his young son, ended in a hung jury. He later pled guilty to voluntary manslaughter and agreed to a term of 15 years in state prison.

—Larry Charles Gary, whom the detectives arrested in Miami, was convicted of two counts of first-degree murder and sentenced to LWOP.

—Ramon Sanchez, the college student who was chased on the freeway, pled guilty to voluntary manslaughter and was sentenced to 16 years in prison. His 14-year-old brother was convicted of second-degree murder and will be released from the California Youth Authority when he is 25 years old.

—Slick, who was suspected of driving down East 94th Street in his Cadillac and killing Erick Johnson with a shotgun blast, was released from custody. The day of the preliminary hearing, the key witness to the homicide, who had previously identified Slick as the shooter, suddenly backed out and refused to testify.

—Angelic Davis, who admitted stabbing her brother to death, pled guilty to voluntary manslaughter and was sentenced to 12 years. The judge recommended that the state prison system evaluate her mental condition and consider sentencing her to a state psychiatric hospital.

At the end of the summer, after Razanskas determined that Winn no longer needed a supervisor and they split up, she worked with another partner for about six months. She then was selected to join a new LAPD-FBI task force, a plum assignment for a young detective. Eight South Bureau Homicide detectives were paired with eight agents from the FBI's Los Angeles office to investigate unsolved murders in South-Central. It was a one-year assignment, and she now is back in the South Bureau rotation, catching cases again.

Epilogue

The other team of detectives Razanskas supervised also has split up. Armando Reyes is now a homicide detective in the Rampart Division. Reyes' former partner, Paul Masuyama, is still at South Bureau and still searching for his father.

As for Pete Razanskas, he has outlasted the two lieutenants who contended he was burnt out. One lieutenant retired and the other transferred out of the unit. Razanskas, who has been with the LAPD 24 years, has no plans to retire.

ACKNOWLEDGMENTS

This book could not have been written without the cooperation and support of Lieutenant Sergio Robleto, who headed South Bureau Homicide when I conducted my research. At no time did Robleto attempt to limit my access or dictate what he wanted me to write. Before I began, he told me, "I'm not asking you to sugarcoat it. All I ask is that you lay it out like it happened. People should know what goes on here." I was truly fortunate to have found a lieutenant who had the courage and the confidence in his detectives to give a writer such free reign.

Pete Razanskas and Marcella Winn were a pleasure to spend time with and to write about. I will never forget their many courtesies. Razanskas' incredible memory, his knowledge about homicide and his willingness to teach me made my job much easier. And because of his sense of humor, getting called out in the middle of the night and working 24 hours straight was never a chore. I also greatly appreciate Winn's honesty and frankness, her patience and the way she took time out to answer all my questions, no matter how much pressure she was under.

I want to thank Saundrea Young of Loved Ones of Homicide Victims, who allowed me tremendous freedom at the center. She helped me understand homicide from the perspective of those left behind—the families. I also owe a debt of gratitude to the members of Loved Ones' early Saturday morning support group and their therapist, Robert Bennett. They welcomed me into the group and the members shared their lives with me. I constantly marveled at their courage and selflessness as they put aside their own troubles and helped new members come to terms with the loss of a loved one. I have the greatest admiration for all of them.

Barney Karpfinger is an astute reader, a sage adviser and an honorable man. I cannot imagine a better agent.

Michael Shapiro's constant support and his enthusiasm were, as always, a tremendous help. He is a true friend.

Laurie Bernstein, my editor, provided invaluable insight and critical judgments.

My editors at the *Los Angeles Times* were gracious enough to grant me a leave of absence to write this book.

I thank all the people who read the manuscript: Bernard Bauer, for his eagle editing eye; Sam Freedman, for his excellent advice; Ruth D'Arcy, for her guidance, her counsel and her belief in me over many years; James Shapiro, for his scholar's touch; and Ed Boyer, for his historical perspective. I also would like to thank my sister, Leni Corwin, a computer wizard who, like a hostage negotiator, talked me though many crises when I was unable to negotiate the intricacies of word processing.

My wife, Diane, a detective's daughter, vowed she would never marry a cop. But during the research of this book, and beyond, she had to endure a detective's hours and a detective's life. Yet the phone calls at 3 A.M., the nights and weekends away from home, the last-minute changes of plans, never fazed her. For her encouragement, her sense of humor, her keen editing ear and her unflagging support, I am especially grateful.

Source Notes

This book is a work of nonfiction. No names have been changed; no incidents have been altered.

The vast majority of the book is the result of my own reporting, the time I spent with Detectives Pete Razanskas and Marcella Winn.

A number of sources, however, were extremely helpful when I was researching the historical sections of the book. Lonnie G. Bunch's history of Los Angeles' black community, *Black Angelenos: The Afro-American in Los Angeles, 1850–1950,* was invaluable.

Joe Domanick's book about the Los Angeles Police Department, *The LAPD's Century of War in the City of Dreams,* was an excellent resource, as was Martin Schiesl's essay: "Behind the Badge: The Police and Social Discontent in Los Angeles Since 1950."

Interviews with criminologists Marc Riedel and Albert Cardarelli and FBI statistician Gilford Gee helped me understand the changing nature of homicide in America.

Introduction

While the murder rate among adults 25 and older: James Alan Fox, "The Calm Before the Crime Wave Storm," *Los Angeles Times,* October 30, 1995.

Source Notes

"Totally inappropriate and unacceptable": Author interview with Vernon Geberth, March 1995.

Prologue

About a third of the households: Lucille Renwick, "The Myth of South-Central," *Los Angeles Times,* January 3, 1993.

Chapter 4

From 1910 to 1920, the black population: Lonnie G. Bunch, III, *Black Angelenos: The Afro-American in Los Angeles, 1850–1950* (California Afro-American Museum Foundation, Los Angeles, 1988), p. 29.

White residents, including a group of Ku Klux Klan: Bunch, p. 35.

A. Philip Randolph . . . Demanded that defense contractors end discrimination: Bunch, p. 38.

The unemployment rate in South Los Angeles: *Understanding the Riots: Los Angeles Before and After the Rodney King Case* (*Los Angeles Times,* Los Angeles, 1992), p. 10.

From 1963 to 1965, 60 black Los Angeles residents: Robert Gottlieb and Irene Wolt, *Thinking Big: The Story of the Los Angeles Times, Its Publishers and Their Influence on Southern California* (G.P. Putnam's Sons, New York, 1977), p. 376.

Almost 75,000 blacks moved out: Miles Corwin, "L.A.'s Black Flight," *Los Angeles Times,* August 13, 1992.

Chapter 7

Statistics on clearance rates, per capita murder rates and murders by race: "United States Homicide Patterns: Past and Present," in *Crime in the United States 1993* (Federal Bureau of Investigation, Washington D.C., updated 1995).

During the past 15 months, more than a dozen witnesses to homicides: Author interview with South Bureau Homicide source.

Source Notes

Chapter 10

Alprentice "Bunchy" Carter, leader of the Slausons: Elaine Brown, *A Taste of Power: A Black Woman's Story* (Pantheon Books, New York, 1992), pp. 118–120.

The Panthers and US were bitter rivals: Alexander Cockburn, "The Fate of the Panthers; Black Panthers Infiltrated by the F.B.I.," *The Nation,* July 2, 1990; Ronald J. Ostrow, "FBI Pitted Ron Karenga's US Against Black Panthers," *Los Angeles Times,* November 26, 1975.

The origin of the Crips: Bob Baker, "Homeboys: Players in a Deadly Drama," *Los Angeles Times,* June 26, 1988.

The LAPD tripled patrols in Westwood: Sandy Banks, "The Legacy of a Slaying," *Los Angeles Times,* September 11, 1989.

Los Angeles replaced Miami: "Los Angeles Surpassing Miami as Cocaine Capital of the U.S.," *St. Louis Post-Dispatch* (*Reuters News Service*), September 3, 1989; Ronald L. Soble, "Indictments in New York Point to L.A. as Cocaine Hub," *Los Angeles Times,* August 25, 1989.

California now ranks near the bottom: Carolyn Nielsen, "Wilson's Tax Cuts Clouding Horizon," *San Francisco Examiner,* May 30, 1995.

But in California almost three-quarters of state prison inmates: Statistics provided to the author in February 1996 by the California Department of Corrections.

Chapter 14

Parker felt it was important to discourage: Joe Domanick, *The LAPD's Century of War in the City of Dreams* (Pocket Books, New York, 1994), pp. 110–112; Martin J. Schiesl, "Behind the Badge: The Police and Social Discontent in Los Angeles Since 1950," in Norman M. Klein and Martin J. Schiesl, eds., *20th Century Los Angeles: Power, Promotion, and Social Conflict* (Regina Books, Claremont, Calif., 1990), p. 155.

"One person threw a rock": Gottlieb and Wolt, p. 378.

Gates deemphasized or dismantled many of Davis': Jim Newton, "Ed Davis' Influence Still Strong in LAPD," *Los Angeles Times,* May 5, 1996.

In 1980, the city paid $891,000: David Shaw, "Media Failed to Examine Alleged LAPD Abuses," *Los Angeles Times,* May 26, 1992.

Lawrence Powell, had been accused of brutality: Domanick, p. 371.

A dozen LAPD patrol captains were attending a training seminar: Ted Rohrlich, Richard Serrano, and Rich Connell, "Riot Found Police in Disarray," *Los Angeles Times,* July 13, 1992.

During his last six months in the Marine Corps: Paul Feldman and Robert J. Lopez, "Fuhrman Case: How the City Kept Troubled Cop," *Los Angeles Times,* October 2, 1995.

Chapter 18

Community activists call for an invasion: Bob Pool, "Symbolic Siege," *Los Angeles Times,* September 21, 1994.

"To describe an unfortunate death situation": Robert Shapiro, "Using the Media to Your Advantage," *The Champion,* January/February, 1993.